# TEENAGERS
## THE EVIDENCE BASE

MATILDA GOSLING

Swift

SWIFT PRESS

First published in Great Britain by Swift Press 2025

1 3 5 7 9 8 6 4 2

Copyright © Matilda Gosling 2025

The right of Matilda Gosling to be identified as the Author of this Work has been asserted in accordance with the Copyright, Designs and Patents Act 1988

Typeset by Tetragon, London
Printed and bound in Great Britain by CPI Group (UK) Ltd, Croydon, CRO 4YY

A CIP catalogue record for this book is available from the British Library

ISBN: 9781800752399
eISBN: 9781800752405

'A brilliant resource for parents navigating the teen years. This essential guide combines the latest research with evidence-based strategies to help you understand and support your teenager through their formative years. Discover practical advice on strengthening parent-teen bonds, guiding friendships, managing mood swings and fostering a positive body image. This comprehensive resource equips parents with tools to handle the complexities of adolescence while offering guidance on shaping your teen into a well-rounded, resilient adult. With a compassionate approach and practical strategies, *Teenagers: The Evidence-Base* turns the tumultuous teenage years into a period of growth and connection'

Stella O'Malley, author of *What Your Teen is Trying to Tell You*

'I found myself smiling and nodding throughout this book as Matilda guides us through the weather patterns of the teen years using an excellent range of research sources. There are entertaining anecdotes from her own parenting, but the real genius is finishing off each chapter with advice bullet points: perfect for all those times we find ourselves in need of guidance but we're busy and tired and we can't for the life of us remember what we've read'

Rachel Richards, host of *Teenagers Untangled*

'A brilliant, must-have book'

Milli Hill, author of *The Positive Birth Book*

'As a mum to three and now a grandma, the teenage years come with their unique challenges. In a world that seems to get more stressful for them by the day, navigating the hurdles before we stumble over them is always a wise move. *Teenagers: The Evidence Base* will help parents and grandparents to do just that.'

Sharron Davies, British Olympian and author of *Unfair Play*

'An amazing resource, meticulously researched and full of wise and interesting advice on dealing with teenagers, especially useful for parents on the frontline'

Professor Suzanne Franks, author of *Get Out of My Life...
But First Take Me & Alex Into Town*

'An invaluable resource for parents of teenagers, offering both reassurance and practical guidance. It delves into the science and addresses key concerns such as risk-taking, conflict and social media – topics that weigh heavily on many parents' minds... highly recommended for its compelling blend of research and real-world application'

Dr Bettina Hohnen, Clinical Psychologist and Senior Teaching Fellow at UCL, and author of *The Incredible Teenage Brain*

'A tour de force. Matilda Gosling, building on her unique reputation as the integrator of scientific evidence with parenting advice, has produced a most valuable summary of developmental, psychiatric and neuroscience knowledge about the teenage years in a language accessible to all to offer sound advice to parents facing the inevitable challenges of supporting young people growing up in the twenty-first century. A book that will help all parents who want to base their parenting on facts rather than fiction'

Professor Peter Fonagy, National Clinical Advisor on Children's Mental Health, NHS England

*For all the teenagers*

# CONTENTS

*Introduction*   1

**1**   A recap and an introduction to teenagers   5
    *Key parenting evidence*   5
    *Who is this evolving human?*   10
    *Forging an identity*   19
    *Chapter summary*   23

**2**   Your relationship with each other   27
    *Shifting dynamics*   27
    *Strengthening your relationship*   31
    *Managing conflict*   41
    *Maintaining your equilibrium*   51
    *Chapter summary*   55

**3**   Other connections   59
    *Friendships*   59
    *Love and desire*   67
    *The online world*   74
    *Chapter summary*   88

**4**   Mind, part 1: mood and maturity   93
    *Mood*   93
    *Maturity and independence*   100

| | | |
|---|---|---|
| | *Secrets, revelations and lies* | 108 |
| | *Chapter summary* | 115 |
| **5** | **Mind, part 2: mental health and resilience** | **119** |
| | *Anxiety and sadness* | 119 |
| | *Gender identity* | 129 |
| | *Resilience and healthy stress* | 137 |
| | *Chapter summary* | 144 |
| **6** | **Body** | **149** |
| | *General health during puberty* | 149 |
| | *Appearance and body image* | 156 |
| | *Girls and boys* | 161 |
| | *Sexual harassment* | 163 |
| | *Chapter summary* | 167 |
| **7** | **Risk and reward** | **173** |
| | *Reasons for risk-taking* | 173 |
| | *Sex and porn* | 179 |
| | *Drink and drugs* | 193 |
| | *Managing risky behaviour* | 197 |
| | *Chapter summary* | 204 |
| **8** | **Equipping a future adult** | **211** |
| | *Building a well-rounded person* | 211 |
| | *Permission to fail* | 225 |
| | *Chapter summary* | 227 |
| *Acknowledgements* | | 231 |
| *Endnotes* | | 233 |

# INTRODUCTION

We have a deep-seated cultural myth that teenagers are unfathomable. They're akin to a different species who leave behind them a slipstream of havoc. We're taught this by angst-ridden coming-of-age films and novels, and the wry grenades lobbed our way by older generations while we're wrestling our toddlers – 'Just wait for the teenage years.'

The truth, as with most things, is more complicated. This book draws together evidence about teenagers, with the intention of replacing myth with knowledge and stereotype with data. It weaves together research studies with expert knowledge from the fields of adolescent psychology, biology and neuroscience, family systems, relationships and others to offer parents a clear understanding of what it means to be a teenager today, how they develop, the hazard points and developmental opportunities, and how best to support them as they navigate their labyrinthine and very personal route to adulthood.

This book is for everyone with an interest in teenagers – but it's predominantly written with parents, step-parents and other caregivers in mind, using the shorthand of 'parents' for ease. If you're a teacher, adolescent psychotherapist or someone else who wants to understand the teenage mind, and assuming you're happy to filter out some of the more parent-specific ideas, there's plenty of information in here for you, too.

Chapter 1 offers a brief recap of key cross-cutting evidence on good parenting – as originally set out in this book's predecessor, *Evidence-Based Parenting* – with thoughts on how to apply these research findings to the particular context of teenagers. The chapter summarises modern adolescence and how teenagers forge their eventual adult identities. Chapter 2 looks at parents' relationships with their teenagers, encompassing the shifting dynamics that are inevitable during the teenage years, how to manage conflict and how parents can maintain their equilibrium through any turbulence. Chapter 3 addresses other connections in the form of friendships, love and desire, and the online world.

Teenage minds are sufficiently complex to warrant two chapters. Chapter 4 encompasses mood, maturity and independence, and the increasing propensity for cards to be held close to teenage chests. Chapter 5 explores anxiety and sadness, gender identity – whatever your views on the wider debate relating to sex and gender, this is increasingly affecting teenagers' lives – and resilience, including the need for teenagers to experience healthy stress. Chapter 6 focuses on the body, covering puberty and general health, appearance and body image, and the biologically and socially driven differences between girls and boys. Chapter 7 is about risk and reward. It looks at why teenagers might take risks, sex and porn, drink and drugs, and how to manage risky behaviour as a parent. Finally, Chapter 8 covers equipping a future adult, including how to support your teenager to become a well-rounded person, the importance of giving them permission to fail and how to help them become a perfectly imperfect adult.

The word 'teenagers' is a mild misnomer. I've used it to encompass the body of research on adolescents, most commonly referring to those between the age of ten and adulthood. I've chosen this terminology because 'adolescents' is a little clunkier and colder than the word 'teenagers'. You can assume when reading that the cited research covers pre-teenagers as well as teenagers themselves. Some of the studies relate to a narrower age range – early adolescents, for example – and where this is important to any conclusions inferred from the research, I've made it clear.

Some of the caveats I made in *Evidence-Based Parenting* remain true for *Teenagers*. Having a link between two areas – increased time on social media, for example, and worse mental health – doesn't mean that one element necessarily causes the other. Often, two linked factors will feed off each other, or be driven by some other, underlying cause (such as less time spent outside, independent of adult oversight) – or, most likely, represent a complicated mesh of different links and relationships, much of which we don't yet have enough information to begin to unpick.

In recognition of the fact that teenagers have a rightful need to guard their privacy, I've only attributed stories when they're not personal. I've therefore anonymised stories belonging to friends and family when they stray into the private realm.

In some other ways, *Teenagers* takes a different approach to *Evidence-Based Parenting*. There's much less in the way of common experience by the teenage years, and teenage outcomes are partly driven by earlier parenting and life experiences. They're also more likely to be fired in the crucible of trial-and-error parenting, as well as by myriad other ingredients, often outside parents' control. There's less ability to learn from other parents during our children's adolescence – they have increasingly different personalities, interests, relationships and experiences, and our teenagers are less likely to share the intimate details of their lives. Moreover, rapid changes mean that what worked to smooth ruffled feathers six months ago may have no hope of working today.

## TEENAGERS: THE EVIDENCE BASE

Anyone who's read my first book will know that I don't believe in a sweeping, one-size-fits-all approach to parenting younger children. For teenagers, this is even more true. For this reason, I've focused more on understanding individual differences and fortifying human relationships – underpinned by the evidence-based but generalised idea (I didn't promise not to make exceptions) that all teenagers need guardrails in the form of parents' boundaries.

# CHAPTER 1

# A RECAP AND AN INTRODUCTION TO TEENAGERS

## Key parenting evidence

In some important ways, being the parent of a teenager isn't so different from being the parent of a younger child, however much you might struggle to believe it if you're waiting anxiously for your child to get home safely and wondering if those are alcohol fumes you smell when they do. In *Evidence-Based Parenting*, I explored some cross-cutting parenting approaches that are useful across many different situations – several of these can work across the ages, too, and I'll set them out briefly in this section.

The starting point is you and, if they're in your child's life, the other parent. You are the centre of gravity for your child: the axis around which they spin, whatever else might be happening in their lives. It may be that they're going through a break-up, or they're experiencing the giddy feeling that comes from the end of exams, or the hormonal shifts and brain changes that come with puberty are making them feel Lana Del Rey levels of melancholy. Having a warm, centred, available parent helps them to navigate everything else within their lives, even if they're working very hard to make you believe they're independent. This gives you, as their lodestar, permission to prioritise your well-being, first and foremost – if you're sleeping well, exercising, making time to throw pots or read novels, or doing whatever else it is that props up your own mental and physical health, your teenager will be better off.[1]

And it's a good idea to make sure your relationship with your partner (if you have one) is in reasonable shape, if you can.[2] All relationships go through rough patches, at which point couples' counselling can be useful[3] – or, more affordably, you could try watching videos put out by individual and organisational experts like The Gottman Institute on YouTube.[4] A research review has found that online relationship education, even without support from professionals, can be helpful.[5] It goes without saying that the source of this education should be someone with credentials – and perhaps not the influencers telling you to build your relationship with your partner by jointly cleaning your chakras.

Learning how to handle your emotions, if you're someone quick to feel anger or sadness, is likely to be useful for your teenager, as is helping them to do the same.[6] One way to do this is to be clear to your teenager that their emotions are genuine, whether or not you believe they're warranted, and merit discussion.[7] If my teenager rages at me that she shouldn't have to unload the dishwasher when she needs to revise for her mock exams, we can discuss – perhaps at a slightly calmer moment – the underlying pressure on her from multiple sources and other reasons she might feel angry. At the same time, I can hold the line that she needs to contribute to family life and make it clear that her anger can be expressed without shouting at me. (Or I can get cross with her. The original driver for researching this book was that I get things wrong, regularly.)

There are things to avoid as a parent and as a family. Conflict can be constructive,[8] but not if it's at unhealthy levels.[9] If the exchanges of insults between you and your teenager have reached Premier League calibre or family dinners are marked by rows, it's probably time to take action. Household chaos is another area to minimise, where possible.[10] It's measured by a lack of family routines, lots of noise, background TV and an absence of calmness, among other things.[11] Routines are important for teenagers, independently of household chaos measures.[12] It's probably fair to say that chaos varies by time of day and occasion. My home's more chaotic on a weekday morning – with the radio on, cereal bowls clustering on every worktop and regular yells of 'Has anyone seen my [schoolbag/Chromebook/scientific calculator/right shoe]?' – than it is at 8 a.m. on a winter Saturday, when the dog and I are the only ones up, and I can quietly watch the sunrise over a cup of coffee.

Harsh discipline goes on the Avoid List, too. This means trying not to threaten your teenager and to avoid yelling at them if they don't behave as you would like. I'm sure most of us are occasionally guilty of both these things – in my experience, it's very hard not to shout when the dog has just run off with the third pat of butter in a week after it's been left carelessly on the edge of the countertop. (The dog has a table-height snout and is terribly trained.) But harsh discipline is linked to teenagers both feeling and behaving worse than they do without it.[13]

Also on The List is psychological control.[14] This can be linked to short-term compliance[15] but tends to lead to a longer-term increase in problematic behaviour.[16] Psychological control entails making your teenager feel guilty about what they've done or said. It should probably be distinguished from being clear about the consequences of their actions – for example, if you've asked them only to eat and drink downstairs, but they ignore you and then spill hot chocolate indelibly into the carpet (this is a real example, a reminder of which I get to witness every time I go to bed or come down to breakfast), it seems reasonable to be clear about the outcome without getting overly guilt-trippy. I probably failed on this last point.

Psychological control is also measured by withdrawing your affection or attention – for example, by withholding eye contact from your child – if they've upset you, by using threats to induce anxiety, and dismissing or minimising what your teenager has said to you. My maternal grandmother had a catchphrase that beautifully illustrated this last point, which she would wheel out every time my mother or I said anything that didn't conform perfectly to her world view. 'Oh, don't be so ridiculous.' I remember being cut down by those five words and how small that made me feel – and how much I resented that feeling.

Enmeshment – which happens when relationships are interlaced to such an extent that boundaries are lacking – warrants attention if you think it might be an issue in your family.[17] You might be contributing to an enmeshment scenario if you want to know everything about your child's life, if you expect them to have the same opinions as you, or if you rely too heavily on them for emotional support. You can help to avoid enmeshment by respecting your teenager's boundaries and ensuring they have plenty of opportunity to assert their independence (see Chapter 4).

## LINKS BETWEEN HOME ENVIRONMENT AND TEENAGE TRAITS[18]

| AUTHORITATIVE HOMES | AUTHORITARIAN HOMES |
|---|---|
| • Responsible<br>• Self-assured<br>• Competent | • Dependent and passive<br>• Less adept and assured<br>• Intellectually incurious |
| **PERMISSIVE HOMES** | **INDIFFERENT HOMES** |
| • Immature<br>• Irresponsible<br>• Conforming to peers | • Impulsive<br>• Risk-taking<br>• Prone to delinquent behaviour |

A more positive step you can take is to aim for an authoritative parenting style.[19] This means loads of warmth coupled with plenty of guidance and limits (see Chapter 4). Authoritative parents show their love, give their teenagers good dollops of support when they need it and set boundaries (for example, by ensuring their children don't stay up all night gaming and allow themselves enough time to do their homework). Another model known as 'sensitive attunement' has been suggested by researchers. This is similar to authoritative parenting, and involves being positive and respectful when engaging with your teenager, keeping an eye on their behaviour and communicating openly.[20]

Being able to communicate well with your teenager includes talking about your opinions and your feelings,[21] while being careful not to step into the degree of emotional support that can characterise enmeshment. I might tell my daughter I'm excited about a new research project, nervous about an upcoming presentation or still grieving the loss of my dad. I won't tell her if I'm experiencing a rocky relationship patch, or tell her about my grief in a way that would make her feel it's her responsibility to give me comfort.

Finally, consistent discipline is important,[22] as is flexibility[23] and being confident in your abilities as a parent[24] (despite your teenager's potential attempts to convince you otherwise. There's only a very small link between how parents view their parenting and how their teenagers perceive it. Parents are more likely to believe they're parenting well than their children are to think so.[25]) This book can give you the evidence. Only you know how to apply it in your particular circumstances with your unique teenager. You're well qualified for the job of seeing this human into adulthood. Also, as I said in my last book, it's OK to mess up from time to time – and undoubtedly important for your teenager that you do. That way, they can see that fallibility is part of the human experience.

## Who is this evolving human?

For some parents, the teenage years roll in like a gradually shifting weather front. The skies may occasionally cloud over but they remain, for the most part, clear and predictable. For others, storms ebb and flow, rocking family stability and leaving parents desperately nostalgic for a small, warm body wrapped around them in the shared peace of a bedtime story. The humdrum reality for most of us is that it's sometimes so tempestuous that it's impossible to remember the calm – and at other times, in moments of plain sailing and satisfying glimpses of our future adult, we struggle to remember the turbulence of the shifting seas.

The teenage years, though, are unlikely to be marked only by squalls. Many of us have absorbed the 'storm and stress' model of adolescence through popular culture, but more recent research suggests it's unhelpful as an exclusive lens through which to view teenage development.[26] Rebellion and defiance, which are often marked by a sudden, 180-degree revolution from calm to chaos, aren't necessary for healthy development,[27] while teenagers' emotional shifts are gradual[28] and personality changes are small.[29] The extent to which the storms engulf teenagers varies, too, in accordance with the people and ideas around them, with adolescents showing different levels of internal and external struggle depending on the country in which they grow up.[30]

There are also risks attached to typecasting teenage behaviour and feelings in the way that the storm and stress model invites us to do, as parents' stereotypes are linked to their teenagers' later behaviour.[31] In other words, your beliefs may get confirmed by your child. If I expect my daughter to erupt when I ask her to put away her clothes, towel, shampoo, candles and seventeen mystery face products after she's had a bath, I'll probably sound exasperated when I ask her, making said eruption more likely. (Resetting my expectations here may be challenging – history does have a habit of informing our predictions.)

And these stereotypes do not hold true for teenagers as a whole. Recent international research has found that teenage behaviour tends to be more positive than it is negative, and this is true across different cultures.[32] The storm and stress model, on the other hand, foretells pretty dreadful behaviour. Dr G. Stanley Hall, who originally coined the term back in 1904, suggested that adolescents are cruel and lazy, and that they lie and steal.[33] They may be and do all of these things from time to time – but most humans are surely guilty of the first three, at least on occasion. The model also leaves out the many upsides of the teenage years – among much else, it's a time of curiosity, creativity and feeling deeply.

Another area in which our commonly held ideas about teenagers prove inadequate is in the link between brain development and risk. The stereotype is that teenagers' brains are too immature to be able to make sensible decisions about rock-jumping or that little white pill their friend has slipped them at a gig. But teenagers' approach to risk is driven more by the way they process information that comes from the world around them than it is by immaturity. They become more sensitive to rewards, other people's emotions and social feedback, and this sensitivity is related to the risks they take.[34] Chapter 7 has more information on this.

Some incredible things happen over this period. According to *Scientific American*, the 'computational bandwidth' of the brain increases by a factor of 3,000 between a child's birth and the time they reach adulthood.[35] It's little wonder teenagers sleep so much. The number of synapses in the brain increases around puberty and starts to decline again a little while afterwards. The structure of synapses also reorganises itself at around this time, which can disrupt key processes – for example, the ability to recognise other people's faces or to work out what they might be thinking.[36] Adolescence is also a period during which children develop the ability to think about thinking. This isn't just biological – it's probably driven by a pressure to fit in and by the emergence of crushes.[37] These new ways of thinking drive creativity and a fresh perspective on the world.[38]

There's a popular idea among people who write about teenagers and young adults, and a research literature to back it up, that proper maturity isn't reached until the age of about twenty-five.[39] But a recent paper drew together four datasets containing information about more than 10,000 children and young adults, and found that by one measure of maturity – executive function, which covers skills such as self-control and flexible thinking – teenagers tend to stabilise to adult levels between the ages of eighteen and twenty.

This paper argued that earlier research showing later maturity was based on theory, rather than real-world observations, or looked at an overly narrow range of measures.[40]

These years are marked by an increasing drive to be autonomous and to try out different ways of being so, while each teenager's social world aligns itself with that of their peers.[41] Teenagers may seek more independence from their parents due to hormonal changes, brain development and desire for a sexual partner.[42] The clay has started to harden on their general personality by this stage,[43] but the effects of puberty continue apace.

Parents, sometimes harshly and occasionally with charm, start to be given the cold shoulder. My own mum swears I was horrible between the ages of nine and eighteen, which makes me want to yell at her that she's ruining my life and slam the bedroom door shut. It's normal for a teenager to try to separate from you and to do this in a way that hurts. Here are some things I have been told in the years immediately before or after the teens are reached: *Get out. I don't want you in here. I hate you. Can I leave home when I'm sixteen? Why are you such a control freak? Why are you so difficult? Leave me alone. Don't touch me.* There's also the go-to *Could you NOT?*, which is remarkable in its applicability to almost every situation (and all the more cutting as a result). It's bruising. It's horrendous. When you are operating on little sleep or under high stress, it can feel soul-flattening. But it's standard. It means your teenager feels safe enough to push you away.

More likeably, when I was badgering my daughter (amusingly, and with GIFs) about taking up football, she texted me, 'Bye bye x'. End of conversation; gate locked; drawbridge raised. When attempts are made to shut communication lines down, it's parents' job to keep them open – if only with a flickering, intermittent connection – because teenagers, whatever their instincts say, will be lost without them.[44] I can probably dial down the football badgering, though.

If you're feeling excluded from your child's life, it might be time to manage your expectations. Rare, surface-level chats don't mean that something is amiss, necessarily.[45] You might also need to remind yourself of the natural self-absorption of teenagers, and that there's probably no malign intent behind their words or actions – even if you've just picked them up from a party or ironed their school uniform to a thudding silence in place of any acknowledgement. Defensiveness is best avoided, but you can certainly be assertive if you think some better parental treatment is in order.

There's a disconnect between teenagers' need for parental approval and a commonly held misconception that their parents are thinking about them critically. When you (genuinely) criticise your teenager, they typically feel it deeply, but the parts of their brain that allow them control over their feelings show less activity in brain scans than when you're discussing more neutral topics.[46] In other words, your child isn't being deliberately difficult when they scream at you for saying they've left the bathroom in a mess – instead, the parts of their brains that would allow a more measured response aren't quite in alignment yet.

It's hard to guess what a teenager might be thinking and feeling. An uncommunicative, grouchy toddler is probably the wrong temperature, tired, hungry or in need of some attention. A teenager in a similar mood, on the other hand, might have one of a hundred things going on. Perhaps their hormones are raging. Perhaps they're feeling excluded on social media. Perhaps they want more space but don't know how to get it. Perhaps they've suddenly decided you're not as nice as Toby's mum. Who knows? You don't, and probably never will. It's possible – even likely – that *they* don't know. The uncertainty can make it hard to work out how to respond.

An invisible wall often prevents teenagers sharing their emotions with their parents, and parental uncertainties can be compounded by rapid shifts in mood.[47] What teenagers do with their feelings can vary by sex – girls may be more likely to engage in parental battles when they feel angry, whereas boys can hole up in their room.[48] (This is, of course, an average and therefore a generalisation. I've witnessed room-cave tendencies in girls.) The psychotherapist Philippa Perry suggests you imagine your teenager experiencing emotions in colour, while you experience them in monochrome.[49]

There's a yawning gulf between what parents and teenagers think they understand about each other and what they actually understand. One study team placed fifty families, each with two parents and a teenager, in a lab. They videoed these families talking about areas on which they disagreed. Researchers then took family members into separate rooms, played them the video discussion and asked them to describe what they were thinking at each moment of the playback. They were also asked what they believed other family members to be thinking. Three quarters of the time, they were wrong.[50]

There are some clues you may be able to use to work out how your teenager is really thinking and feeling, assuming they're not keen to share. One thing you can do is to look at your child's behaviour – they can be more likely to act up when they feel deeply unhappy. Another is to consider how you're feeling when you're talking to each other. A teenager's emotions may be transferred, subtly and unconsciously, to the parent.[51] If I'm feeling frustrated and on edge when talking to my child about her maths revision, it may be that she's feeling this way about her upcoming exam. You can also think about whether your child's basic needs are being met – do they have reasonable, age-appropriate levels of autonomy, are they supported to feel competent and to deal with the challenges they face, and do they have decent enough relationships with the people around them?[52] This point about decent relationships is notwithstanding the fact that you'll probably be held at a slight distance while your child attempts to do their job of separating from you.

As well as misconstruing each other's thoughts, teenagers and their parents tend to have quite different perceptions of the relationship. This is true even of something simple like how much time they spend with each other. Using a dataset of several thousand teenagers, one American study found that teenagers think they spend about fifteen hours a week in the company of their mums – whereas the mothers think they spend twenty-four hours together.[53] In other words, mothers' estimation of the amount of time spent together is 60% higher than that of their teenagers. (Twenty-four hours, to me, sounds like loads – which makes me wonder, of course, where I have gone wrong.) And some parents believe their teenagers no longer care what their parents think about them. They do care, though, despite their increasing orientation towards their friends.[54]

Differences in perceptions extend beyond thoughts, feelings and relationships to things as mundane (yet important) as how chaotic your home life is. If you believe you live in order and calm, and you have plenty of family routines, it may be worth asking your teenager what their views are on these things. Teenagers may see these matters more negatively than their parents and, if so, they risk having worse well-being than they would if they saw these aspects in a more positive light.[55] Asking this question might help you to work out what would help your teenager to perceive the environment at home more positively.

One task for parents during this period is to let teenagers experience (safe, legal) things for themselves, despite the potential to be hurt, and to be there for them as needed. Learning by experience informs teenagers' future behaviour.[56] My daughter probably isn't going to listen if I warn her that one of her friends can behave viciously towards her. She's much more likely to look out for future warning signs once the so-called friend has brought her unpleasantness fully into the light. There's more on this in Chapter 8.

Teenagers' life satisfaction is linked to how admiring their parents are of them, according to one international study, as measured (for example) by their parents letting them know they're good at lots of things.[57] There's probably a fine line here between letting your child know they are competent, and that you like and admire them, and slipping into unhealthy levels of child worship. There's a protective shield built into parent–teenager relationships here, as the generational gap means you're destined never to understand certain decisions – and therefore unlikely to descend into uncritical exaltation. I will never comprehend, for example, why my daughter would choose to wear the inch-long acrylic nails that prevent her from heading out to the climbing wall. We are, in some ways, from two different species.

Teenagers can mark their increasing independence through emotional autonomy. They show new levels of defiance at decisions they dislike, backed up by a mint-fresh realisation that adults can be wrong about an awful lot of things.[58] Parents get rudely toppled from the lofty pedestals on which they previously stood. At the same time, their younger teenagers may be showing a contradictory hankering for the trappings of being much younger than they are – they want to be cosseted, to enjoy their leisure time and to avoid the responsibility of chores or picking up after themselves (you may need to push the chores, constantly and tirelessly, to avoid you having to do everything on their behalf – as your beloved no doubt intends).

Volumes of research on teenagers have been published over the last 100 years or so, but in some fundamental ways, our understanding of teenagers hasn't shifted. Anna Freud, a psychoanalyst and daughter of Sigmund, wrote in 1936:

> Adolescents are excessively egoistic, regarding themselves as the centre of the universe and the sole object of interest, and yet at no time in later life are they capable of so much self-sacrifice and devotion. They form the most passionate love relations, only to break them off as abruptly as they began them. On the one hand they throw themselves enthusiastically into the life of the community, and on the other hand they have an overpowering longing for solitude… They are selfish and materially minded and at the same time full of lofty idealism… At times their behaviour to other people is rough and inconsiderate, yet they themselves are extremely touchy. Their moods veer between light-hearted optimism and the blackest pessimism. Sometimes they will work with indefatigable enthusiasm and at other times they are sluggish and apathetic.[59]

But this description risks us seeing teenagers as a uniform group. The reality is they vary hugely. Some go through extreme emotional swings. Others do not. And in the time since, as we've seen, the storm and stress model has developed and was then shown to be inadequate. But most parents will recognise at least intermittent squalls. And those parents at the Severe Weather Warning end of the teenage spectrum may benefit from knowing that the portrait their child displays to other adults is probably the person they will become. If your child is sullen and uncommunicative with you but friendly, polite and funny in the company of Auntie Joan, it's this more appealing version that's likely to constitute their adult self.

This is no reflection on you – you are their safe harbour who (sometimes to mostly) allows the full range of their feelings to be tested and expressed. There's a Kevin the Teenager sketch by comedian Harry Enfield in which Kevin's friend Perry is over for tea. Kevin, having just bellowed at his mother, is impossibly polite to Perry's mum when she calls the landline asking to speak to Perry. Perry picks up the phone and roars, 'WHAT? No, I don't want to. No. It's so unfair. I hate you.' He slams the phone down, gesticulates at it wildly and then smiles fondly at Kevin's mum. 'I've got to go now, Mrs Patterson. Thank you!'[60]

Be optimistic. If your child was once charming but is no longer – at least not to you – the chances are that, one day soon, they will be again.

## Forging an identity

Teenagers tend to try on various identities before they commit to a set of values and beliefs.[61] They might define themselves by the sports they play, their favourite music or the clothes they wear, but also by deeper things – what it means to live a fulfilling life, what job they might want to do, or how they want to treat others and be treated themselves.

I used to dance slightly frantically between identities as a teenager – I'd change my handwriting every few weeks, as it never seemed to represent quite how I viewed myself, and my chosen career would change almost weekly. I wanted to be a doctor (hindered by my dislike for science and a nausea when I consider what happens beneath human skin), a lawyer (I wasn't keen on following structure or tight processes), an artist (foiled by insufficient talent), a diplomat (I'm terrible at arguing for things I don't believe in) and a politician (criticism destroys me). Everything was the right fit until it was the wrong one. But there was such promise and opportunity attached to every new identity cloak – the pleasure came from stepping lightly into each one to see how it felt.

One theory of identity development proposes three main approaches to its formation. Teenagers might rely on outside information to help them construct an identity – they try different options according to the world around them and make changes if they come across information that conflicts with their sense of self. Others might construct their identities based on those of their parents or other authority figures. A third set of teenagers avoid any thoughts of identity until they're forced to – if, for example, they have to choose a set of A levels that will naturally shut off a large number of future careers. These teenagers acquire an identity that's forged more by randomness than it is by self-determination.[62]

It's fair to say the first two groups are probably the healthiest. Exploration of identity is easier for teenagers whose parents are authoritative and give them plenty of room both to try things out and to get to know themselves.[63] You might see your teenager's friendship groups shifting rapidly as they explore their identity, or perhaps you witness their interests changing – one week they're at the boxing gym and the next it's all about track and field or quilting. Changes in friendship groups may reflect ongoing processes of identity development. These shifts can make teenagers feel unhappy and isolated – older friendships tend to offer more support than newer ones, and growing apart from long-standing friends can feel incredibly difficult.[64] If your child doesn't seem unhappy, though, these changes in friendships and interests are probably nothing to worry about.

A difference between our own experience of identity development and that of our children, unless we're very youthful, is the effect of social media. In one view, social media allows teenagers to try out different personas. They can simultaneously be an Instagram artist and a Reddit intellectual. But at the same time, social media drives teenagers to conform to global trends and may distract them from the very important task of self-reflection and insight. It also bears the risk of making identity experimentation fossilise into something that's hard to shrug off – unlike the echoes of a conversation in the school canteen, there's a permanent record: a public transcript of every conversation and fleeting statement.[65]

Your influence is likely to be limited unless your child is one of those who adopt their parents' identities as their own. Your teenager's friendships will, almost certainly, influence their identity more strongly than you do.[66] There may be areas, though, in which your influence is unwittingly exasperating to your identity-flexing teenager – if they're trying to separate from you, any traits you have that they want to adopt become a source of deep frustration (they are yours, but they want them for themselves). At the same time, any traits you have that they've rejected become irritating, too.

We become a ball of vexation, as far as our teenager is concerned. My daughter might become annoyed by me listening to classical music while cooking dinner. (She hates it! It's so boring! *Why* would I want to listen to anything created by *dead white men*?) At the same time, she might deeply resent the parts of me she sees in herself – perhaps she's developing an interest in an author or subject I love, so we reach a tacit understanding that we Will Not Discuss my own thoughts about it. And we will certainly not discuss the Kurt Cobain poster on her wall, even if he is a dead white man.

A key role for adults when it comes to identity development is encouraging teenagers to experiment and explore.[67] You're sailing a boat propelled by a healthy following breeze when it comes to your input here, as teenage identity experimentation is embraced by society as normal.[68] My daughter's probably going to be more comfortable trying on a new identity if I'm accepting and curious (but not, of course, annoyingly so) than she is if I express surprise that she's moved on from last month's interests and presentation.

There are certain areas in which you might need to be more careful – those in which peer-influenced identity can lead to poorer outcomes for your child, or where your child is closing off the ability to change their mind later. The key point about identity is that it's fluid. The end of the teenage years seems to be more important for identity development than any earlier time,[69] and there's evidence to suggest that identity development continues into adulthood.[70] Helping your teenager to keep their options open is therefore vital.

Parents also need to be cautious when it comes to negative identity labels. If teenagers see themselves as being a 'risk-taker', for example, they can take on the mantle of this label in how they permanently see themselves.[71] The same point no doubt applies to other negative labels – if your child sees themselves as 'troubled', say, or 'anxious'. The risks of children identifying with mental health conditions are explored in Chapter 5. It's all too easy to ascribe labels linked to our negative assessment of our own traits, too – 'He's scatty, like me' or 'She gives up on things easily, like I do.'

Again, keeping things open is likely to be useful – the danger comes when negative ideas get internalised and made concrete, or when identity becomes crystallised too soon.

# CHAPTER SUMMARY

## Teenagers

- **The myth of storm and stress.** The legendary teenager who rages, tears apart relationships and pushes the edges of every boundary might exist, but they're not the norm – and if this is what you witness in your teenager, it won't be the same from day to day or month to month. Healthy development doesn't depend on the emotional turbulence that many of us have come to expect from teenagers, and any storms tend to blow themselves out. Teenagers' later behaviour can be informed by stereotypical beliefs their parents hold about them – if you have negative expectations of your child, they're more likely to end up acting these out. Adolescent behaviour tends to be more positive than it is negative, overall.
- **Brain changes.** Risk-taking is related more to the way that information is processed by teenage brains than it is to brain immaturity. Brains change tremendously over this period, and these changes may – among other things – affect teenagers' ability to work out what other people are thinking. They develop the ability to think about thinking during these years, generating a torrent of creativity. They reach adult levels of maturity, according to some measures, between the ages of eighteen and twenty – though some studies show brain development continuing beyond this point. There are some aspects of your teenager that a combination of genes and earlier life experiences will already have crystallised, and over which you may now have little influence.
- **A drive towards independence.** Your teenager isn't rejecting you when they try to put clear water between you (or, more accurately, they are rejecting you, but this is normal and necessary). They

need to learn to function without you in the world. At the same time, it's your job to keep communication lines open, however much your teenager's trying to shut them down – they still need you. Teenagers' natural propensity over this age range is to orient themselves more towards other people, and those who are the same age in particular.

- **Different perspectives.** When the perspectives of parents and teenagers diverge on an issue, it's teenagers' feelings that – perhaps unsurprisingly – are most likely to inform their outcomes. It's easier for teenagers to learn from experience than it is from our well-meaning advice.
- **Shifting feelings.** It's hard to work out what a teenager is thinking and feeling if they're not willing to share this with you. If they're acting up, they might be feeling unhappy. Your own feelings when you're talking to your teenager – frustration, anger, hurt, sadness – may provide clues as to their own internal state.
- **Identity development.** Identity exploration is a normal and natural part of teenage development. Teenagers can try on different identities according to the information they get from the world around them. Some keep those aspects that fit with their sense of self and reject others. Other teenagers may adopt the identities of their parents, while the identities of the rest are driven more by circumstance and being forced to make choices that close options down. Social media has a potentially huge (and, as yet, not fully understood) influence on teenagers' identities. Parents' influence is likely to be secondary to that of friends. Identity development continues beyond adolescence into adulthood.

## Ideas for parents

- **Look inwards.** Prioritise *your* well-being. You probably have more time now your child's a little older – use it wisely on things you enjoy. Learn how to manage your feelings if you're quick to react to things. Be optimistic if you find your relationship with your child challenging – things will improve again, in all likelihood. Don't worry too much if you face temporary setbacks in your relationship with each other. At the same time, you may need to lower your short-term expectations.

- **Look outwards.** If you have a partner, make sure your relationship's in a tolerable state. Couples' counselling or YouTube relationship education videos can be useful if it's not. Work to minimise conflict in the family if it's at unhealthy levels. Try to have household routines and minimise chaos, if you can.
- **Focus on how you relate to each other.** Aim for an authoritative parenting style, balancing warmth with limits. Make sure both you and your teenager are able to have boundaries. Acknowledge your child's feelings – this doesn't mean you have to agree with them or validate how they express these feelings – and discuss your own, ensuring you're not looking to your child for emotional support. Encourage your child to experiment and explore different identities, and to keep options open. Avoid harsh discipline and psychological control. Take guesswork out of it – you're unlikely to be able to pinpoint with any accuracy what your teenager is feeling. Consider asking your teenager what their perspectives are on things like family routines and household chaos.

Remember that everything else follows from your relationship with each other. Challenge any stereotypical beliefs you may have about your teenager's behaviour and development. Be assertive, not defensive, if your teenager's treatment of you needs work. Be consistent, but not to the point where you can't be flexible. Have confidence that you're the right person for the job of seeing your teenager safely into adulthood. Know that you'll make mistakes, and that this is fine – and is probably better than making none.

# CHAPTER 2

# YOUR RELATIONSHIP WITH EACH OTHER

**Shifting dynamics**

There's a moment when you realise that, at some forgotten juncture, you carried your child for the final time, read them their last chapter of a bedtime story or saw the end of an easy, uncluttered relationship in which there were no feelings or information they were trying to hold back. The new world order may be no worse. It may even be better – you can talk about ideas and share humour that's not just related to bodily functions. But it's certainly different from the one that preceded it.

There are many factors that change the shape of your relationship with your teenager, one of which is a necessary shift in power – when your child is younger, you have the lion's share (although, ideally, you'll have given them enough freedom that this power is flexed delicately), but your relationship needs to become one of greater equality by the time your child reaches adulthood.

I was apprehensive about my children's entry to the teenage years, due to the cultural myth of storm and stress that had woven itself into my knowledge of how much I hate conflict. But endless battles don't need to be a defining feature of your relationship, and manageable levels of conflict can be positive. It can serve as a useful mechanism to help teenagers to separate from parents and to reset the relationship to one that's more equal. I remind myself of this in mantra-like tones when bracing myself to ask my daughters to walk the dog or re-do the washing-up so the pans are cleaner than when they started.

There's a tension in the research here, though. The value of conflict is seen through gradually equalising the parent–child relationship, but boundaries and limits – which challenge this fragile equality – are still important. What are parents meant to do with this information? We're meant to be less controlling, but only sometimes. Research on teenage delinquency suggests it's probably a matter of degree – high and low levels of parental control are linked to worse outcomes for teenagers, but there's a sweet spot in the middle.[1]

Teenagers' desire for greater independence is part of the broader shift in power. This drive towards self-determination can make parents feel their authority is under threat or that they're no longer needed by their child. You are needed, of course – much as it might be hard to remember when you've just been told firmly that you're getting in the way of successful homework completion or a stomach-churning baking experiment. But these doubts and authority challenges may be at the heart of the less appealing elements of parents' changing relationships with their teenagers, as the mismatch in expectations undermines trust and underpins feelings of separation.[2] Teenagers' and parents' expectations about freedom are better matched by the end of adolescence, resulting in improved relationships.[3]

There are several other ways in which parent–child dynamics change during this period. An experimental study involving a stressful situation showed that parents' support reduced production of the stress hormone cortisol in younger children, but had no effect in adolescents.[4] Teenagers believe that trust between them and their parents dwindles between the early teenage years and the end of school, and they feel more alienated from their parents.[5] Feelings of closeness between teenagers and their parents, while high, also decline over this period.[6] This may be for the best – you need to know how to support a child who is struggling to make friends, but you might benefit from not knowing exactly how your eighteen-year-old spent their Saturday night.

But despite teenage moves to separate – and, perhaps, evidence to the contrary – teenagers tend to like and feel close to their parents.[7] And while some teenagers perceive relationship difficulties with their parents over adolescence, others may sense improvements. Overall, though, there's a sharp fall between the ages of twelve and sixteen in the proportion of teenagers who believe their parents are both supportive and powerful, and an increase in those who perceive turbulence. A course correction then takes place – relationships tend to improve again between the ages of sixteen and twenty.[8] I keep this nugget in mind during moments when it's harder to find perspective.

Much of the popular narrative about parent–teenager relationships misses what's good. When your child's older and has a tendency to duck affection, a proactive hug can take your breath away; and the intellectual challenge of a dinner-table debate brings an entirely new dimension to your relationship. I enjoy my daughters' company now, most of the time, in a way that I could never have imagined when they were younger. The narrative also misses the things you won't be sorry to leave in the past – you no longer have to be woken by a small finger worming its way into your ear at 5 a.m., or to swim through hairbergs and slicks of Lynx at the local leisure centre. And it misses the many positive ways a parent can shape their teenagers' well-being and worlds. Parents still tend to have the greatest influence on their children's decisions, despite the increasing importance of friends,[9] and are central in shaping their attitudes.[10]

Even when things are really hard – or perhaps especially when they are – it can be worth looking for the upsides of your changing relationship with each other. Aggressive or immature teenage behaviour often leads parents to respond harshly or to become distant with their teenagers, whereas more positive traits such as curiosity and self-assurance can lead parents to be warm and flexible.[11] These patterns lead to positive or negative feedback loops. Looking for the good things, or for underlying explanations for the bad, may help to interrupt any negative cycles. If my teenager is having a row with a friend, or going through something else that's making her unhappy and sulky at home, I can (and frequently do, despite my best intentions) interpret her behaviour as a mark of her disdain for me and respond defensively. If I can search for the positive moments and for the possible underlying reasons for her behaviour, I'm less likely to want to give myself space by withdrawing from our relationship with each other.

A bedrock of your changing relationship is likely to be found in the push–pull forces drawing you towards the requisite balance when your child reaches adulthood. Independence and privacy are important to teenagers; they also need you to be able to set appropriate boundaries and to understand that you are non-negotiably entitled to know, within reason, what they're up to. The teenage years may well become a dance fashioned by the rhythm of these forces, with the parent and child both trying out different stances until each can accept the other's moves.

## Strengthening your relationship

My relationship with my daughters is sometimes golden. This is more common when we're all happy, and there are no massive stressors looming on our collective horizons. At other times, it frays at the edges. This might be because I am on edge, or my partner is – as a wise acquaintance once said to us, the two of us are the emotional thermostat of our family. I write this paragraph at a moment of research deadlines and hormonal changes, having spent too long at lunchtime clearing up unheeded breakfast crumbs and a colony of empty tea mugs, and knowing that the emotional temperature is going to be fiery this evening if I remain irate. My daughters, of course, are capable of throwing their own grenades into our relationship.

Your relationship with your child is likely to evolve gradually over the teenage years, as well as fluctuating in temperature and nuance from moment to moment. The psychiatrist Professor Daniel Siegel has written of his relationship with his daughter, 'She, and we, have moved from eye rolls and intense emotional wrestling over issues of what she wears, how long she stays out, and what movies she can see and with whom, to finding a mutual space of respect where we can say what we are concerned about and she can state what she needs, what she wants, and what her thinking is regarding these day-to-day decisions as well as major life choices.'[12]

Having a good relationship with your teenager doesn't just benefit you both directly. Its knock-on effects include the extent to which other strategies you employ to help your child are likely to work. A Swedish study that tracked 1,500 teenagers, for example, found that a positive emotional family climate made parenting strategies more likely to boost teenagers' well-being. Emotional climate was measured by the extent to which teenagers agreed with statements like, 'When I am angry, sad, or worried, my mother/father can make me feel better,'[13] which seems like a pretty good measure of their parents' relationship with them. A good relationship, then, is a cornerstone for other aspects of bringing up your child.

The strength of your relationship, crucial though it is, isn't the only thing that matters. It may be that your relationship is aggravated by the lines in the sand you draw on areas such as behaviour and safety – and it will be your knowledge of your teenager's needs as well as the amount of flex in your relationship that determines how you navigate these. Everyone's lines are different – I'm a pushover on my own personal boundaries, meaning I spend more of my week than I would like giving lifts and running errands, but get fierce about sleep and nutrition. The key thing, though, is that your teenager needs some limits – and these, perhaps surprisingly, can be good for your relationship. Research has shown that parental maintenance of firm, rational boundaries is linked to positive relationship outcomes – for example, low levels of conflict and high levels of teenage willingness to share information – even in the later teenage years.[14] There's more about boundaries in Chapter 4.

I realise this section may read as 'Be perfect and absorb whatever comes at you, even when it's the size and consistency of elephant dung.' It needs to be seen, though, through the lens of setting a minimum bar for your own treatment. You don't need to be an emotional punchbag for your child, nor to have constant composure. The information here should be considered alongside the sections on dealing with conflict, and on setting and maintaining boundaries. If you don't like how your child is treating you, you can be clear about what you expect from them, then walk away and close the door. They will almost certainly benefit from this, as will – in the medium term, if not through the immediate cascade of rage – your relationship with each other.

The other thing to remember when reading this section is that authenticity is key. According to Perry, a lack of this can rupture your relationship with your teenager.[15] Some of these ideas may not feel right or authentic to you – in which case, avoid them. Your child will notice if you're being bright and brittle in your attempts to keep your relationship on a steady course, which will undermine your efforts to do so. It's relatively easy to create a beautiful, polished veneer of seeming perfection; it's harder to talk to your child genuinely, in a way that meets their basic needs but through which you remain true to how you feel.

The quality of your relationship with your child is more likely to withstand their efforts to separate if you had a good relationship with them at the start of adolescence.[16] Of course, you have to work with what is possible in the moment. I know the impact of early separation on children, but I can't do anything now about the six weeks of maternity leave I took with my younger daughter or the regular overseas research trips I made when they were both small. I can only work with the here and now.

So what helps parents to maintain or strengthen their relationships with these growing humans whose brains are shapeshifting in ways we cannot imagine? The way we communicate with them is, of course, critical, and listening well is a central plank of this. A study about conflict, for example, found that teenagers and their parents were more likely to be satisfied if they'd taken time to listen to what the other party was saying and to validate each other's point of view.[17] Another study found that teenagers were less likely to tell their parents about experiences of discrimination if they believed their parents wouldn't listen well or would react badly.[18]

Listening well means being available – and not, as I am prone to do, rushing constantly from one task to the next without finding quiet spaces in which your child can start talking. The psychologist and teenage expert Dr Lisa Damour recommends taking a newspaper editor approach to your teenager's stories in order to listen well, imagining that you're listening to a first draft of a piece as your child is talking to you. 'Here's your task,' she explains. 'As soon as your reporter comes to the end of the article, you have to craft its headline. In other words, you need to distil a long and detailed story down to its compelling essence.'[19]

Another aspect of listening well involves being open to conversations in which your child wants to tell you what you're doing wrong.[20] This doesn't mean you need to place yourself in parental stocks while your child lobs verbal rotten eggs at you. You may, of course, choose to defend your original position once you've heard and acknowledged their feelings about the matter. If my twelve-year-old tells me she's unhappy that her phone apps stop working an hour before bedtime, I can explore what this means for her (perhaps her friends continue to play a game without her), empathise with her feelings about it, then reiterate my position on screens and sleep while agreeing with her about how frustrating she must find it.

Parents and their teenagers tend to have different views of what to talk about, which may be a contributing factor to those mealtimes when everyone's knackered and proffered topics get instantly shut down by a knitted-browed teenager. Following a teenager's lead can be helpful – it may be that they don't want to talk at all, or that there are things they want to chat about that you haven't considered. A study of more than a thousand teenagers found that topics they'd like to discuss with their parents include their relationship with them, as well as their parents' pasts.[21] If your teenager doesn't want to talk, you can make it clear you're available if and when they need it – and perhaps do something as simple as bring them unbidden cups of tea.

Speaking to the side of your teenager you want to see is something you can try when the less pleasant version has turned up to the conversation. It's a bit like a German weather house, which is a contraption that depicts the weather through two figurines. One emerges when it's fair and the other when it's wet. You can't see them both at once. In your conversations with your teenager, you may sometimes see the bad weather figurine – but if you speak to the one that represents sunshine and warm winds, it's more likely to make an appearance. Similarly, reframing how you see your child – trying to see them as friendly and socially minded, not grumpy and malign – may help you to communicate better with each other.[22] This may be hard, at times. (Me: 'Could you take the dog out for a walk, please?' My teenager: 'Stop having a go at me!'). It's a strategy that requires more patience than I usually possess.

Being present is another important step – trying to work out what's happening in the moment, and assessing your child's internal state as well as your own. According to Siegel, 'Being present for others means we resonate with what is going on in their inner worlds, creating the essential way we feel their feelings. This feeling felt sensation is at the heart of how we can help one another feel seen, safe, soothed, and secure.' Linking back to the point I made earlier about authenticity, you can also describe to your teenager what is happening in your mind – this means your thoughts and feelings, your hopes, and what you believe your child is trying to communicate.[23]

Physical presence is important, too. Your child may pretend otherwise, but teenagers tend to feel more secure when they know physically where you are and how they can find you.[24] Considering what your child might be thinking and feeling is a key element of being present. Parental empathy can lead to better relationships, and having a better relationship makes it easier to feel empathetic.[25]

Parents' empathy is also linked with lower physical signs of stress in their children.[26] The psychologist Rick Hanson suggests going beneath the surface of your interactions with your teenager if they are being irritating or dismissive towards you, to try to work out what might be causing them to act in this way. This process can spark compassion towards your child.[27] (Or not. Perhaps there is no deeper meaning, and your shiny new adolescent is simply being an arse.)

Asking lots of questions of your teenager is best avoided. This is something I find very hard not to do, even when the grunts I receive in response imply that I'd be better off meeting my own need for connection by calling a friend or my own mum. That said, you can use judicious gentle questioning alongside explanations, and acceptance of different opinions, to open up your teenager's world. The aim is to accept your child for who they are, while helping them to form and articulate their own world view.[28] They may be utterly wrong, but they have their whole lives ahead of them to re-evaluate these positions in line with accumulated wisdom and experience. Your role can therefore be more about healthy disagreement and acceptance of difference than about attempting to turn their opinions upside down.

Another way to connect is to try quietly reading the same books as them, if reading is something they're into, or listening to their music – if you can do this without annoying them, it gives you an avenue for discussion that follows their interests. Media and technology are good scaffolds for parent–teenager relationships. One study found that sixteen- to eighteen-year-olds in the United States typically swap five or six messages a day with their parents, and that these messages tend to be neutral or positive. Given how little time parents and teenagers spend together without anyone else present, the study team pointed out that these messages are likely to be an important way for them to communicate with each other.[29] This study was published in 2020 but used data from several years earlier. It's therefore possible the number of daily messages swapped between parents and teenagers has gone up significantly in the interim. (The UK average is pushed up, no doubt, by my younger daughter, who sends an endless string of messages each saying 'Mum!' if I haven't responded to her original missive within 2.7 seconds.)

A different group of scholars published a study in which nine in ten parents and teenagers said they've wrapped media into family traditions – they might, for example, play video games together on Christmas Eve. These traditions can help family members to feel secure and committed, and to have a sense of belonging. Eight in ten parents in this study used media to talk about serious issues with their teenagers that might not otherwise come up. Media use was linked to families getting along with each other better and communicating effectively.[30] Media can also be enlightening. I discovered, while watching *The Traitors Australia* with my daughters, that an Australian accent is impenetrable for British–Irish girls born a generation too late to have trained their ears on *Neighbours* and *Home and Away*.

Mealtimes are important, too. A survey of around 26,000 Canadian teenagers found a link between frequent family dinners and emotional well-being, as well as better behaviour and greater life satisfaction. The more habitual these dinners were, the better the teenagers' outcomes. Some of the positive effects were explained by the way parents and teenagers communicate with each other.[31] Presumably, communication is better if you have plenty of opportunity to practise over the shared ritual of breaking bread or eating endless plates of pasta – and teenagers are better off when they and their parents communicate well with each other.

Another thing that can help to strengthen or maintain your relationship with your teenager is to be wary of giving advice. This is almost impossible for me – I find even my sleep to be interrupted by dreams along the theme of 'Here is a problem! Let me find you a solution!' A teenager may not want advice. They may want to talk through their problem fully before starting to think about solutions, or to have their feelings about this problem acknowledged by you ('That sounds stressful – no wonder you felt upset') before any solutions are proposed. If your teenager talks about a problem with you, it's worth checking whether they want any help with it before you wade in with your (doubtless excellent and informed by decades of experience) tuppence worth.

Relationships can be damaged by something known in the research literature as 'inhibitory gatekeeping'. In a two-parent couple, this means one parent restricting the other's access to family life. In a study that gave me pause for thought, inhibitory gatekeeping attitudes were measured by agreement with statements that included: 'My spouse doesn't really know how to do a lot of household chores... so it is just easier if I do them' (he knows perfectly well, but see the next statement); 'I have higher standards than my spouse for how well cared for the house should be' (mild understatement); and 'I frequently re-do household tasks my spouse has not done well' (again, yes). Behaviours were measured by things of which I'm less likely to be guilty – taking sole charge of a child's feelings, medical care and discipline, and taking solo decisions on their behalf. If you read any of the behaviours or attitudes with the discomfort I did, your relationship with your teenager may be improved by opening the gate you have constructed.[32]

Humour, as with all relationships, is a great way to fill your reservoirs of shared warmth. Your relationship with your child can also be helped by apologising when you've got something wrong.

My partner is excellent at modelling this if he's been overly gruff or reactive with our girls. He'll often acknowledge the rupture and repair the situation with levity, while not undermining the significance of his earlier behaviour. An overly harsh response may be linked to how you are feeling in yourself. One study measured mothers' heart rates, blood pressure and negative emotional responses during an interaction task with their teenagers; when mothers were less reactive, they parented well and their relationship with their teenagers was better.[33] This may be a partial explanation as to why some of the general advice described in Chapter 1 on looking after your well-being is important. Parents are less likely to be emotionally reactive if they're feeling OK than if they're bearing a heavy burden of stress.

This need to look inwards brings us nicely on to the issue of parental flaws, which teenagers find themselves increasingly able to recognise as they hurtle towards adulthood. On the one hand, knowing their parents' limitations is important for teenagers – it helps them to see that they do not have to aim for perfection and supports their growing sense of independence. On the other hand, some research suggests worse outcomes for teenagers whose parents take the greatest tumbles from the thrones upon which they were once seated.[34]

I am hopeful, though, that this finding is based on teenagers recognising the faults of the older generation because they have bad relationships with their parents or due to objectively crap parenting, not because their parents have been honest about getting it wrong. My own children are all too aware of my neuroses and failures. They've seen me repainting the front room by hand three times in the space of a month because the shades weren't quite right. They have witnessed my control freakery over lights burning when there's nobody in the room and thermostats that have been whacked up while I wasn't looking. They're aware of a fractured end to the business I co-founded and ran for twelve years, which saw many relationships fall apart and people disappear from their lives. They know that I can't stop, even when I want to rest – something I desperately hope they won't end up mirroring. (Evidence suggests this isn't currently a risk.)

Finally, relationships – like parents – are never going to be perfect, and you may have to bear occasional ruptures in them. I had a moment of clarity when I realised my children were coming back from school, watching TV or talking to their friends – occasionally doing some homework, but basically taking a gorgeous chunk of uninterrupted leisure time. I was finishing work around six, tidying up the snacks they'd made and their bags and shoes strewn over the floor, throwing out the empty packets they'd left in the cupboards and the rubbish they'd left on the side. I'd then feed the dog, unload the dishwasher, put on a load of laundry and start cooking dinner. This would be interspersed with requests for them to put the occasional thing away ('Can you just get off my *case*? I just want *five minutes* to sit down without you *bugging me*') and complaints about what I was making for dinner ('You know I hate jacket potatoes/curry/eggs/gnocchi/chickpeas. Why can't you make something [one of two dishes] I actually like?').

My children are lovely. This anecdote does not back this statement up. Standards slip, parents get distracted or too busy to put the short-term structures in place that will save them time in the long term – or they can't face the conflict they know will ensue from mentioning these structures. But there will be, as I found, a point at which your reservoirs of patience run dry. Feeling like the household servant was the moment my final puddles drained away. There was short-term friction while I reminded my family of their responsibilities and my humanness. It was necessary pain.

## Managing conflict

Conflict plays an important function. It helps teenagers to separate from their parents, which they need to do to become healthy, functioning adults. It forges healthier patterns of communication, and can (honestly – The Research Says So™) strengthen your relationship with each other.[35] When teenagers feel safe to express their rage or other negative feelings with a parent, they can practise how to manage these feelings and how to be flexible. This isn't much fun in the moment, especially for the parent. But if adults can create a sense of safety for the teenager during any arguments – perhaps aiming for them to understand you'll still love them at the end of it and that you won't ground them for eternity – and both parties feel able to express a range of feelings, they tend to end up with a more balanced, reciprocal relationship with each other.[36] This is the long-term goal to remember, anyway, when you've just absorbed some potshots for undercooking the rice or for breathing too loudly.

It's estimated that one in ten families, at most, have to deal with deep-seated and increasingly serious arguments with their teenager – and for many of these, any difficulties are an extension of earlier challenges.[37] Most families, though, experience at least a degree of friction during the teenage years and, unless you have a highly unusual teenager, you'll have to deal with conflict from time to time (or even frequently). Assuming you've avoided the temptation of booking a one-way ticket to Rio, this section may help you to navigate these periods with an understanding of what may be driving the conflict and your options for handling it.

Here's a comforting fact to start us off. The amount of conflict between parents and their children falls over the teenage years. Among adolescents, it's worst for ten- to twelve-year-olds. If you're at the start of your teenager's journey, you're probably at the nadir right now. The intensity of conflict goes up, though, through to mid-adolescence, or thirteen- to sixteen-year-olds – so while you might fight less with your child, those fights *will* get worse. In both conflict rates and intensity the changes are small, leading a big review of studies to suggest that the supposedly heightened levels of conflict that come with a teenager are mythical.[38] This evidence provides further support for the inadequacy of the storm and stress model.

While fighting is unusual in parent–teenager relationships, bickering is common.[39] I can bicker endlessly with my daughters about laying the table, getting them to clear up after themselves or walking the dog. (Sample conversation. Me: 'Can you put away your breakfast things, please?' Her: 'Oh my God.' Me [imitating, because I'm a bad human]: 'Oh my God.' Her: 'Can you just *stop*?') There's more conflict between mothers and daughters, and between fathers and sons, over the teenage years than between opposite-sex pairings.[40] I write this, uneasily, with quite a few relevant years left to go.

In more positive news (for me, smugly, from the other side of it), conflict peaks in younger siblings at a younger age than it does in a family's oldest child – in first-born children, it tends to come to a head between the ages of twelve and fourteen, whereas it's nine to eleven for younger siblings. Conflict may hit younger children earlier because it spills over from arguments between parents and the oldest sibling. In even better news, conflict ebbs more quickly in younger siblings, probably because parents' baptism by fire from their oldest helps them to learn how to manage conflict effectively for the child or children who follow.[41]

At the roots of much family conflict are teenagers' attempts to assert their independence.[42] They might want to see their friends after school tonight while believing their homework can wait, to set the griminess standards for their bedrooms at Fungus the Bogeyman levels or to live their busy lives without the inconvenience of household chores. The flashpoints come at the intersection of parental demands and teenagers' perceptions that these demands impinge upon their expanding rights to make decisions that personally affect them. Detonation is sometimes postponed to the point at which a teenager has quietly not met certain requirements – to be home at a particular time, perhaps, or to remove the twenty-three dead plants they have relocated from their bedroom to the worktop downstairs (to use a personal and contemporaneous example).

There's more conflict when teenagers believe parents invade their privacy or are intrusive in other ways. There's a risk of getting sucked into pernicious negative feedback loops here, as teenagers are more likely to perceive privacy invasion when there's a lot of conflict.[43] There's also more conflict when parents use psychological control (for examples of this, see Chapter 1) in an attempt to influence their children's thoughts and feelings, and less when parents are supportive of their children's autonomy.[44] This autonomy still needs to be balanced with limits, as conflict is lower in families in which parents are authoritative.[45] Fine-tuning these limits is a matter for individual families, with a bit of trial and error probably needed. This is explored further in Chapter 4.

Conflict is often centred around mundanity, not ideas, according to the research. And with the exception of homework, which requires more negotiation and management over the transition to secondary school and the subsequent period, bones of contention don't tend to change much across the teenage years.[46]

Patterns to quarrels are often long-lasting. One study of conflict between parents and teenagers divided them into groups according to whether they were placid; explosive, with intense rows; or squabbling, involving regular, low-level conflict. When I hear the word 'placid', I think: 'That sounds spectacular. How can I have a more placid relationship with my teenagers?' Sadly, placidity has already disappeared into the mists of possibility. These groups tend to be stable over time – meaning that if you are already in the squabbling or explosive groupings, your best efforts aren't likely to shift this much.[47]

There are, of course, downsides to conflict – and not just for your short-term sense of harmony. Teenagers who fight a lot with their parents, for example, are more likely to be depressed as adults.[48] Some of this relates to the nature and intensity of the conflict. Showing a lot of anger, for example, is linked to worse outcomes for teenagers.[49] People fight differently with family and friends – with family, they're more likely to get angry and less likely to make amends.[50] There's an irony here. It's easier to lose friends than family members, so we work harder to maintain relationships with them – and we don't work as hard for the people who are ever-present, at least until the nest has been flown.

The impact of conflict on teenagers, and the nature of it, varies according to their character and current state of mind. Empathetic teenagers, for example, are more likely than others to be negatively affected by conflict.[51] And while extrovert teenagers are more likely than their more internally focused peers to be constructive in an argument by problem-solving, they're more likely to get into arguments in the first place – and less likely to withdraw from them.[52]

You may be able to offset some of the negative effects of conflict through the quality of your relationship with your child. Conflict doesn't dent teenagers' well-being when parents demonstrate stable, high levels of warmth.[53] If there's not too much of it, conflict may even lead to better-adjusted relationships in these families.[54] This finding suggests that if fighting is inevitable, which it pretty much is, you can mitigate its impact by being warm (which is, of course, hard to do when you're fighting a lot).

Potential impacts of conflict on parents include dented mental health and worse relationships with other family members. Parents get stuck thinking about conflict in a way teenagers don't, possibly because they attach more meaning to it.[55] Alternatively, they may just be atrocious at it (hi). My children can erupt at some tiny, perceived infraction – like asking them to take their random detritus upstairs now, not later – and within five minutes be asking what time dinner is or chatting away about their day. The same flare-up will see me trying to shake myself out of a slightly frozen state in which I can be absorbed for hours without a lot of effort to shift myself out of it.

The adolescent psychologist Professor Laurence Steinberg has suggested that the impact on parents explains the strength of the persistent myth about teenagers and conflict, driven by a parental aversion to low-level bickering and a greater propensity to linger on negative feelings. 'The popular image of the individual sulking in the wake of a family argument may be a more accurate portrayal of the emotional state of the parent, than the teenager,' said Steinberg.[56]

And what about doing conflict well? There are some foundations you can lay to keep you both steady through inevitable disagreements. Some of the general advice outlined in Chapter 1 is likely to help here; according to one group of expert scholars who study conflict, a 'friendly, nonthreatening' family climate may be the most helpful thing to manage conflict with teenagers.[57]

Some of the foundational groundwork may be things you need to do alone. For parents who sometimes find it hard to control their irritation, for example, anger-management strategies – working out the best time of day for you to have difficult conversations, say – can reduce repeated conflict with teenagers.[58] I know, for my part, that I need strategies to manage the mental to-do lists I'm constantly creating in order not to feed these through into conflict with my girls.

You could also try to avoid correcting what you perceive to be character flaws like laziness. As the authors of the excellent book *Get Out of My Life: But First Take Me and Alex into Town* put it, 'Parents who try very hard to prevent warped character development in an obnoxious teenager are usually wasting their time. They are fighting a battle that they have already won or lost. They just don't realise it.'[59] Working out how to respond to your teenager's criticism of you is another way to select your scuffles strategically. They might be telling you something important but phrasing it clumsily. (Or, again, they may just be being an arse.)

Another preventative measure is to normalise differences in opinion. You can teach your child that disagreement is part of life and that it's possible to disagree constructively.[60] In the words of comedian, diversity expert and Stonewall co-founder Simon Fanshawe, 'Safety comes from the ability to disagree well, not from the absence of disagreeing. And disagreeing well means you find ways of living, loving and working with them even though you disagree, because above that you have a purpose in common, [which is your] relationship.'[61] Tolerance for different points of view is declining in many settings (see Chapter 8), so it's all the better if we can model this at home. Disagreeing with someone else's *opinion* doesn't mean we don't accept them as a *person*.

You can also have pre-emptive conversations with your teenager about small, relatively unimportant things that build the trust you need when you come up against something more significant. They might want to stay at the park for an extra half hour after their usual curfew on a summer's evening, perhaps. At this point, you can chat to them about why they want to do it (their friends are staying late and they don't want to miss out), what it looks like in practice (the evenings are light, so they'll still be home before dark) and how you can feel more comfortable with it (they'll get the bus home with a friend). These kinds of constructive negotiations make a teenager more willing to accept a firm safety limit on a bigger issue, like going to an overnight festival when you don't believe they're old enough.

Once you get to the point of impending conflict, it's worth taking a step back and asking yourself if this is a battle in which you're willing to sacrifice key flanks of your armies. This means avoiding, if you can, conflict that's unlikely to go anywhere other than on and on, like a modern-day battery advert with nobody on hand willing to let the exhausted bunny rest. It also means engaging with the part of your brain that automatically says 'no' – is the matter at hand likely to have a negative impact on your child, their safety, or your resources and well-being?

If not, you may want to bypass the quarrel so you can focus any potential skirmishes on the issues that really matter. But if it's a pivotal point and you've made the decision to engage, strategy makes a difference. Reflecting on what you want to achieve may be useful. Thinking about what's likely to support your relationship with your teenager or to promote their well-being is more likely to be helpful to you both, and to avoid repeating cycles of negative behaviour, than simply aiming for compliance.[62]

Taking a problem-solving approach to conflict – for example, working together to find the root cause of the problem and coming up with potential solutions – is linked to having fewer disagreements in future.[63] Points of conflict can be made more constructive through a focus on emotions. One study identified a hot topic among parents and their teenagers that had led to recent, intense conflict; sibling needling would be the main contender for me. Family pairs were then given six minutes to try to resolve the dispute. Adults and teenagers were coded according to their coping behaviours in one of four ways: problem-focused coping ('Why don't we try setting two alarms?' or 'You can stay up for an extra half-hour if you read rather than watch TV'); regulated emotion-focused coping ('It concerns me when you don't take care of your things' or 'Sometimes I'm too hard on you'); angry or hostile emotion-focused coping ('I hate it when you do that' or 'He always starts it'); and avoidant coping ('What's for dinner tonight?' or 'It's not your business').

Teenagers didn't much differ in their coping styles by sex, but mothers were more likely to focus on emotions, and fathers to problem-solve. (As I've already alluded to, this is not the case in my household. Even good friends have told me: 'Sometimes, you just need to listen and not come up with a solution to everything.' I wonder if this extends to writing parenting books.) Teenagers had more influence than parents over whether the conflict got resolved, and using adaptive strategies – problem-solving or emotion-focused coping – was linked to decent mental health.[64]

While compromise seems like a tidy solution to conflict, it may be more a marker of relatively equal adult relationships than of lopsided parent–teenager ones.[65] Conflict between parents and teenagers tends to be ended by one party going on the attack, giving in or walking away; or through constructive problem-solving.[66] Giving in, from the perspective of the parent, isn't recommended if your child has been aggressive and hostile – it can make them more likely to act this way in future (with other people, as well as with you), as doing so gets them what they want. It also makes you more likely to give in to similar behaviours in future to escape what you know to be the inevitable escalations from your teenager.[67] If you've capitulated to a teenager using insults to avoid stacking the dishwasher, the next time they start to argue with your request to do this again, you may give up on the request rather than subject yourself to the verbal onslaught.

A key step, if tempers are fraying, is to try to take the heat out of any discussions. You don't need to be visibly angry to get your point across. If you're obviously irate, it's more likely to make your child enraged, which makes you angrier, and so on.[68] Parents and teenagers are more likely to do and say things that escalate conflict when they're driven by fury; when they feel sad, on the other hand, they tend to be more conciliatory (parents) or avoidant (teenagers).[69] If you feel angry, you could try to process it away from your child, perhaps by talking about it with their other parent, if relevant, or with a friend. You're more likely to try to assert your parental power when you feel angry, and less likely to be able to reason with and respond to your child.[70]

You can calmly put consequences in place, if they're needed, as an alternative to shouting or other forms of being visibly angry – for example, telling a fifteen-year-old who has come home drunk that they will not be allowed to go to the party next weekend, as you need to make sure they are safe and understand your expectations. If you're not able to do this calmly, be honest – you could say something like 'I'm too angry to talk about this at the moment. We'll talk later, when I've had a chance to calm down.' If your child is the one who is upset, you could offer some time away or a cup of tea before you discuss the matter at hand.

Assuming anger isn't getting in the way of a constructive collision of differing viewpoints, you could try switching perspectives. You might describe how you believe your teenager sees the situation and ask them to let you know what you missed. You can then ask them to hop over into your psyche and do the same. This shifts the conversation into a place in which nuance and understanding are possible, rather than one in which both of you are grimly determined to win. Humour, if you can find some embers of it within the fire of your conflict, is often worth a try, too.

If a friction-riddled discussion with your teenager isn't feeling constructive, you should end it swiftly. There's little to be gained from circling round the same topic and rehashing stale arguments. If an altercation turns into a power struggle, it can whip up other issues and resentments into a single, merciless weather system. The authors of *Get Out of My Life...* advise, 'It is now, immediately, that parents must end their participation. To continue is to be sucked into a trap that inevitably causes matters to go one way – downhill. The parent can have one last line, but one line only: "Emily, you are to be home by 11.30."'[71]

It's worth being the one to end the conflict – at an appropriate moment – even when it's not quite at the full-on tempest end of the spectrum. Conflict becomes harder to resolve if the discussion at hand is ended by the teenager, not the parent. Teenagers can absorb unhelpful ways of managing conflict if they see their parents are happy to let them continue or even escalate. Modelling an end to conflict can help teenagers learn how to navigate balancing their own needs and wishes with those of other people, and how to handle feeling angry or sad during difficult conversations.[72]

Once a conflict is over, and if words were uttered that you regret or messages delivered in a way that was unnecessarily sharp, some repair may be needed. I know the word 'entitled' has slipped past my lips more than once in the agitation of the moment, which – while it may have been credible in relation to a particular deed – risks attaching itself to my tender teenager's self-image. You could have a post-argument chat, once tempers have cooled and if your teenager is open to it, in which you both try to be honest about how you feel without attaching too much blame to the other person – and at the same time try to be open to what the other is telling you. Avoiding reopening the argument itself for round two is a key aim here. If your child isn't willing to speak about it, you could bring them a cup of tea and ask what needs to happen to repair things between you. If a row has been cataclysmic, you will also need to make efforts to help you both get past it. Hanson advises, 'It's counterintuitive, but the fastest way to restore your own power and the fastest way to get a good result from others is to admit the maximum reasonable fault and then move on.'[73]

I'm not sure who's better at holding a grudge, me or my daughters, but it's a close-run contest. We're excellent at it. As I mentioned before, though, most teenagers move past any arguments quickly, and adults may feel cross with them about something that's no longer in their minds. My challenge here is to avoid leading or getting dragged into competitive sulking. This seems to be best handled by reminding myself about the short-fused nature of the teenage brain, which can't be helped; being clear with each other about responsibility – theirs and mine; apologising for my part and discussing what needs to change to make things better for both of us; and then heaving my unwilling attention onto something else.

The good news is that teenagers get much better at conflict as they journey through adolescence. As their ability to exercise self-control and to understand other people's perspectives evolves, teenagers become more likely to solve any problems constructively.[74] Sunnier days are ahead.

## Maintaining your equilibrium

Raising a teenager can be wonderful and rewarding. It can reflect the saccharine memes that go round on social media. It can also be miserable and lonely and take its toll. This toll can take the form of reflected moods – you can catch good moods and bad ones from your teenager, so you're slightly dependent on how they're feeling (as they are on your own state of mind).[75] Even a small, surly interlude with one of my daughters can trigger a cascade of negative feelings in me – sadness that she's unhappy; then anger that she's being grumpy when I haven't done anything wrong; then a swirl of worry as I try to work out if I have done something wrong, but missed it; then back to gloom as I decide that I must have misstepped, if only I could work out how. The research for two parenting books has convinced me that this mood chain is deeply unhelpful.

Some parents are reminded by their teenagers of the end of their youth and the fact that they are now, unless they had children young, middle-aged.[76] Many have to deal with difficult feelings driven by healthy emotional separation from their children. Teenagers' independence has to be matched by their parents' ability to let go. This letting-go process is facilitated by my daughters' ability to let me know exactly what I do badly – singing, wearing clothes ('Mum, don't take this the wrong way, but you have a terrible dress sense'), choosing music and chewing, among many other things – but these reminders don't always contribute to my sense of equilibrium.

There are some hidden costs to parenting. One study looked at empathy – which, most of us would agree, is a useful, brilliant trait – and found some mixed results. Parents who feel very empathetic towards their teenagers have more self-esteem and a greater sense of purpose than other parents, but they also have higher levels of chronic inflammation. This may be because there's a physical cost to taking care of others, or because their own needs in areas like sleep and exercise get deprioritised.[77] But it's not selfish to centre your needs. As shown in the last chapter, it's better for your teenager if you're OK. The suggestions drawn from my first book and summarised in Chapter 1 about looking after your own well-being are a good starting point. There are also some steps you can take that are more specific to being the parent of a teenager.

One is to maintain your own boundaries. This means not doing everything for your teenager, a side-effect of which is to help them build their own independence and resilience. Doing too much for your child can disrupt their developmental need to separate from you, leaving them in a shiny, pressure-free limbo that prevents them from experiencing the healthy stress they need to thrive in their future adult lives. If you're not burning yourself out on your teenager's behalf, it helps you to avoid feeling resentful when they fail to notice all the lifts you give them, the laundry you do for them, the sheets you change for them and the errands you run for them. I'm not saying don't do any of these things, but there's a balance to be found here.

Challenging your assumptions is helpful. Parents who believe that adolescence is a time of storm and stress – that their teenagers will inevitably rebel and be difficult – are more likely to suffer from burnout, possibly because these beliefs make them overprotective of their children.[78] And, as we've seen, these ideas can elicit precisely the behaviour parents are seeking to avoid. You can also keep in mind what you love about your teenager. Mine are funny, smart and interesting, and are brilliant friends to those lucky enough to be in their inner circle. They're kind to our dog, even if they could walk him more. They've been excellent at identifying the security weaknesses in our house by wriggling in through small, unlatched windows when they've forgotten their keys. And, most of the time, they are bloody lovely.

You may also want to keep in mind, during trickier moments, that any attacks on you are not personal, much as they might feel like it. (I need to keep returning to this line to remind myself of it.)

Your teenager is simply going through the natural, inevitable process of separating from you. And you are the right person to manage this process – you know the bones of your teenager.

Finally, it's important to maintain your own interests and activities, or rebuild these if you have let them slip over the years before you were safely able to leave your child alone. This is important in the here and now, for feeling OK. It is also protective. Your child will leave home in the coming years, and it will be an empty, difficult time without your own clearly defined, curious and rewarding life to buffer the absence.

# CHAPTER SUMMARY

## Your relationship

- **Changing patterns.** The teenage drive for independence – coupled with slightly more intense conflict – can shift the balance of power between teenagers and their parents over adolescence. Parents could help younger children calm down in a way they may no longer be able to do with teenagers. Teenagers' feelings of isolation and separation from their parents increase as they get older, and they feel less close – but they do still feel that closeness, however diminished, and they still like their parents.
- **Changing relationship quality.** Relationships tend to deteriorate over the early teenage years and then bounce back. But all parent–child relationships are different – and some of them improve over adolescence. Parents get new things from the relationship, like deeper discussions or newly found shared interests. Relationships tend to be better in the teenage years if they were already strong.
- **The vital importance of your relationship.** A good relationship helps you both individually, and has many knock-on effects – for example, making other parenting strategies more successful. Other aspects also affect your relationship, including maintaining boundaries. You can catch each other's moods, both good and bad.
- **The purpose of conflict.** Conflict helps to reset your relationship to be one of greater equality, which is a necessary part of the separation process. It allows teenagers to express their negative feelings safely with a trusted adult, and to learn how to manage these feelings when they're with other people. Teenagers' efforts to assert their independence lie beneath a good portion of any conflict.

- **Other conflict facts.** Around one in ten families have to deal with entrenched, worsening conflict with their teenagers. Conflict is worst in volume for early adolescents, but gets more intense through to mid-adolescence. However, changes in conflict levels and intensity are small, implying that dramatic stereotypes about teenage conflict are exaggerated. Parents get more fixated on conflict than their teenagers, perhaps explaining some of this hyperbole. Conflict tends to be worst between mothers and daughters, and fathers and sons, and conflict levels for second-born siblings peak at a younger age.

## Ideas for parents

- **Aim for balance.** Don't be afraid of conflict, but don't run towards it. Exert control, but not too much of it (and never psychological control). Avoid asking lots of questions, but use gentle questions wisely – alongside acceptance of different opinions – to open other perspectives for your teenager. Centre your own needs, and don't burn yourself out on your teenager's behalf. Maintain your interests and activities, or rebuild them if you've let them slip.
- **Don't take efforts to separate too personally.** Most parent–teenager relationships go through this process – and on the rare occasions they don't, there may be something more worrying going on (for example, family members being enmeshed with each other). It may also help to remember, if your relationship's going through a tricky patch, that it will probably improve once they reach sixteen or so.
- **Look for the good.** You're more likely to parent well if you notice your teenager's positive traits and see past the negative ones. And if you talk to the version of your teenager you want to see, they're more likely to show up. Challenge stereotypes. Think about what you love about your child.

- **Remember what works when it comes to parenting, as this can also help your relationship.** You need to set boundaries and know what your child is up to, while not intruding too much on their privacy. Your own boundaries are also important, including ensuring you don't get used as an emotional punching bag. Effective listening is key, as well as making efforts to understand your teenager's point of view on issues over which you disagree — perhaps reflecting back to them what you understand their position to be. Be emotionally and physically present. If your teenager isn't keen to talk, try letting them lead conversations and/or make it clear you're available to talk when they're ready. Eat together when you can.
- **Manage conflict well.** Create a sense of safety for your teenager when you argue with them, so they know they'll still be loved. Avoid being visibly angry — if you feel enough anger that you can't avoid being hostile, step away and resume any interaction when you feel calmer. Keep in mind outcomes that are likely to support your relationship with each other or promote your child's well-being. Focus on how your teenager is feeling. Try problem-solving or emotion-focused coping. Calmly put in place consequences as needed. Try switching perspectives with each other. Don't give in to your child if they've been aggressive or otherwise hostile. Swiftly end any conflict that's going nowhere with one final line.

    Head off some of the causes — don't invade your teenager's privacy or act intrusively in other ways. Make amends if you've acted badly. Don't get stuck in a loop of thinking about conflict — your teenager has probably already forgotten it. Make it clear that disagreements are part of life and that it's possible to disagree constructively. Be flexible and build trust in small, easy ways to make disagreement easier to manage when it comes to something bigger. Choose your battles wisely.

- **Make the most of technology.** Keep in touch when you're apart via text. Wrap media into family traditions, like film nights or weekend video games.
- **Beware giving advice.** If your teenager brings you a problem, consider empathising or asking what they would like to do about it. If you're desperate to give suggestions, ask if your teenager would like your thoughts before you wade in.
- **Give yourself regular reminders of the research on adolescent development from Chapter 1.** Remember, if your teenager's acting like a thorn in your side (or more accurate and ruder versions of this idea), they probably can't help it. Don't try to correct what you perceive to be character flaws. That ship has probably sailed.
- **Think about other factors that might contribute to improving your relationship.** Make sure you're not erecting an invisible wall between your child and the other parent, if relevant, through any beliefs that you're more competent. Use humour. Apologise when you've got things wrong. Don't be afraid to let your child see your flaws.
- **Be authentic.** Abandon suggestions that make you feel you're being false with your child, as it can damage your relationship with each other.

# CHAPTER 3

# OTHER CONNECTIONS

## Friendships

A common pastime when I was a teenager was to watch tribes at my all-girls' grammar school divide and reform like murmurations at sunset. I was often on the outside edges of these alliances, propped up by the security of a non-school best friendship. The groupings at school made for compelling viewing. There were the leaders – the girls steeped in a charisma that everyone recognised but nobody could pinpoint or reproduce. There were the deep bonds that survived the chaos around them, the dances made between different groups, the power plays, the elevations to inner circles and the tumbles from favour. By the time I'd moved close enough to enter the social fray – I relocated when I was fifteen from a tiny, tidal island to a bigger one with actual people and a bus route not far from my school – the sense of drama had abated, and I happily took a position within the relatively calm formations that remained.

There's been little experimental study made of what social isolation does to humans, for good reason – I can't imagine an ethics board signing off a trial in which one group of teenagers gets assigned a smashing friendship group, and another has to cast down their eyes and cut off contact from those around them. Studies on rodents have shown that isolation in adolescence damages brain development and mental health.[1] The natural experiment of the Covid pandemic also showed that social isolation and loneliness were linked to depression in teenagers, and that the length of time for which they felt lonely was more relevant to their well-being than how intensely they felt that loneliness.[2]

Non-experimental evidence tells us that support from friends in the teenage years is linked to future resilience[3] and to various measures of well-being, including happiness, mood and quality of life.[4] These studies lend additional weight to the rodent evidence on social isolation by suggesting that friendships influence teenagers' brain development.[5] The power of other teenagers is immense and encompasses all sorts of areas. Teenagers are more likely to act in a socially minded way, for example by volunteering, if they see their friends doing the same.[6] Friendships may also influence teenagers' engagement at school by motivating them and showing them the value of doing well in education.[7] If I'm remembering my GCSE years correctly, there's also a competitive element.

Some of these effects can, of course, work the other way – if friends aren't motivated to do well, for example, your teenager may not soak up the fuel of ambition to succeed themselves. Teenagers are much more sensitive than adults and younger children to the influence of their peers and to how they're perceived by other people. Each new cohort has a list of slightly ridiculous rules that they must meet if they want to fit in with the tribe. To be socially acceptable in early 1990s Colchester, you had to keep your coat unzipped and unbuttoned in winter, and to carry your textbook-laden schoolbag – if it had a double strap – on one shoulder. Long-term spine health was a mere bagatelle, and exhortations towards it only underlined the necessity of the single-shoulder approach. I still find myself looking round uneasily, anticipating external judgement, if I wear a rucksack using both straps. Teenagers in 2020s Brighton have an aversion to coats, even on mornings where the ground is laced with frost and you can see your breath. And I'm sure you can spot individual differences in dress sense if you're in the know. I am not, so I can't.

Being susceptible to the influence of peers during the teenage years helps us to make friends and protects us from being cast out by the tribe.[8] Choosing joggers over jeans is fairly benign, and it's much easier to navigate adolescence if you fit in. But there are some darker elements to peer influence. It can amplify risky behaviour – having a risk-worshipping passenger in the car makes teenage drivers more likely to overtake and less likely to stop, for example.[9] Eating disorders and other mental health conditions spread through friendship groups.[10] Social contagion between teenagers can even lead to mass fainting episodes and other physical symptoms.[11] There's evidence to suggest that the increasing number of teenagers identifying as trans is driven, in part, by peer influence (for more on this, see Chapter 5).[12]

There may be other challenges, too, relating to teenage friendships. As teenagers start to tell their parents less, they share more with their friends – meaning some will be shouldering burdens that they have no idea how to manage. A teenage friend of mine, Anoukh, had a pathological fear of dirt in case it turned out to be contaminated blood. It's something that I now understand was probably linked to obsessive-compulsive disorder but, at the time, none of us had the first clue how to help her manage it, beyond providing reassurance that each mark on the school stairs was probably mud or spilt hot chocolate. This responsibility for things that should be in the adult realm creates pressure for teenagers and may give them a misplaced sense of culpability for their friends' outcomes. Friendships are, though, broadly essential and positive for teenagers. Friends may even be more protective against poor outcomes than parents.[13]

Temporary ruptures can result from children's interests developing at different times. A few years ago, one of my daughters wanted to spend increasing amounts of time sitting and chatting with her best friend, Emily, while Emily grew increasingly fraught at the lack of structure when they saw each other and wanted to return to the safer world of Beanie Boos and dragons. They disconnected from each other for a while, but found each other again later when they were in a similar place.

Sharing feelings encourages teenage friendship success, perhaps because it reveals vulnerabilities – in the form of their worries, say, or who they fancy – and being vulnerable requires trust. A German study looked at emotional competence and friendships over time in around 300 teenagers, from the start of secondary school (aged twelve) to just over three years later. It found that teenagers who shared their emotions more at the start of the study had a greater number of reciprocal friendships ten months later. These friendships made teenagers even more likely to share their feelings by the end of the study. In other words, the act of sharing was linked to the development of friendships, and having friends increased the likelihood that these adolescents would talk about how they felt. The study authors concluded that disclosure makes people feel closer and more committed to each other.[14]

Intensity, of course, is a marker of teenage friendships, especially for girls.[15] I remember observing pairs of best friends at my school in the manner of an amateur anthropologist. They would mirror each other's language and mannerisms, bow their heads in deep discussion at break time to the exclusion of all else, spend entire weekends together, then have an enormous fight and retreat to the classroom factions that best supported them. They'd later make up (at which point, you'd better hope you'd said nothing even vaguely unkind about one best friend while comforting the other) and the cycle would start over. They were like Shakespearean love affairs, with less death.

Boys are more likely to develop intimacy through shared activities than they are through self-disclosure.[16] But there's a gap between what boys do and what they would like. On the whole, they want to be able to share personal information with their good friends, but the intimacy they have in the early teenage years tends to wane.[17]

Girls, too, can suffer from their chosen approach. Their greater inclination to share secrets and intimacies leaves them vulnerable to the process of 'co-rumination',[18] through which they get pulled into repeatedly fixating on a particular problem. Co-rumination has been linked to mental ill health[19] and to the spread of mental health symptoms among friendship groups.[20] Despite these negative impacts, the tendency to co-ruminate appears to get reinforced through short-term mood improvements driven by teenagers having a close friend validate their emotions and by the feeling of closeness generated by these high-intensity discussions.[21] If you were a teenager worried about an exam, say, and you were feeling sick and sleeping badly, you might get temporary relief from a friend who shares this fear and makes you feel understood – but going over and over these concerns would make you feel worse over time, not better.

You might hope, as a concerned bystander, that the limitations of same-sex friendship groups can be overcome by mixing them up. Mixed-sex friendship groups, though, are less stable than same-sex ones, and unsupervised time in mixed-sex groups is linked to later risky behaviour such as smoking and drinking. This instability might stem from a lack of experience and knowledge about how to navigate friendships with the opposite sex when teenagers are used to hanging out with same-sex peers.[22] My friends with brothers were certainly more comfortable in crossing the no man's land of the school gym at joint discos with the boys' school, while everyone else remained in awkward, stereotyped clusters of the familiar on the edges of the room. Sisters of brothers were also the ones who flocked together at the bottom of our adjoining school fields to share cigarettes with boys – and, no doubt, much else besides.

It's not just close friends who play an important role in teenagers' development. A review of studies found that support from a wider network, such as classmates, has a stronger link to positive mental health than support from close friends. This might be because close friends are more likely to co-ruminate, which partly offsets their positive contributions, or because having steady support from a wide network of peers is helpful and gives teenagers a sense of predictability.[23] They are also influenced by teachers, coaches and other mentors.[24]

Times will arise, of course, in which your child has arguments with their friends, gets frozen out of a group or comes up against other challenges. Friendship quarrels are more common than rows with acquaintances in the teenage years, but they become less frequent with age.[25] They're also not, necessarily, to be feared. Arguments between teenagers of a similar age often require negotiation to settle them, as power can't be wielded in the same way as it can within a less equal relationship – your child's best friend can't threaten to withdraw privileges in the same way that you can. This friendship-driven negotiation is important to teenagers' intellectual development.[26]

Teenagers themselves usually have pretty solid ideas about how to deal with friendship issues. Some South Australian researchers ran focus groups with teenage girls to discover what advice they would give friends who were having friendship difficulties. The girls gradually came up with a list of practical solutions to manage conflict within their groups, which they ranked in order of importance. Top solutions were developing a wide friendship group to give themselves options when something goes wrong; working out what is important and what to let go; walking away from conflict when it becomes unmanageable; and trying to talk to anyone who is causing upset, away from the rest of the group. The girls also advised avoiding gossip and meanness, both in person and online, for self-protection.[27]

Parents can be wary of their teenagers' friendships, but this caution is often misplaced. It's been informed, to a large extent, by literature that's overly focused on risk and by (likely inaccurate) suggestions that friendships jeopardise parents' relationship with their teenagers.[28] These parents may also be influenced, no doubt subconsciously, by a reminder of what they've lost – our chances to form significant new friendships fade as we get older.[29]

Parental mistrust of children's friendships may also be driven by a misplaced belief that our offspring are blameless when rules are flouted by a group. My friend Luke's fourteen-year-old daughter, Katie, illustrated this beautifully when she had a sleepover with five friends one Friday night. Luke went to ask them whether they'd prefer pasta or pizza for dinner. He walked into a thick haze of vape fumes, which Katie tried to pass off as smoke from her scented candles. Luke asked for a private chat, at which point Katie wept, apologised and said two of her friends were the culprits – they'd insisted on vaping inside, she said, and nobody else had taken part. Luke collected the two vapes in question, then congratulated himself on handling the situation smoothly and relatively without embarrassment for Katie. The two vapes were later proclaimed as empty duds by his more knowledgeable wife and, three weeks later, Katie's younger brother discovered her vape stash while rifling through her cupboards for his own nefarious reasons. Luke is no longer quite as naïve as he once was.

If you find yourself bristling at the influence of the other young wolves on your teenage cub, there are a few things to bear in mind. The first is that these relationships are essential to them. They may well believe that their friendships are more important than their connection with you. If you try to disrupt or interrupt these bonds, it's your own relationship that's likely to suffer.[30] The second is that banning friendships is, counter-intuitively, linked to a higher chance of your child having friends with delinquent tendencies in future.[31] The third is that what your child gets from their friendships doesn't take away from what they get from you, unless their orientation towards their friends is extreme.[32] You might give your child love, stability and values, while their friends give them a social life, a sense of safety in numbers and others with whom they can share their high spirits.

You can take comfort from the fact that while the middle-adolescent years are a time to push at rules and to elevate the views of their friends over those of their parents, older teenagers are more balanced.[33] Until they reach this point, keeping an eye on where they are and who they are with – making sure you're not being controlling about it – is linked to having fewer high-risk friends.[34] There's more about monitoring in Chapter 4.

In terms of other active input to support your child's friendships, there's not a huge amount you can do beyond making it easy for them to see each other to an extent that doesn't get in the way of school, homework or family relationships. I have myriad flaws as a parent, to which either of my daughters would happily attest, but I've only said 'no' to friends coming over if it's for a sleepover on a school night, or we're away or having friends to stay. I much prefer their friends now they are older, too. The meaner ones seem to have been left behind – or perhaps they've grown out of any unkind tendencies – and you can have a more interesting conversation with a fifteen-year-old than with someone who is six, sweet (or not) as they might be.

Catering, though, has not got easier. My children choose not to eat meat. One friend can eat no raw dairy or cooked cheese, though cooked butter and milk are fine (with the suspicious upshot that she can eat cakes and puddings, but not most savoury dishes). Another will eat cooked tomatoes, but no raw ones. Someone else can eat no spice, and so the list goes on. They occasionally all come round at once, at which point I leave out a loaf of bread with some toppings, or go to meet one of my own friends and leave the catering to my partner. Sometimes, parenting is about pragmatism.

## Love and desire

This section risks being quease-inducing for the average parent, as does the linked section on sex and porn in Chapter 7. The idea that our children are stepping into the terrain of desire and love may be uncomfortable. It's worth understanding the ages at which things change, though, so we can keep a watchful eye – from a comfortable distance – being ready if needed to pick up the pieces, or to step in to prevent a coercive or age-inappropriate relationship.

The emergence of desire in adolescence isn't only biological. It's also driven by society, culture and values.[35] According to one research review, teenagers can experience love at the age of thirteen or fourteen; for many, of course, this will be later. Even older teenagers, though, have trouble telling the difference between love and lust.[36] (I know people in mid-life for whom this is still an issue.) Lust is the craving for sex. Love, on the other hand, is often marked by feelings of elation. Teenagers in love have high levels of energy. They yearn for the object of their affections and can think about them obsessively.[37] On the romantic side, we have Romeo – 'It is the east, and Juliet is the sun. Arise, fair sun, and kill the envious moon.'[38] On the crashingly empirical side, love is driven more by dopamine reward systems than it is by Romeo's fume of sighs.[39]

Unless teenagers are dating because of social norms or other pressures, desire is a precursor to a relationship. It forms part of the wider spectrum of sexuality, which is also made up of arousal, sexual function and behaviours.[40] Testosterone isn't just a male hormone – it plays an important role in attraction in both sexes. Male testosterone peaks in autumn and female testosterone peaks around ovulation, so desire may follow these patterns.[41] There can be a difference, too, in the way that sexuality presents itself in the two sexes, informed at least in part by media and wider culture. Girls may be more focused on how they feel about their own attractiveness, whereas boys' sexuality focuses on the person to whom they're attracted.[42]

The cliché about unrequited love burning brightly (while your teenager no doubt ignores the kind, attentive and eminently more suitable person who makes themselves available) turns out to be grounded in science. The feeling of rejection can trigger increasing ardour through – sorry to be horribly unromantic again – an increase in dopamine and other hormones caused by a sense of abandonment and stress. A sense of delayed reward – the beloved might, after all, awaken and reciprocate your teenager's smittenness – keeps the brain focused.[43] I remember pacing along the sea wall as a fourteen-year-old, desperately thinking about the boy I believed myself to love. I'd probably have been reluctant to be told about the biological processes that were driving it.

Teenagers whose desire, or love, is reciprocated may start going out with each other. Dating at this age isn't just for fun. It helps teenagers to do a number of things central to their development, including building their identity and changing their relationships with family and friends.[44] Teenagers talk endlessly about their romantic entanglements with their friends, for example, which helps bond them to each other.[45] There are underlying currents to teenage romantic relationships that distinguish them from their friendships. These include heightened emotions, more social discomfort and an exclusivity[46] – assuming you're not in an environment like my primary school, where it was common to have four boyfriends or girlfriends simultaneously (no Essex jokes, please). There's more fighting between teenage partners than there is between teenage friends,[47] and there are heftier mood swings involved, too.[48] Love shares some elements with drug addiction – the increasing desire for more of it, the sometimes inappropriate behaviour, the withdrawal symptoms that follow its end.[49]

There are often imbalances in status and power, with romantic partners trying to change or control the other person either to overcome the differences between them or to ensure they measure up in the eyes of other people.[50] The most obvious example is the film *Grease*, in which Danny encourages Sandy to metamorphose from a sweet, square conformist into a Lycra-clad, chain-smoking femme fatale who burnishes his reputation. My parental antennae are twitching at the idea that my daughters might ever encounter a boyfriend or girlfriend who attempts to change them, but the chances are that they will – and that they'll attempt to bend others towards their own yardsticks in return.

One thing to have changed since most of us were growing up is a cultural shift from traditional ideas of dating towards teenagers sleeping with their friends. According to one group of scholars, friends with benefits are 'relationships that combine friendship and sex in ways that may be not only confusing for youth but leave them open for exploitation and heartache'.[51] Casual sex can cause teenagers to become attached to the other party through the release of attachment-linked hormones, such as oxytocin, during orgasm – attachments that become hard to break and that have knock-on emotional impacts when they're not reciprocated or they end.[52]

There are other harmful aspects of relationships, too, for which it is worth keeping a beady parental eye open. Teenagers may feel pressured into a relationship or into having sex by their friends.[53] Social media and technology, of course, are a risk. While they can support teenagers' relationships with each other, they also provide an avenue for more concerning behaviours, including harassment, stalking and control.[54] There's more on technology later in the chapter, and on porn and sexting in Chapter 7.

The amplification of damaging stereotypes is another risk, especially if it links to any controlling or degrading behaviours by partners. An international study in five low-income city areas in the United States, Peru, Scotland, Belgium and Kenya found that heterosexual dating stereotypes persist everywhere. Girls are seen as passive and innocent, whereas boys are perceived as active and dominant.[55] There's more about teenagers who may be lesbian, gay or bisexual in the section on sex in Chapter 7; there's far more research on same-sex attraction in relation to sex and sexual health than there is on romantic relationships, which probably gives its own message on bias.

Teenagers' limited relationship experience means they may not spot the signs of an unhealthy relationship – when there's a lot of conflict, for example – and will require support from adults to understand what a healthy version looks like.[56] They find it especially difficult to recognise jealousy or possessiveness, which can be confused with the idea their partner is in love with them.[57] If teenagers are experiencing violence or abuse in their relationships, they're more likely to tell their friends than an adult.[58]

Even healthy relationships will come to an end for most teenagers. My old friend Ruth (not her real name) had her first relationship when she started university, and they were married the following summer. I've lost touch with her, so I don't know if that was her only romantic entanglement, but I suspect – based on her strong faith – that it was. Most other people have to deal with the inevitable conclusion of romantic relationships that die on the vine, and this is a particularly hard job for teenagers. They're living through a time of keenly felt emotions, and they lack practice. Teenage heartbreak can be more serious than we imagine.[59] I was nineteen before my heart was properly broken, when it shattered. No amount of friendship, rebound flings, exercise or nights out could fix it – it needed, instead, time.

If your teenager has been dumped, they may be in love with the person who ended things for months – or even years – afterwards. There is often a time of protest, during which your inconsolable teenager will try to win back their former girlfriend or boyfriend, sometimes humiliating themselves in the process. This may be an instinctive response that's common across mammals when important bonds get ruptured, rather than a socially driven choice. It's generally followed by resignation and/or despair. Break-ups can also generate rage, shame and jealousy, among other strong, hard-to-handle feelings.[60]

One expert recommends avoiding all contact with the person who has ended the relationship, if it's possible to do so. Obviously this doesn't work if they attend school together. Doing things that are generally good for mental health, including getting outside and eating well, are also recommended, as is trying out new activities. Your child may be the one to have ended a relationship, and to be facing inappropriate or even scary behaviour from the person they have jilted.[61] If this is the case, they'll need a different kind of support. And even if there's no pushback, they may subsequently experience doubt or distress over their decision to end the relationship. Your child may need support with fictional relationships, too. I remember going on a blind date with a young man called Tom, whose intensity made me uncomfortable. I was politely chilly to the follow-up emails he sent (this was before mobiles were common) and turned down the offer of a second date. I later got a message saying, 'I get the feeling I'm more into this relationship than you are.' Teenagers can be deeply weird.

There is an overlap between talking to your teenager about love and desire, and talking to them about sex (see Chapter 7). While parents may want to delay talking to their teenagers about these things (Me! I want to delay or, if possible, avoid this!), having these conversations has been linked to better outcomes, including safer sex[62] – though too much focus on risks is linked, counterintuitively, to teenagers taking more of them.[63] And while they may run screaming with their fingers in their ears if they think you're about to talk about relationships or sex, research with eighteen- to twenty-five-year-olds shows that most people wish their parents had talked to them more about the emotional parts of relationships, including how to initiate a relationship, how to avoid getting hurt (this seems rather hopeful) and how to deal with endings.[64]

So what else do you need to communicate to your child? A common missing element of parent–teenager relationship talks is the good side of love, desire and sex, including healthy relationships, love and enjoyment.[65] You could try to get across an idea of what a healthy romantic relationship looks and feels like – they are fun, people are kind to each other and the relationship isn't marred by power imbalances. You could also, subtly, seize on relationships you see in films and on TV as examples of more and less healthy relationships, and use them to help your teenager learn the difference between a partner showing healthy interest and straying into the rocky waters of possessiveness.

Health in a relationship isn't just about treating each other well – it's being aware what each person wants, and not being afraid to step away if the balance of good feelings and discomfort is awry. I had a boyfriend as a teenager whom I jilted after a month – he was a warm-hearted, thoughtful and interesting human being, but I wasn't attracted to him. I felt so awful at his reaction to the dumping that I took him back, and it took me another nine months to work up the courage to end things. This, with the benefit of hindsight, wasn't good for either of us, and I wish my more experienced adult self had been around to let the teenage version know I wasn't a terrible human for causing a lovely boy some temporary distress.

One guide for parents recommends they discuss various questions with their teenagers. 'What's the difference between attraction, infatuation, and love? How can we be more attracted to people the less interested they are in us? Why can we be attracted to people who are unhealthy for us? How do you know if you're "in love"? Why and how can romantic relationships become deeply meaningful and gratifying? How do they contribute to our lives? How can the nature of a romantic relationship and the nature of love itself change over a lifetime?'[66] I hope my daughters are more philosophical thinkers than I am by the time they reach the end of their teenage years, as I have not the first clue how to begin answering most of these. If not, I can probably rely on the emotional literacy of their dad to do the heavy lifting.

You'll influence your child, too, in ways of which you're barely aware.[67] You'll normalise a particular model of relationship through your own, or through its absence. You'll communicate values and ways of being through the areas to which you give your attention. If your teenager witnesses a friend telling you that you're useless, for example, and you gloss over it, they'll learn it's normal to be treated that way in relationships, including romantic ones. You can normalise acceptance, too, of different sexual orientations. This is something of which I've been aware since the earliest days – if a hypothetical future relationship comes up, I talk about potential boyfriends or girlfriends, as I want them to know they can have either.

One final note on romantic relationships is that they're probably better for your child than your protective instincts might lead you to believe. Teenagers' well-being tends to be supported by being in relationships, according to a review of studies.[68] But they aren't the only template for what happens in future. Adults are more likely to believe they need to invest emotionally in their relationships – by communicating openly and addressing disagreements, among other things – when they've grown up in a warm, supportive home.[69] And we all know, however unwillingly, that those who are prepared to put in the work are more likely to be rewarded by happy, more resilient liaisons.[70]

## The online world

Young people connect online for many of the reasons they connect in real life. These include getting to know other people and staying in touch with their friends.[71] Several mechanisms wrapped into the use of social media go beyond simple scrolling, clicking and posting. These include making comparisons with other people – I have more friends than this poster, or this other one is more beautiful than me and wears more expensive clothes; self-disclosure – I will let people know that I'm feeling vulnerable this morning; and impression management – I'll share a carefully curated set of photos that makes my life look fabulous.[72] Teenagers also use social media to share intimate thoughts and feelings with their friends.[73]

My daughters spend swathes of time navigating through a tide of messages, which have replaced the endless but narrower attachment to the landline that marked the teenage years of many parents. (Our teenagers won't know what it is to answer a phone by reeling off a string of numbers, with no idea if you're about to enjoy a conversation with your best friend or to make polite conversation with your grandmother.) This shift has been happening for a while. As early as 2009, more teenagers were using text messages to communicate each day than were meeting up with friends out of school.[74]

It's hard to know how much time teenagers spend on their screens, as measures of it in studies are made by researchers who are stumbling around in the dark. They often focus on teenagers' or parents' estimates of how long they spend on screens, which are notoriously inaccurate, or they measure actual engagement on a single device – but how accurate is measuring time spent on a smartphone, say, when many teenagers are also using tablets, school Chromebooks, televisions, games consoles or family computers? Bearing these caveats in mind, a 2021 American survey found that eight- to twelve-year-olds average five and a half hours of screen time a day. The equivalent figure for thirteen- to eighteen-year-olds is more than eight and a half hours. Time spent on screens increased by 17% for both age groups in the two years between 2019 and the time of the survey.[75] These figures don't include screen time at school or as part of homework, which is likely to have shot up since the start of the pandemic, when schools had to pivot towards technology as a teaching tool.

Eight and a half hours a day spent on screens, excluding time for schoolwork, is an extraordinary figure. There's a phrase in German that roughly translates as 'One donkey calls the other one long-ears.' I spend most of my workdays in front of a screen, and I'm not averse to passing an evening laying waste to the latest Netflix drama. I'm therefore all too aware of my extended lugs, long face and large teeth in relation to this statement. But screen time isn't necessarily bad, and I don't just say this to justify my own heavy usage (although it does make me feel slightly better about it). Very little is wholly good or bad, including the online world. There's been lots written on negative mental health impacts of screens in general, and social media in particular, which I'll explore further below. I'm going to start, though, with what's good about screens when it comes to teenagers.

When teenagers talk to their friends online, it can help them to feel that they belong. They feel connected to these friends through the wispy web and tangible hardware that convert their voice, face and finger movements into meaningful sounds and images on a screen. These connections don't need a physical presence, so the resulting sense of belonging can be more permeating than one that's generated in real life – teenagers may not be able to see their friends that much at 9 p.m. on a school night, but they have the option to get in touch online. Phones carry all sorts of meanings for teenagers. A phone connects them to other people, it helps them to be independent and it delivers a level of social status.[76] Other benefits of being technologically connected include improved self-esteem linked to the social support and sense of belonging that social media can kindle.[77]

There's another friendship dimension here that easy narratives about the ills of the internet often miss – the online world enhances elements of real-world friendships. There is intimacy that comes from online disclosures. Social media helps teenagers to show they care about each other, whether that's through the like of a post or a deeper demonstration of support, and to arrange physical meet-ups.[78] If my teenager is using a WhatsApp group to arrange to meet her friends on the beach on Saturday afternoon, rather than having to write down weekend plans three weeks in advance with a parchment and quill like her parents used to, then technology is supplementing her friendships – not taking away from it. As one pair of scholars puts it, 'In contrast to early online applications, which were seen as refuges from real life, today's online environments reflect, complement, and reinforce offline relationships, practices, and processes.'[79]

Being online offers teenagers a sense of control over their interactions with other people. This is especially handy for those who might find real-world communication tricky. One study found that people who feel greater levels of social anxiety seek out self-disclosure through online social networks, perhaps because they can spend time planning their disclosures and are able to post on a platform that makes them feel safe (whether their perceptions of safety match the reality, of course, is a different question).[80] The online world can also help teenagers to develop new skills, especially if they're creating things rather than just consuming content passively. I have no idea if there are unintended outcomes of this – I haven't seen any in the research – but in my family, we distinguish between screen-screens and 'constructive screens'. The latter might include maths games, design apps, Duolingo, logic puzzles, YouTube videos that teach you how to draw using perspective, video editing, photo editing, writing projects… The list is almost as extensive as the range of apps on offer. There are, quite feasibly, future careers that can be fashioned from spending time on constructive screens – and, if not, there's productive enjoyment in the here and now.

Onwards, now, to the downsides. I'll start with some of the more straightforward ones before looking at the big issue of mental health and the conflicting evidence we have about it. People disclose more deeply when they see somebody in person,[81] so online benefits of self-disclosure may have been overstated. There are also risks in doing so – we have a rule of thumb at home (of which I need to take better account myself) that you shouldn't put in screenshottable format anything that you wouldn't want to be shared without your permission. If your teenager sends a Snapchat to Will calling Anton a wanker, and Will screenshots this then wheels it out when he and your teenager have had a fight, the ramifications are far greater than if the word 'wanker' had been whispered to Will in the corner of the school canteen.

The potential effect of social media on attention has led one psychologist to warn that children who spend a lot of time on devices 'will be neurobiologically incapable of reading *War and Peace* as an adult. Not lazy or unmotivated. Incapable.'[82] When my daughter reveals that she couldn't get past the first page of du Maurier's *Rebecca* – which she tells me is Taylor Swift's favourite book, a fact that may or may not be related to her decision to take it out of the school library – I've pondered whether Swift might have had the same issue if she'd grown up with a similar amount of screen time. Digital devices may also prevent teenagers from learning to sit with their boredom or mustering the necessary resources to conquer it.

We don't know for certain, though, if the online world negatively affects attention, or if links are explained by other factors. It might be that teenagers who have short attention spans spend more time on social media, for example, as the ceaseless changes to the feed meet a desire for constant stimulus. One American study of several thousand teenagers measured symptoms of attention deficit hyperactivity disorder (ADHD) when they were in the equivalent of the UK's year 11 and assessed them again two years later. The researchers found that those who didn't have significant ADHD symptoms at the start of the study were more likely to have developed them in the intervening period if they'd spent more time on digital media, and the chances of them doing so increased for every additional digital media activity in which they frequently engaged. Even with this change over time, the researchers warn that we can't know if one causes the other.[83] We can probably employ a certain amount of logic here, though. I checked X twice while writing this paragraph.

In a tangentially related link to attention, we're not yet sure what the connections are between the online world and adolescent brain development. A review of the literature has found a mixture of positive and negative links between the two, but there's not enough information yet to work out exactly how these fit together or what the long-term implications might be.[84] We're more certain about rest. There are relationships between poor sleep and time spent on screens, particularly before bedtime.[85]

Where the research gets interesting, for me, is in how it relates to teenage mental health – which has been plummeting in line with an increase in time spent on devices. In the United States, the proportion of high school students who experience persistent feelings of sadness or hopelessness increased from 28% in 2011 to 42% in 2021 – a trendline that was increasing even before the pandemic.[86] It's clear that there is a teenage mental health crisis, which is explored further in Chapter 5. Some experts, including the social psychologist Professor Jonathan Haidt, have held social media pretty much fully responsible.[87] For those who believe social media has caused poor teen mental health, reasons include constant exposure to idealised images that may lead teenagers to believe they are lacking; reinforcement of negative ideas about the world; and a tendency to look inwards instead of focusing on connections to the world around them. Time spent on social media might be replacing time they could spend on things that support their well-being, like sport or drama.[88] Social media also has the potential to magnify negative emotions.[89]

But the evidence base is, at best, mixed. One study of British fourteen-year-olds showed that depressive symptoms are worse the more hours per day teenagers spend on social media,[90] but another, of ten- to fifteen-year-olds from North Carolina, found no meaningful link between mobile phone ownership, social media usage and teenagers' well-being.[91] Even where positive links are found, the causal direction might run the other way – teenagers with poor mental health may be more likely to avoid real-world interactions and to get lost down online rabbit holes.

The research literature is full of these contradictions. Two scholars tried to deal with this by pooling the findings of different reports, with the intention of removing the potential bias of individual studies. They found that, while digital technology is negatively linked to teenage well-being, the effect is minuscule – explaining less than half a per cent of the variation in how teenagers feel.[92] A different review of studies found a small link between use of social media and symptoms of depression in teenagers, but it found a wide variation in results, suggesting we can't draw clear conclusions from the data.[93]

So what's going on? Are the pressures of social media and a move away from the real world driving a mental health epidemic in teenagers, or is this crisis being driven by something else entirely?

Or does the answer, as is so often the case with these things, lie somewhere between these two perspectives?

One possible explanation is that while there's no strong effect on mental health at an individual level, a culture skewed towards an online world is an unhealthy place in which to grow up. An environment shaped by teenagers using a lot of social media may be one in which it's common to make comparisons with other people and to find oneself lacking. Another explanation is that there is, genuinely, no substantial and significant link between the online world and mental health. A third is that a relationship exists, but it's not a straightforward one so hasn't been captured in the data. It seems reasonable to argue that very low and very high levels of social media use, for example, could be associated with poor mental health, while moderate users experience a boost – those at the low end could live in resource-poor families or, perhaps, controlling ones, while those at the high end may find it hard to control their use or are employing social media as a distraction from difficult lives.[94]

Another potential reason for the rather mixed findings, which are weighted slightly more towards the argument that there's no clear link between social media and mental health (sorry, Professor Haidt), is that the effects vary according to the use, the user and the messages they consume. While mindless scrolling makes some feel better, for example, it has the opposite effect for others.[95]

Those who are prone to negative thoughts about appearance and body image are likely to come out worse than those who aren't.[96] This may explain, at least in part, why girls – who tend to be under more appearance-related pressure than boys – experience poorer outcomes. A study of around 800 young women of college age in the United States found that TikTok is linked to body dissatisfaction, as it causes users to survey their own bodies and to compare themselves unfavourably with other people. These effects were found even when users saw body-positive material, which was designed to do the opposite.[97] Online effects may vary, too, with individual sensitivities. I fit within the category of human who can get into endless spirals of worry if I know someone has read my message but not responded. Have I offended them in some way? Do they not like me? My partner fits within the category who shrugs, assumes they are busy and moves on. Neither is necessarily right (his is certainly healthier) – but it does mean that we are differentially affected by the messages we exchange with others.

A teenager caught in a self-harm algorithm and being swept ever deeper into messages of despair is going to come off worse than the slightly shy Dungeons & Dragons kids who have found their tribe in a corner of the internet. The online world is likely to be terrible for those who become dependent on it, who get caught up in contagions (of which more below), who get bullied and belittled within it, or who use it to replace sunlight, movement and real-life connections. It's likely to be pretty good for those who use it to amplify their real-world friendships, gain knowledge and skills, and pursue interests, and, importantly, are able to use it lightly. These mixed effects may explain why the research findings are so murky.

A final point about negative online outcomes relates to social contagion, which is the spread of attitudes, moods and behaviours through social networks – in this case, online ones. Where online contagions relate to mental health conditions, they have become known in the research literature as 'mass social-media induced illness'. This phenomenon has been observed in all sorts of areas, from eating disorders through to behaviours – Tourette's-like tics have spread through social media, for example. Algorithms play into contagions by prioritising posts on topics in which users have already shown an interest. Their exposure then escalates, and they create their own relevant content – thereby passing on the ideas or behaviours to other people.[98]

While sites such as TikTok have publicly committed to remove content that promotes anorexia, videos that supposedly show the opposite – those that raise awareness of its consequences – remain. On the surface, this seems positive, but a case-report study has shown a possible link between anti-anorexia content and disordered eating – the videos show calories consumed and what it means to suffer from the worst forms of anorexia, which may lead vulnerable teenagers to emulate the condition.[99] Contagions may therefore occur despite efforts to rein them in. There are other areas in which recognition of possible risk is only just beginning – for example, in the case of teenagers who question their gender. We do not have solid research on this yet, but early information suggests an internet role in spreading feelings of distress about being male or female.[100]

One scholar has proposed that social contagion is not the only means by which apparent psychological symptoms spread online. In some cases, she suggests that 'Munchausen's by Internet' may be at play, with adolescents demonstrating psychological symptoms due to a need to be recognised by other people – even if they are strangers – and to receive care from them.[101]

What all this rather mixed information means for parents depends, really, on your child. You may want to set early, stringent rules around device use (assuming that sailing boat hasn't already left harbour) while you see how they respond to the apps, information and connections available to them. It's easier to relax rules if things are going well than it is to tighten them if they aren't. It's then a matter of monitoring for red flags. You might start to worry if your teenager is spending a lot of time on screens, if they're unhappy or sleeping badly, or if screens have replaced elements of real life to a level that feels potentially unhealthy to you – if they're no longer seeing their friends or pursuing hobbies, say. Being aware of their vulnerabilities can be helpful, too. Those who have been bullied online are more likely to use the internet problematically in future,[102] and teenagers with mental health or neurodevelopmental conditions may be more vulnerable to this, too.[103]

Early rules you might want to put in place include no screens in bedrooms or at mealtimes, no screens beyond a particular time in the evening (to help sleep), and leaving an option for device checks to make sure your teenager is safe. Obviously these are more appropriate for younger teenagers than older ones – but hopefully by the time your teenager is at the point where rules are inappropriate, they will be able to manage things safely and independently. Parental monitoring and rules can curtail social media use[104] and make teenagers safer online.[105]

Rules, as with so many other areas, depend on your teenager. One of mine has had her devices confiscated from her bedroom a sufficient number of times that she's got smart enough not to get caught. I know it. She knows I know it. We both know I'm not up for the battle. If you have a teenager who is into gaming, the culture for which tends to be more of a nighttime one, you may choose to have slightly more flexible evening screen rules, if your child is sleeping well. One study found that the type of rule mattered, and that teenagers are more likely to abide by rules that block particular apps such as Snapchat than they are rules about when and where devices can be used.[106]

The Internet Matters website recommends ensuring your younger teenagers are set up with parental controls on their devices, as well as activating these on your home broadband. You can also set up safe searches on key websites and apps, including Google and YouTube.[107] But recent evidence suggests that blanket advocacy for parental controls may be misguided. A review of forty studies has found that having this kind of restriction without communication can have negative impacts, including less knowledge about online risks among children. Parental controls are more likely to work when put in place alongside consideration of children's needs and abilities, and where they're part of ongoing conversation and negotiation about screen-time approaches.[108]

It's important to check age ratings on apps. Early conversations are key – for example, on the benefits and risks of social networking, and the elephantine memory of things posted on the internet – and, importantly, how to stay safe online, including blocking people where necessary and ensuring contacts are known in real life before allowing them to become virtual friends or followers. Setting clear boundaries on your child's device use is essential.[109] For older teenagers, you'll probably have fewer rules, but you'll still want to make sure they've set their privacy settings high, know that few things disappear from the internet, and understand some simple rules of engagement – respecting others, blocking abusive comments, not engaging with or meeting up with strangers, and being careful about what they download.[110]

Talking about the online world, according to Internet Matters, means having short, relevant and regular conversations with your child, and choosing a good moment – over a meal, perhaps. It also means sharing information yourself and really listening to your child – asking open-ended questions, holding off with follow-up questions if they're speaking, and being patient and calm. It suggests covering online reputation, including digital footprints and treating others in the way you would if they were in the same room as you (assuming your teenager isn't one for violent in-person tendencies, of course); critical thinking, including recognising that others may be posting false information; how to deal with issues such as online bullying or coming across inappropriate content; personal safety; and how to get the best out of the online world.[111]

These talks should include algorithms and their manipulative nature. Teenagers really don't like the idea that someone or something might be manipulating them. At the same time, it's worth being clear that they might get pulled further online because that's how their devices have been designed, and it's best for them not to get too self-critical about that.

You might also want to think about how you'll deal with transgressions if rules are broken. Taking away their device, according to experts, is not the way to go. Doing so removes some of their ability to connect with their friends, which is vital at this age.[112] It may have a knock-on impact on your relationship with your teenager as well. Another reason is safety – teenagers may not tell their parents about risky online experiences if they fear the app or device in question being taken away.[113] And even if you do remove their phone or another device, they'll probably still have access to technology – if they're really desperate to seek it out – through school devices or those belonging to their friends.[114]

I'm going to say a word likely to drive terror into the hearts of those of you whose own device use could do with a bit of a revamp: modelling. Parents who use media heavily are more likely to have teenagers who do the same.[115] If you're taking screens to bed with you, or scrolling Instagram while someone is trying to talk to you, or replying to WhatsApp messages when you're watching a family film, it's going to be hard to convince your child to do otherwise. I haven't just written this paragraph for my husband, but I'm assuming he'll read it (hi, Pete).

There are two other quick notes drawn from expert suggestions that may be useful. One is flexibility – if you ask your child to come off their device and they request another five minutes, asking why might be better than a blanket no. It is built into the design of many games that you can lose a huge chunk of time if you exit them at a point before you can save. Your child may be asking for an extra few minutes to save an hour of game time, not to push boundaries. The other note is that it can be worth drawing in other family members – a favourite uncle or aunt, say – who can keep a gentle and respectful eye on your teenager's social media accounts.[116]

Finally, research suggests that teenagers are not the keenest on their parents posting about them online, so that might be something to avoid.[117] It says nothing about writing about them in a parenting book, though. I've been very careful, but it would probably be better for them that I never revealed even a morsel of their existence. At least if this sells well, it can contribute towards their future therapy bills.

# CHAPTER SUMMARY

## Friendships

- **Impact of friendships.** Human studies suggest friendships are linked to future resilience and well-being, while rodent studies show that social isolation in adolescence damages brain development and worsens mental health. Friendships are linked to socially minded behaviour, to risk-taking and to motivation levels at school. Teenagers start to tell their parents less as they disclose more to their friends, meaning that the recipients of their secrets may be dealing with issues they're ill-equipped to handle. Friendships can be more protective against poor outcomes, though, than family.
- **Nature of friendships.** Teenagers are uniquely oriented towards other people of a similar age. Boys' friendships can centre on shared activities, while girls' friendships are centred more around the intimate sharing of thoughts and feelings – something of which boys would like more. Girls are more at risk of co-rumination – obsessive, ongoing fixation on a particular problem – which can lead to the spread of poor mental health among friendship groups. Same-sex friendships tend to be more stable than ones that are mixed, and are less linked to later risky behaviour. Arguments happen more between friends than they do between acquaintances, but they're less common as teenagers get older.

## Love and desire

- **Emergence of sexuality.** Biology, society, culture and values combine to instigate the first flushes of desire. Teenagers can struggle to understand the difference between lust and love. Adolescent sexuality – like adult sexuality – consists of desire, arousal, sexual

function and behaviours. Girls can be conditioned to look inwards towards their own attractiveness, whereas boys focus more on the objects of their desire.
- **Desire in practice.** There's a basis in science for people being attracted to those who are 'hard to get'. Reciprocal desire can lead to dating, which has a number of functions – including identity development, the adjustment of parent–child relationships and the building of friendship bonds through exhaustive romantic discussions. There are overlaps in feelings and behaviour between drug addiction and being in love – but romantic relationships are, on the whole, good for teenagers.
- **Nature of relationships.** Romantic relationships, as opposed to friendships, drive more intense feelings, more mood swings and greater social discomfort in teenagers. The exclusivity of romantic relationships is another dividing line. Teenage partners fight more with each other than they do with their friends. Status and power imbalances are common.
- **Risks.** Casual sex causes a release of hormones, meaning that teenagers attach themselves to the other person. This precipitates hard impacts if there's no emotional reciprocation or an entanglement ends. Teenagers may feel unduly pressured into having sex with friends. Social media provides an avenue into harassment, stalking and controlling behaviours. Gender stereotypes – such as girls being passive and boys being dominant – can underpin unhealthy behaviours. Teenagers don't have enough experience to know when relationships may be harmful – when they're marked by jealousy, for example, or too much fighting. Heartbreak is practically inevitable.

## The online world

- **Reasons to connect.** Adolescent online connections are driven by similar underlying factors to real-world ones – getting to know people and staying in touch with friends. There are a number of other functions of social media, including making comparisons with other people, disclosing personal information and managing how others perceive them.

- **Screen time.** Estimates of screen time made by researchers are probably inaccurate, as it's a difficult thing to measure. One approximation for thirteen- to eighteen-year-olds is that they spend on average eight and a half hours a day on screens, excluding schoolwork and homework, and this amount has been rising rapidly.
- **The many upsides.** Screens aren't wholly good or bad, and there are numerous benefits. These include a sense of belonging, connection and independence, and an ability to connect at times of the day (or evening) when teenagers would usually have few opportunities to see friends in person. Some of these benefits can bolster self-esteem. Social media can enhance real-world friendships through self-disclosure and resulting intimacy boosts – a sense that their friends care about them through post engagement and the ability to plan real-world meet-ups. Being able to choose carefully when and how to engage can offer teenagers a sense of control over their interactions, which is particularly useful to those who are shy or who otherwise find real-world communication challenging. Screens can help teenagers to develop new skills.
- **The corresponding downsides.** There are risks to online self-disclosure – there's a record, and screenshots can be taken even of supposedly disappearing content. There may be effects on attention spans and teenagers' ability to sit with boredom, and there are possible negative (and positive) links with brain development. Teenagers who spend more time on screens, particularly near bedtime, risk sleeping badly. There's evidence of links with poor mental health, though effects are ostensibly small and complex, and may be indirect. It's likely that some users experience a boost and others experience negative impacts. There are particular

risks attached to those who are exposed to negative messages about appearance and body image, and those who get caught up in destructive algorithms. The internet also has a role to play in social contagions.

## Ideas for parents

- **Don't be afraid of your child's friendships.** They're beneficial, overall, and links with risky behaviour have been overstated. Your child is probably just as much to blame for any nefarious actions as their friends are, and it's your own relationship that's likely to suffer if you try to break any friendship bonds.
- **But keep an eye on where they are and who they're with.** If you can do this in a non-controlling way, your child's likely to have better outcomes.
- **Talk to your child about love and desire.** Key things to communicate include the good side of relationships (not just the risks), what a healthy relationship looks like and red flags. Communicating about sex is covered in Chapter 7.
- **Keep a careful lookout for unhealthy dating behaviour.** Your teenager may not know what's normal and acceptable. They may fail to recognise when there's too much fighting or when they're being controlled or coerced (or, perhaps, if they're doing these things to other people). If your teenager is being abused in any way, they're more likely to tell a friend than an adult, so your senses may need to be well tuned.
- **And watch out for heartbreak.** Be aware that your teenager may be in love for months, or even years, after a relationship has ended. Consider subtly trying to get them to do more things that are good for their well-being and to open up their worlds – eating well, getting outside and trying new activities. If possible, try to steer your child away from contact with their ex.

- **Model healthy relationships.** Make sure you're not silently communicating to your child that it's acceptable to be treated badly.
- **Base your screen-related rules around the needs and propensities of your teenager.** If your child is still young, it's worth setting early, tight rules that you can relax later, if appropriate – perhaps including a screen cut-off time, keeping screens away from bedrooms and mealtimes, and regular parental device checks (so you can make sure they're safe online and not accessing inappropriate content). Parental controls should, ideally, be put in place with plenty of communication or they risk backfiring. A teenager who is into gaming may be prevented from playing with friends if your evening cut-off time frustrates it; tight rules are less appropriate for a teenager approaching adulthood. Regular conversations about internet safety and algorithm-driven manipulation are important for all teenagers. Don't remove devices as punishment, as this can have unintended consequences such as riskier online behaviour and damage to your relationship. Model healthy screen use yourself.

# CHAPTER 4

# MIND, PART 1
## MOOD AND MATURITY

**Mood**

One challenge in being the parent of teenagers is that I'm never entirely sure which version is going to emerge. Will I get the soft, sleepy, cuddly version, the – hopefully not literally – high-as-a-kite version, or the version that thinks her parents are lower than a snake's belly and must be treated as such? One I often encounter is the stubborn-as-a-mule version, who is prepared to argue that penguins live in the Arctic or that *Stranger Things* is no scarier than *Teletubbies* if it allows her to get one over on another member of her family. This obstinacy is a trait that was inherited from both parents, and the emergence of which I should have foreseen. I had a text exchange with my younger daughter, who'd run off with my charger cable, that went something like this.

    **Me** (texting, possibly unreasonably, from my basement office):
    'I need that cable. Can you bring it down now, please?'

**Her**: 'It's on the kitchen table.'
**Me**: 'Can you bring it down please?'
**Her**: 'Why?'
**Me**: 'Because I need it. And you were meant to bring it back to my office, which is where you took it from.'
**Her**: 'No, I was meant to bring it back in from the car.'
**Me**: 'Now, please.'
**Her**: 'You'd have it by now if you stopped dictating what I do.'

I am guessing she meant dictating in the Stalin and Mussolini sense, not the 1950s secretary sense, which felt a touch extreme given that I just wanted to charge my phone using the cable she'd taken. This argumentativeness can flicker into excitement, happiness, then an obvious desire for solitude within the space of minutes. Teenagers' mood fluctuates more than the mood of adults or younger children. Their brains become more sensitive to social rejection[1] and the pleasure they feel from taking risks,[2] while the part of their brain that regulates feelings develops more slowly.[3]

We can probably assume that most parents aren't going to quibble about their teenagers' excellent moods, so this section focuses more on the negative ones. It's important to make the point again, though, that traditional ideas of constant conflict, rages and terrible moods aren't backed up by evidence – we need to be careful that our expectations aren't colouring our actual experiences with our teenagers.

I find other people's negative moods hardest to handle when I don't understand where they've come from, as I'm prone to thinking they must be personal. The chances are, though, that any glumness or irritability really isn't about you – or, at least, that it's not just about you, as your teenager's experiences elsewhere are probably affecting their mood, which spills over into how you engage with each other. One study used daily diaries from 130 pairs of teenagers and their mothers to test links between what happens at school and at home. It found that conflict at home went up and parenting practices got worse on challenging school days.[4]

Conflict is certainly related to mood – unsurprisingly, teenagers report worse moods when there's been a lot of squabbling.[5] A friend remembers a row with his daughter precipitated by his statement that she couldn't go to a party with her friends, as there was going to be no adult supervision and he'd never met the host. His daughter entered the kitchen in a fury and smashed a vase into pieces. A few months later, she had a similar row with her mother, then did the same thing to a substitute vase. (The second time this happened, the cost of replacing it came out of the daughter's allowance. They've had no vessel-smashing incidents since.) Teenagers who find it hard to regulate their emotions are the ones most likely to convert these feelings into problem behaviour or poor mental health.[6]

Teenagers are particularly sensitive to how they perceive others feel about them, making them respond to situations with more emotional intensity than adults or younger children.[7] This tendency is compounded by the fact that these perceptions are often wrong. If teenagers at an early stage of puberty see a neutral face in a photograph, the amygdala – which is one of the regions of the brain responsible for emotions – lights up in a way that the brains of their post-puberty peers don't, suggesting they're more likely to see hostility that doesn't actually exist.[8] (Me: 'How did it go today?' My teenager: 'Oh my God, can you stop pressuring me?')

One reason for teenage reactions that baffle our adult brains is the way that information reaches the amygdala. According to the psychiatrist Professor Daniel Siegel, there's a slow, rational route to the amygdala that adds a veneer of thought and reason to any transmission that runs through it, and a fast route that bypasses rational analysis. Teenagers' brains take the fast route more often than adults' brains do.[9] So it's not necessarily that your teenager is disregarding the streams of impeccable logic and insight that you're bringing to a conversation – instead, they may simply be unable to process what you're saying. At the same time, other systems that contribute to teenagers' ability to manage their emotions, including their hormonal systems and other ways that their brains are wired and balanced, haven't yet reached maturity.[10]

Social rejection leaves teenagers prone to anger, anxiety and depression.[11] A thirteen-year-old who has just spent a school bus journey alone because nobody wanted to sit next to him, for example, may react badly when he gets home to something that appears totally innocuous to his parent. Or a fifteen-year-old may be tight-lipped for hours if she asks a question and her mum fails to look up from her phone.

A way to navigate the minefield of teenage emotions is to model successful management of your own. You help your child to understand what's suitable and appropriate when it comes to steering your way through the emotional world. Part of this modelling means talking about your own feelings. But as we saw in the section on conflict, it's become culturally normalised for mothers to discuss feelings and fathers to discuss solutions to problems, and we need to ensure that teenagers know men are able to talk about how they feel. My dad could do this in some ways – he'd talk fluently about something at work that had made him furious, a family event that had given him great pleasure or an exciting new project. He couldn't talk about sadness or fear, though – and this made it incredibly hard for me, later on, to know how to talk to him about his terminal cancer diagnosis. (His answer: Nothing to see here! Move along!)

According to the research literature, validating your child's emotions is a key part of emotional management[12] – though acknowledging them might be a better description, as you're not necessarily trying to suggest your child is right. My partner makes a fair point here – 'Why should I validate them if they're being a royal pain in the arse and when they've got absolutely nothing to be complaining about?' And some experts believe that being overly prescriptive about things like this risks making the parent–child relationship feel inauthentic.[13] There are two important responses to these points. The first is that you don't need to be validating the pain-in-the-arseness. 'I can hear that you're feeling upset about this, but I don't like the way you're talking to me. We'll discuss it later.' It's the emotion behind any action that you're acknowledging, rather than the ways in which the emotions are expressed.

The second is that acknowledging emotions works. A study of eighty pairs of teenagers and their parents, for example, found that parents who are emotionally dysregulated are more likely to invalidate their children's emotions, which in turn makes the children themselves emotionally dysregulated, and more likely to have both mental ill health and behavioural problems.[14] I'm prepared to do a bit of (occasionally reluctant) validation if it means a happier child who's less likely to act up in future. Damour paints this function as 'emotional garbage collection', through which you allow your teenager to offload some of the intense things they're feeling onto you. Knowing you'll take their feelings seriously and can describe what they're feeling back to them helps them to keep a handle on everything.[15]

Being a teenager's emotional rubbish truck will naturally have an impact on parents' own mood. I don't have endless capacity to absorb someone else's negative feelings, however much I love them – sometimes I need space. Work meetings in another city can be very handy, I find. When it comes to rudeness, experts offer conflicting advice. On the one hand, picking up on it risks exacerbating it, and it may be better to deal with it at a later moment. Alternatively, you could give your teenager three options in the face of rudeness: being friendly, being polite or letting you know that they need some space. You could also choose to remove yourself from the conversation (perhaps by leaving the room) until your teenager can discuss things with you more calmly.

There's a persistent flashpoint in my house over laundry and the unending piles of it that seem to emanate from one daughter's bedroom, and which she often saves up until she's run out of clean socks. In a sample snippet, I watched her dump three loads' worth of laundry into the bathroom bin one evening, then told her that I'd put a wash on but she would need to hang it up before school the next morning. She stuck out her chin. 'I won't have time.' 'You need to make time,' I replied, wearing the Unamused Face that I only roll out in extremis. 'This laundry's going to take a while to get through, it's yours, and you need to contribute to getting it done.' Her reply? 'That's not my priority at the moment.' With hindsight, I should have bowed out of the conversation at this point, with the suggestion that she put the laundry on herself when it became a priority to her. She likes to wear clean clothes. It wouldn't have taken long. The summary of the lengthy conversation that actually followed resulted in me being asked why I was being so difficult, and her 'hanging up' the laundry the next morning by heaping it in a single pile over the airer.

In situations of lesser conflict and when teenagers make it clear they want space, leaving them alone can be a fruitful avenue when they are in the swirl of heavy emotions. If they've had early support to manage their feelings, they may be skilful at it by now. Art has the power to mirror mood, and they may have found a way to channel their emotions through music, books or TV. I found refuge in the American navel-gazing show *My So-Called Life*, or in skimming stones into the sea, or in dissecting kaleidoscopic emotional minutiae with friends.

You might decide to use your teenager's emotions as a prompt to help to build your relationship with each other or to help them to grow and develop. This depends, of course, on them not brick-walling you – but if they put up barriers to stop you talking to them, you can make small signals that you're around if they need it. You might respond to obvious unhappiness by bringing them an unprompted hot drink or by making their favourite dinner. Sending a text to ask how your teenager's doing can be a way to get them to open up, if they're otherwise unwilling to speak. It removes the pressure of eye contact, and allows them time to think up a response and to execute communication-by-emoji, if that's easier for them. If how your teenager is feeling remains a mystery, you could try asking how their friends are feeling about an upcoming exam, say, or about a new person who has joined their friendship group. This distance might make it easier for your teenager to talk and for you to latch onto some clues about their own feelings on the matter in hand.

There are two things worth keeping in mind when it comes to teenage mood. The first is that there isn't necessarily a darker truth running under the surface of their emotions – feeling things deeply is a normal part of teenage development. And it's worth remembering that the most unexpected things can cause the barometer of a teenage mood to rise from *stormy* to *fair*. I bought some crutches following a knee injury. Nobody could remain unhappy while nicking them to swing around the house, and these crutches entertained my daughters for far longer than any birthday present ever did.

## Maturity and independence

My mum gave me a card for my sixteenth birthday that she found highly amusing. It depicted a cartoon mother saying to her teenager, 'Why don't you leave home now while you still know everything?' My mum was right – I did know everything then, as far as I was concerned. I knew how to cook a half-decent meal, pull a pint, structure an essay, mend a puncture on my bike and beat everyone I'd ever met at the card game Slam. Thanks to my grandparents living on a farm with a dirt track snaking its way to the main road, I even knew how to drive a car. The fact that I had no legal piece of paper saying I was able to do so was a mere technicality.

What I have learned in the interim is doubt. This is a feeling that the average teenager is loath to express, even if they feel it deeply underneath.

A challenge in interpreting research about autonomy is that academic studies often examine different parts of it, or define the concept in disparate ways. This makes it hard to combine the evidence in a way that allows conclusions to be generalised. One of the two main ways of defining autonomy relates to independence, and the second to the extent to which teenagers act on their interests, goals and beliefs. Other ways of defining autonomy relate to emotions – whether teenagers feel themselves to be independent; to values – the extent to which they have their own ideas and beliefs about the world; and to behaviour – to whether they can make decisions independently and look after themselves. Behavioural autonomy includes the ability to resist social pressure to act against one's better judgement. A sixteen-year-old who is unable to resist his mates egging him on to chug the bottle of cider, despite not wanting to and knowing it will make him hurl, probably doesn't have behavioural autonomy yet. By that measure, nor do many twenty-one-year-olds.

The relationship between teenagers and their parents transforms as the younger generation becomes increasingly independent. At the same time, negotiations between parents and children over their autonomy help them to achieve it. In other words, the process of achieving independence (and other aspects of autonomy) changes and is changed by relationships. Your relationship might shift, for example, if you see your teenager increasingly comfortable making thoughtful decisions, just as the shape of your discussions about whether they can stay out late on Friday nights affects how independent they start to feel. An unassailable truth is that teenagers mature at different rates.[16] You might have a pair of best friends, one of whom is ready for unsupervised trips into town months before the other. There are some averages, though. Boys tend to mature later than girls, for example, which means they can struggle with the demands made of them.[17]

There are four main ways that parents affect their children's behavioural autonomy, according to some scholars. The first is whether they model how to make competent decisions. Do you spend your £50 birthday present money on something you really wanted, or will it disappear in a scratchcard-induced puff of smoke? The second is whether they encourage their teenagers to make independent decisions themselves. Do you sit down with your teenager to talk through their GCSE options, and what they see as being the upsides and downsides of the different decisions they need to make, or do you suggest their choices for them? The third is whether they reward decisions made when teenagers are not with their families. Do you commend your teenager for making a sensible decision to get adult help when their friend was vomiting outside a pub, or do you tell them off for getting into that situation in the first place? The final element is one we've discussed already in Chapter 1, and that's whether parents are responsive to their teenagers while making demands of them (demands are explored a little later in this chapter).[18]

Parents can support their children's autonomy by trying to connect to their teenagers' way of understanding a situation without overly imposing their own point of view, trusting them (unless they have a good reason not to), and avoiding intrusive questions, unsolicited advice and lectures.[19] I've accidentally found an excellent way of fostering my children's autonomy by forgetting at least 50% of the things I'm meant to remind them about for school.

Moral development and concern for other people can be supported by parents who reason at a level that's a slight stretch for their teenagers.[20] You might, for example, express a complex opinion on a conflict in the Middle East while being curious about your child's views. It's good to get teenagers to think about the effects of issues on other people.[21] Lecturing doesn't work.[22] Nor does being controlling[23] – when parents exert pressure on their teenagers about moral issues, their children are less likely to take their messages on board and are more likely to flout the rules. If I scold my child about the need for her to defer to people in positions of authority – which would be rich, given my own reluctance to do so – she becomes more likely to defy her teachers. And that's not going to be good for her education or for the long-suffering people who are trying to transmit their knowledge to her. Gentle guidance is more likely to work here.

One element of the research struck me as not quite ringing true for our very particular twenty-first-century context. A 2019 handbook on parenting quoted older research saying that younger teenagers who make fully independent decisions are at risk of later problematic behaviour, including delinquency.[24] This may very well be true – perhaps the absence of parental input is a proxy for having no limits or guardrails in place, which is certainly linked to poor outcomes for teenagers. But I wonder about more recent research forewarning of future difficulties for cosseted teenagers who haven't had an opportunity to stretch their wings (see Chapter 5 for a more detailed discussion about this). My working theory is that the older studies do not capture our cultural shift towards being extremely child-centred, and a bit more independence at an earlier stage for young teenagers may not be a terrible thing for this particular generation.

Alternatively, the type of decisions assigned to our teenagers may matter more than seeing them as a blanket choice between independence and none. Younger teenagers making decisions about what they wear and how they spend their time seems to be a good thing, according to research, whereas more fundamental decisions are better left a little later.[25] (Teenagers tend to agree with this rationale, too – they're more accepting of their parents' authority in decisions that might involve harm to themselves or other people, but more reasonably reject attempts to brush their hair or make them wear a hoodie with fewer than seven holes in it.[26] Their increasing drive for autonomy in other areas may be partly driven by wanting the freedoms they see their friends being given.[27]) Another possible explanation is that too much autonomy at an early age allows more room for the influence of friends – and, as mentioned in Chapter 2, teenagers can make riskier decisions when they're with their friends than without them.

Parents face a dilemma that's almost impossible when it comes to autonomy, and the details of which are as unique as our teenagers. We understand the consequences of badly thought-through decisions or mistakes and may even have lived some of these ourselves. We've witnessed substance abuse or the curtailing of an education through unplanned pregnancy. We've seen people struggling if they didn't get the grades that matched their potential. Our children's actions and inactions when they were younger carried relatively little weight – but now, when the stakes are higher, we have to take a step back.

This is a reason we need limits to balance our teenagers' increasing autonomy. If you're not invested in raising a monster, you'll need to put in place some rules and then stick to them in the face of any wheedling, tears or attempts to shout you into submission that come your way. (I need to take more of my own advice here. A friend told me that cooking has been reconfigured from a burden to a joy now that her four teenage children each cook a regular family meal. 'Dad and I have been talking,' I said to my daughters, 'and we're going to start making sure we each cook at least one meal a week.' There was a wall of protest so strong it felt almost physical. 'I have mocks for my mocks coming up. I have so much homework. I don't have time. It's not my job. You're ruining my life chances.' We have yet to put this into practice.)

Having rules is not just about making your life easier, though it helps. It's about building your child up for a future life without you, and your guardrails help to give them a sense of security. The setting of limits also helps your child to know they are not alone – they have you looking out for them, however irritating they may find you. The rules you choose will depend on your family and your teenager. They might include rules at home (plates need to be cleared at the end of a meal and put in the dishwasher; clothes that need washing go in the laundry basket, not the floordrobe; the cat needs to be fed; the hallway is for walking through, not a container ship for their detritus), rules for seeing friends (they need to be home by a certain time; no sleepovers on a school night) and rules for health and well-being (no vaping; no screens in bedrooms; no staying up all night gaming).

It can be hard to know which demands are the right ones to make. I'm conscious not to set clear rules around food intake, because of the link between pressure around food and unhealthy eating habits – but, at the same time, how do I balance this with seeing the rapidity with which processed snacks are consumed and the disdain attached to anything containing fibre? My children seem to have a sixth sense for my vulnerability in this area. (Me: 'Please don't have a snack just now – dinner will be ready in a few minutes.' My teenager: 'Why are you always so *controlling*?')

You'll probably need some trial and error in finding the right balance, and making sure you keep your powder dry for the issues that matter. The culture of your family and your teenager's beliefs are likely to matter here, too. If your teenager thinks it's legitimate for you to have authority, they're more likely to comply with the rules you set.[28] Rules can be drawn up jointly and renegotiated as needed. Joint decision-making tends to be linked to better outcomes than unilateral wielding of power by either the parent or their teenager.[29] This works particularly well if you can show your teenager that you are trying to understand their perspective – asking what they think about a proposed limit, for example, and showing you understand why they might find a particular aspect of it frustrating. Doing so (probably) encourages curiosity in your teenager, too.[30]

An approach based on negotiation is ultimately more effective during the teenage years than one that's based on edicts. A study on parents banning friendships found that if parents wield their power in getting their child to end a friendship – if they threaten to ground the teenager or take away their phone, for example – their children are more likely to remain friends with the subject of their parents' disapproval.[31] If you want your child to take on board reasons for rules, 'inductive discipline' – through which you explain reasons for any rules, your values and your expectations of your child – is a good way to go.

Changing your mind about rules that have previously been negotiated is fine. The main thing is that rule changes are based on thoughtful reflection, not on how forcefully your child manages to imprint their will upon your desire, or lack of it, to stick to your guns. If my child knows a full-scale war footing has caused me to change my mind about giving her cash to go to the cinema when she has three unfinished pieces of homework due tomorrow, she'll be more likely to employ the same tactics next time I ask her to unload the dishwasher or remove the death-trap schoolbag she's left on the top step. Sometimes, being the parent of teenagers feels like little more than trying to steer a steady course through waves that appear destined to capsize the ship.

In a related point, you probably want to aim for a central point between tight control and limitless freedoms with your teenager. The dividing line needs revising as your teenager develops and your relationship changes, too. A thirteen-year-old will need very different limits to someone on the cusp of adulthood. You also need to ensure that teenagers have sufficient freedom to be curious and to experiment. Those whose drive for novelty is quashed can become disconnected and disenchanted.[32] An experimental study found that momentary increases in teenagers' autonomy led to more instances of their mothers (but not their fathers) showing 'control' by trying to get their teenager to behave in a certain way, making decisions about them without consulting them and similar behaviours.[33] This implies a kind of dance between teenagers and their mums, where signs of independence are met with unconscious efforts to contain them.

Whatever the discussions, negotiations, treaties and territories lost or gained in the setting of limits, there's a point at which talking needs to end. Perhaps you've been negotiating something and your teenager hasn't managed to change your mind. Perhaps they're railing against a rule they believe to be deeply unfair but you see as essential for their safety. At this juncture, some of the tips from the section on conflict in Chapter 2 may be helpful. Your best bet, though, is probably to withdraw from the conversation by bringing it to a close or, if needed, physically leaving the room. My internal hazard lights flash when I'm being shouted at, making it hard to think clearly. If I can get some distance, it becomes more like I've just stepped into and back out of a vexing television scene. This distance helps me to regain some perspective.

And what happens when rules inevitably get contravened? One approach is to state that a rule has been broken, to say that it is unacceptable and to emphasise that the rule remains in place. It's an imperfect solution – a teenager, after all, can just ignore you. But you can't physically stop a teenager from breaking rules, and threats, lectures and sanctions don't tend to do much (and may well backfire). Layering punishment upon punishment for broken rules can lead teenagers to escalate their behaviour,[34] possibly because they think there's no point trying to behave. Restating the rules and your expectations is likely to work with most teenagers – they mainly want to keep you onside, even if they are pushing at the edges of the limits you've set for them. You may need to go through this process of restating rules repeatedly. And it's probably worth hiding the whites of your terrified eyes through this process. In the words of Tony Soprano, 'Let's just not overplay our hand, because if she finds out that we're powerless, we're fucked.'[35]

Limits that you set are more likely to remain in place if you've coupled any rule-setting with the usual markers of good-enough parenting – warmth and involvement. Your child is more likely to listen to you if you're showing up at the school play, carving out space to talk about what matters to them and making time to watch a film together. There's an important difference between healthy separation and detachment, which is marked by conflict and negative relationships. You can remain relatively close to your child emotionally while they increasingly make decisions independently – this combination seems to lead to the best outcomes.[36]

It's important to have your own limits too, of course. When I say I'm too busy to give my children a lift to school on rainy days, they protest that I always have enough time to exercise at lunchtime. I make it clear that this break is important for my well-being and makes me work more efficiently. They grumble, but they grudgingly accept it.

Part of autonomy means letting go of some of your own opinions and experiences. It's easy to let your history colour how you see your child's choices. As someone who lived on a tiny tidal island until the age of fifteen, then a veritable metropolis of 7,000 people (also an island) until I left home, I get frustrated when my teenagers don't suck up every opportunity afforded to them by living in a city. Free swimming in the grotty-but-warm council pool? Can't be bothered. Karate club? Don't have time. My lesson is that they are not me. I still wish I could drop them into the middle of the Blackwater Estuary in 1992 to help them appreciate the sparkling lights of Brighton. I might even choose not to leave them there.

## Secrets, revelations and lies

I'm going to need to brief my mum before she reads this section, as there were various things I did as a teenager of which (I assume – she may tell me otherwise) she remains blissfully ignorant. I don't think she knew the extent to which I believed everyone was judging me and finding me lacking, or how ugly I believed myself to be, or that I threw away my lunch for two years, or that I developed a dependency on caffeine tablets when I was trying to keep myself awake studying, or that I used to take the blunt end of a knife to my thighs when I felt angry with myself. These were all knotty, sharp-edged sources of shame. I shared nothing of these things with anyone, least of all my parents.

There's a vexation for parents when it comes to the information that teenagers keep close to their chests and what they choose to disclose to us. Our children become increasingly less likely to share information with parents as they get older,[37] and teenagers who tell their parents less have worse outcomes.[38] But parents may be oblivious to how little they really know – they are likely to overestimate how much their teenagers tell them (and discrepancies between parents' beliefs and teenagers' beliefs about how much they let on are also linked to worse teenage outcomes).[39]

Keeping secrets from parents and sharing information are not opposites of each other – they are separate ideas.[40] My teenager might share with me that she had a good afternoon on the beach with her friends but be careful not to mention that they were vaping. Some studies have shown that poor outcomes are linked to teenagers keeping secrets, not how much information they choose to share with their parents. Secretive teenagers may experience poor outcomes because it's difficult to keep secrets, because parents can't respond properly to their needs if they are doing so, or because being secretive makes teenagers less likely to share a sense of belonging with those from whom they're keeping the secrets. There's also a feedback loop between secrecy and delinquency. Being secretive increases the chances of things like underage drinking, which itself increases secretiveness as teenagers don't want their parents to find out.[41]

Other studies have shown that the worst outcomes are linked to teenagers being unwilling to share information with their parents, rather than to being very secretive.[42] The value of sharing information may lie in it strengthening the bond between parents and their children, which can underpin mental health.[43] Either way, though, it seems that keeping communication going about thoughts, feelings and activities – if it can be done in a way that supports teenagers' increasing sense of autonomy – is likely to be a good thing. So what makes it more likely for a teenager to share information and hold back on secret-keeping?

Teenagers may disclose more when their parents are accepting of them.[44] (This, presumably, means being accepting of their child as a person, not of their Friday night binge-drinking habit.) When parents listen well to their teenagers telling them about situations in which they've been hurt or they've broken the rules – as measured by, for example, trying hard to understand what is being said, and giving them their full attention – their children are more likely to disclose similar things in future. There's a link to better well-being, too.[45] If my teenager knows I'm not going to ground her for a week if she tells me that there was a spliff being passed round at a party she went to, I'll know more about what's happening in her friendship group and be better prepared to work out how to help her navigate it (see Chapter 7 for a more detailed discussion about risk).

Patterns of disclosure are influenced by both parents and teenagers, and these processes may feed off each other. If a teenager tells you something you have the potential to judge and you react badly, they are less likely to tell you something similar next time. When you respond positively, they feel more connected and become more likely to open up to you in future.[46] Unsurprisingly, teenagers are more likely to withhold information if they believe parents will disapprove of it – perhaps they've taken up smoking or they're dating someone much older – or if they believe it's personal information over which parents should have little jurisdiction.[47]

There's a broader purpose in withholding information, too, of which teenagers may or may not be consciously aware. It changes power dynamics within a family, and enables a less hierarchical relationship to develop between parents and their teenagers as they hurtle towards adulthood. There needs to be a balance, though, from the teenagers' perspective – withholding information can damage their relationship with you. Alternatively, your teenager may increasingly give you less information because it's normalised that parts of their lives become increasingly private as they grow up, and because there's less opportunity to tell you things. There were plenty of chances for intimate disclosures when I used to lie on my daughters' beds reading them stories – and fewer now that they spend more time out with their friends and, when they are home, more time alone in their rooms.

You may not need your child to disclose their secrets to know what they're up to – the clues may be hiding in plain sight. When my friend Sara was seventeen, she asked if she could go to a club night near London's Victoria to celebrate Bastille Day. Her mum said no, as the club finished at 3 a.m. and Sara's curfew, like Cinderella's, was midnight. In the next breath, she said, 'Jo's having a sleepover on Saturday night. Can I go?' Her mum, not spotting the link between the two requests, said yes. Sara went to the club night, which was fine until she clocked that the evening was being filmed by a French TV channel. She spent the night not dancing, but hiding from the TV cameras in case her presence there ever got back to her mother (who wasn't French, so it was unlikely).

There used to be an idea in the research literature that parents keeping a close eye on their teenagers' whereabouts was linked to better outcomes. But more recent findings are unhelpful here, as different studies give us conflicting messages. Some point towards this early idea still being true. A recent piece of research, for example, found that teenagers have the best outcomes when their parents monitor them while providing plenty of support for their emerging autonomy. They have the worst outcomes when their parents are psychologically controlling or don't keep as close an eye on them.[48] Other assessments have shifted towards the idea that it's what our teenagers choose to tell us that's important, not the information that we seek out.[49] And, under a different lens, trying to keep an eye on your child may actively be damaging – one study found that teenagers give their mums more information when they actively seek it, but at the same time the teenagers start to keep more secrets.[50] As we've already seen, excessive secret-keeping seems linked to worse outcomes for teenagers. As with other cases when the research is mixed, you probably need to make a call based on your instincts and your knowledge of your child.

For my part, there is something about the idea of actively seeking out very personal information that makes me feel slightly queasy – I'm very aware of my children's boundaries, probably because I'm sensitive about my own. I want them to tell me stuff, of course, but only if they want me to know it (which is undoubtedly horribly naïve). My general ambition is to know where they are physically, at least until they're a bit older, as that's about safety – I ask them to check in with me periodically and, if I can't get hold of them, the four of us are on a mutual family stalker app. (This sounds terrifying, but it's incredibly useful, so long as the adults in a family have high levels of trust in each other and you know the other one isn't going to go digging around trying to work out where you are all the time. It means that when one of us is in London, the other one can time dinner without needing to worry about reception blackspots – and when our daughters are out with their friends and I get assailed by an irrational fear that they've been kidnapped, I can set my mind at rest without inflicting my paranoia on my children.)

My other ambition is to make it as easy as possible for them to tell me things. This I'm less good at, I think – I don't create the spaces needed to allow them to come to me quietly and casually, for which I would need to override my need to be constantly busy. Addressing this is on my to-do list – though perhaps the true way of addressing it would be to become the type of person who doesn't have a to-do list.

The final part of this chapter is about lying. It's very normal for teenagers to lie, even as they deny all knowledge of doing so. I may be the exception that proves the rule here – I was able to manipulate situations to my advantage. (Can't sing a note in tune? Pretend you're so nervous in your music exam when you get to the oral section that it's making your ability to self-tune go out of the window. It works every time.) But I really struggled with outright lies – even today, if I attempt to hide how I truly feel about a situation to save someone's feelings, I reveal myself instantly to the people who know me best. It's not an asset if you want to retain friends in the face of an overcooked dinner or their newly decorated peach-and-purple bathroom.

This inability on my part makes it hard for me to handle my children lying. One downside of lying, despite how normal it is, is that it can undermine trust between parents and their children. You might have to do some pretty contorted thinking to persuade yourself that your child has not just fibbed to you. There was a time when I'd just been to the supermarket and restocked the fridge, whose teenager-baiting contents included an eight-pack of cheese strings – vile, but apparently not if your palate has some maturing left to do. Two hours later, the empty package was flapping about on the top shelf of the fridge. Each daughter said they'd eaten only one. The house was empty apart from them, me and the dog. The dog would be a fair candidate were it not for the telling lack of opposable thumbs.

What lying has in common with secrets is an active effort to conceal information.[51] Most teenagers think it's unacceptable to lie, but they see acts of omission as being less problematic than explicitly fibbing.⁵² This aversion to overt lies decreases with age, though – older teenagers are more likely to bend the truth.⁵³ Given how normal lying is, it may be worth not getting too bound up with the lie itself if one is uncovered – instead, it's probably more helpful to you both to focus on the subject of the lie. In my cheese strings example, I might focus on the fact that snacks need to last for more than two hours after one of us has been to the shop. If Luke's daughter has told him that the vape clouds curling out from under her bedroom door are, in fact, scented candle trails (ha), it's probably more productive to focus on the vaping than it is upon the born-yesterday misdirection.

Your own general honesty is more likely to shunt your teenager across into a more truthful track than lectures or punishments. It's also worth learning from history – trust matters but, if you know your teenager has lied about something important in the past, similar scenarios should engender future parental wariness. Information may also be distorted in front of other key adults, of course. I got a call one morning from someone at my daughter's school, who said, confidently: 'Hello, I have your daughter here in the medical room. She says her hay fever is playing up and would like you to bring in her medication.' My daughter having hay fever was news to me, which I passed on to the amused member of staff. When I questioned my teenager later, she said: 'Oh, I kept sneezing, and assumed it must be hay fever, and thought you might have some emergency medicine for me you keep in the cupboard.' I'll leave it to you to decide whether that explanation was more plausible than an excuse to step out of double maths.

# CHAPTER SUMMARY

## Mood

- **The shape of teenage mood.** Mood is more variable during the teenage years than it is at other times of life – and teenagers feel things deeply – but the idea that adolescents spend most of their time in dark rages or sulks isn't backed up by data. If your teenager is in a bad mood, though, it's probably nothing to do with you. Where it is, it's most likely to be driven by conflict. Teenagers can be particularly sensitive to social rejection. Those who find it hard to regulate their emotions are more likely than others to turn a bad mood into problem behaviours or mental ill health. Teenagers can be very sensitive to other people's (perceived) feelings towards them, leading to intense emotions. They are more likely than those of other ages to perceive hostility where there is none.
- **Effects of brain processes.** Adolescent brains take a fast route to processing information – one that may bypass rationality – more often than adult brains do. Hormonal processes and wiring that supports emotional regulation have, at the same time, not yet fully matured.

## Maturity and independence

- **Fuzzy definitions.** A challenge to interpreting research in this area is that studies often use different definitions of the word 'autonomy' or are exploring different parts of it. One way of defining autonomy relates to independence; another relates to agency. Other studies may break it down into emotions, values and behaviour.
- **Intertwined autonomy and relationships.** Increasing teenage independence drives changes in the parent–child relationship, and

negotiations over independence help teenagers to achieve it. Negotiating with a teenager is a good tactic. Lecturing is a poor one. Early signs of teenage independence may (probably subconsciously) be met with parental attempts to exert control.
- **The need to balance autonomy with limits.** Parents have more life experience to enable them to understand the real-world implications and longer-term consequences of decisions, and setting limits helps give teenagers a sense of security. Limits are essential, as is keeping an eye on the age-appropriateness of the decisions your teenager is able to make independently.

## Secrets, revelations and lies

- **An arc towards less information.** Teenagers are less likely to share information with parents as they get older, though sharing information (possibly in the form of being less likely to keep secrets) is linked to better outcomes. The value of sharing information may lie in it strengthening bonds between children and their parents. Parents believe their children share more information with them than they do.
- **Corrosiveness of secrets.** Potential reasons for secrets being linked with poor outcomes are that they're hard work to keep, because it's difficult to meet teenagers' needs if we don't fully know what they are, and because keeping secrets from family erodes their sense of belonging. There are feedback loops between secretive behaviour and delinquency.
- **A balancing act.** Teenagers may want to withhold information to equalise your relationship but, at the same time, know the potential it has to cause damage. Or it may be less conscious than this – there may simply be fewer opportunities to tell you things now they spend more time with friends or in their rooms.
- **Mixed evidence on parental monitoring.** The research is mixed on whether better outcomes are linked to parents monitoring

their teenagers' whereabouts and activities, or whether they're linked to teenagers being more willing to disclose information to their parents. Monitoring has potential risks that include making teenagers more secretive. A judgement call is needed depending on your knowledge of what's likely to work best with your teenager.
- **Impact of lies.** Teenagers lying can undermine trust between them and their parents. Most teenagers believe it's unacceptable to lie, though it's very normal for them to do so.

## Ideas for parents

- **Try to model successful management of your own emotions.** This can help your teenager to learn how to manage theirs. You can also acknowledge your teenager's emotions (without validating inappropriate behaviour that might stem from them). Doing so is linked to better behaviour and mental health.
- **Promote your ability to absorb your child's emotions in a way that protects your well-being.** Take yourself away from a situation and get space as needed. Be clear to your child that you won't accept rudeness, perhaps by giving them an option to engage without it or to take themselves away until they can talk to you more courteously.
- **If your child won't engage, leave pathways to connection open.** You could bring them a hot drink or make their favourite dinner, or send a text to ask how they are. You could also try asking how their friends are feeling about a particular event or issue, if they're stonewalling you about their own feelings.
- **Support your child's autonomy.** Model making competent decisions. Encourage your teenager to make their own decisions in areas in which this is appropriate, with your guidance where needed. Reward the making of sensible decisions, and aim to be

both responsive and demanding. Try not to impose your own point of view on your teenager's decisions, and trust them (within reason, and unless you have evidence that suggests you shouldn't). Make sure autonomy doesn't slip into detachment.

- **Balance autonomy with limits.** Focus your limits on the issues that matter. Change your mind if your teenager makes a decent case for doing so, but not in the face of aggressive tactics. Make limits age-appropriate, and ensure they leave space for curiosity and experimentation. If rules get broken, be clear that it's unacceptable and that the rule remains in place. Don't try to exert your power instead. Set boundaries for yourself, too.
- **Close down conversations when they're no longer constructive.** If you are laying down a limit and there are continuing arguments about it, close down the discussion and leave the room if you have to.
- **Stretch your child's thinking.** Challenge them to think about issues at a level that's just beyond their current capabilities. Don't lecture.
- **Try to listen well when your child's telling you about hurtful or rule-breaking situations.** This means giving your complete attention and trying to understand fully what you're being told. Listening well is linked to being told more things in future and to better teenage well-being. It's also worth avoiding judgement and control in these kinds of situations.
- **If your teenager lies to you, try focusing on the subject of the lie, rather than on the lie itself.** This may be more productive for you both. Modelling honesty can be helpful with a lying teenager – as can learning from experience and being more alert in situations in which your teenager has lied in the past.

## CHAPTER 5

# MIND, PART 2
# MENTAL HEALTH AND RESILIENCE

### Anxiety and sadness

As we saw in Chapter 2, we have a newly anxious, unhappy teenage cohort. Mental health got worse over the teenage years even before this more recent spike in mental ill health,[1] and the acceleration is a worrying trend. We've seen, too, that while screens and social media play a role, it's probably not a straightforward one. Another candidate for the rise in mental health problems is the pandemic, which we know had a negative impact on children's well-being.[2] Loneliness was an important factor in this.[3] But teenage mental health was declining even before Covid, which just gave it an extra impetus. If the reason for this decline isn't simply a rise in smartphones or wider screen use, what else might be going on?

Previous generations of teenagers may have avoided talking about their feelings, perhaps turning them inwards into self-hatred or eating disorders, or outwards into aggression or delinquency. These routes are not, obviously, the way to go. But there's increasing evidence that the pendulum has swung too far in the opposite direction. The new fluency teenagers have in talking about their mental health is supposedly an asset. But scratching the surface reveals a generation who may be identifying with their feelings to an unhealthy degree, getting caught in rumination and negative spirals.

'Do you think I might have borderline?' asked my friend Chloe's daughter, Hannah, one evening. She'd done an online quiz about mental health conditions, which had told her she was showing symptoms of borderline personality disorder (BPD). Statements from the website Psych Central's BPD quiz include 'I often experience a sudden shift in the way I look at myself and my life, and completely change my goals, values and career focus' and 'My views of others – especially those I care about – can shift dramatically and without any warning.'[4] These are pronouncements with which most humans would occasionally agree, and probably more acutely during the turbulence of adolescence. Hannah didn't know this. She just recognised the symptoms this quiz reflected back to her and believed they were linked to a potentially legitimate diagnosis.

It's not just online culture that contributes to teenagers like Hannah increasingly identifying with mental health conditions. There's mounting evidence that school-based mental health interventions are causing harm when they're directed at all students rather than targeted at those who need particular support. While some studies have noted positive outcomes linked to these interventions, particularly when delivered by clinicians rather than teachers or other non-specialists,[5] others have found the opposite. One found that younger teenagers experienced increased levels of depression and physical symptoms after a mindfulness-based intervention.[6] Another tested the effects of rolling out a psychological intervention known as 'dialectical behaviour therapy'. It found that the mental health of the teenagers involved in the programme got worse, as did their relationships with their parents.[7] A review of studies that tested the effects of anti-bullying interventions cautioned that those using cognitive behavioural therapy techniques were linked to worse student mental health.[8]

A Texan study set out to test the idea that teenagers' mental health labels can be harmful. Eleven- to fourteen-year-olds were educated at school about mental health. At the same time, efforts were made to reduce the stigma attached to poor mental health. Teenagers with mental health problems were tracked over the course of two years to see whether they agreed with the statement, 'I have a mental illness.' Those who labelled themselves in this way saw their self-esteem fall; self-esteem improved again in those who later dropped this label.[9]

Drs Lucy Foulkes and Jack Andrews of the University of Oxford have proposed that 'awareness efforts are leading some individuals to interpret and report milder forms of distress as mental health problems'. In other words, well-intentioned attempts to increase people's awareness of mental health may lead them to believe their symptoms mean something more significant than they do. The scholars suggest that this leads to an increase in symptoms – their inflated self-diagnosis becomes self-fulfilling.[10] If a teenager, Ben, believes his school-related worries are a symptom of anxiety, he may think he's better off missing school and doing his work from home for a few weeks. His avoidance of school then blows up his initial worries into genuine anxiety. His teachers and parents try to talk to him about anxiety and how it manifests, making him more aware of it and driving further symptoms.

Awareness-raising campaigns causing teenagers to believe their minor symptoms are a sign of something more serious may be facilitated by a new cachet attached to mental health conditions in certain contexts. Social media, in particular, can lend a seductive veneer to poor mental health. One Christmas Instagram post, for example, shows a simple gold star, with the message underneath: 'it's okay not to feel merry and bright'. Its hashtags include #anxiety, #socialanxiety and #healthanxiety.[11] Or the elegant psychologist Dr Julie is over on TikTok talking about the hidden signs of depression: 'Everything seems fine to others. You do everything you need to do. On the inside… Overwhelmed. Hopeless. Self-loathing. Feeling easily frustrated and irritable. Less confident in conversation. Tearful and sad. Numb and empty. Persistent sleep disturbance leaves you exhausted. But too anxious at night to sleep. Even if others have bigger problems, you still deserve help with yours.'[12] She acts out these symptoms, too, looking vulnerable, fragile and graceful. I can imagine watching that video as a fourteen-year-old and wanting to identify with her.

There's a linked problem here. Mental health is often perceived to mean we feel good – the flipside being that feeling bad is perceived as a sign of poor mental health, instead of a normal and natural process. This means that teenagers can see their worries or sadness as being a sign of something being fundamentally wrong, rather than a normal feeling that they're able to manage. It's rational to feel worried about a test or a big trip, or sad because a friendship has broken up. And it's normal, as a teenager, to feel these things sometimes even when there's no obvious cause. The belief that something is wrong can be aggravated by messages about self-care – if taking a bath with scented candles or drinking a mug of hot chocolate mindfully is meant to make our teenager feel better, why do they still feel bad? They may not realise that self-care isn't going to make normal daily stresses disappear, or that it's normal for these stresses to make us feel things – and that we can use these feelings to make decisions about how to act.[13]

Teenagers catastrophise – or see bad outcomes as being likely – when they lock into seeing their feelings as a marker of something more sinister, and when they treat normal feelings of sadness, anger or worry as a sign of mental ill health. These tendencies often lead teenagers to ruminate – they think about upsetting situations, problems and feelings over and over again. Rumination can lead to depression, whether teenagers do it alone[14] or with their friends.[15] As with so many things, this is probably an area where balance is needed – it can be helpful to think about what's wrong, and to talk about what is wrong with friends – but not if it gets repetitive and obsessive. If it does, teenagers may need parents' support to get out of their heads.

It seems, then, that there is a particularly toxic soup in which our susceptible teenagers must swim. Its ingredients include misfiring awareness-raising campaigns and mental health interventions, internet contagion (see Chapter 3) and the misattribution of normal feelings to something more sinister. This recipe may be enhanced by the salt of teenagers' natural propensity to soak up each other's moods and to grab labels as identities, and by feedback loops prompted by more teenagers discussing their mental health, leading to greater rumination and then mental ill health in their peers. A population-based study in Finland, which analysed data from more than 700,000 people, found that a lifetime mental health diagnosis was more likely in those who had been at school with a classmate diagnosed with a mental illness. The risk was greatest earlier on. If teenagers had a diagnosed classmate, they were 9% more likely to be diagnosed with a mental health condition themselves within a year. If they had more than one diagnosed classmate, the risk of their own diagnosis within the same time frame increased by 18%.[16]

Other possible explanations for rising rates of teenage mental ill health include obesity, inequality, city living, academic pressure and fears about the future of the planet.[17] These things don't explain why mental health started to deteriorate in teenagers in around 2010, though, as many of them predated this – whereas the ideas explored in Chapter 2, combined with the ease with which the internet spreads well-meaning messages about mental health, may help to explain a link with increasing smartphone prevalence that moves away from simple, unevidenced cause-and-effect models.

And there are many other reasons why teenagers may experience hits to their well-being, regardless of recent developments. They are more exposed to stress than they were as younger children. They're also more likely to feel lonely.[18] Teenagers may even see time spent with you – their beloved family – as time spent in social isolation. And even when they're spending time with other teenagers, it's possible to feel alone.[19] Imagine being in a room full of people who are on their phones – there's nobody to chat to if everyone is lost in virtual worlds.

Teenagers are more likely to feel the effects of being excluded by their peers than younger children, and they can't compensate for this feeling of exclusion, as they spend less time with their families.[20] Those who were bullied as younger children are also more likely to experience poor mental health.[21] Being bullied at primary school made me anxious and watchful at secondary school, at least in the earlier years – I was so carefully monitoring the reactions of others towards me that I became awkward, which meant others were less interested in me, precipitating a constant feedback loop. One twenty-year-old study used brain imaging to test the effects of social exclusion and found that social pain lights up the same areas of the brain that are illuminated by physical pain.[22] Being rejected by other people quite literally hurts.

Relationships with or between family members may predict mental health or ill health as well. Teenagers can blame themselves when their parents fight with each other, which is linked to worse well-being,[23] and having a bad relationship with a sibling is also linked to poor mental health.[24] As we've already seen in Chapters 1 and 2, family conflict and household chaos are both negatively linked to teenagers' well-being.

If your teenager feels sad or worried about something specific, there's probably no need to worry – this is a normal and natural reaction. My teenager might feel sad for a long time if she's had an ongoing row with her best friend, say. The point of concern crystallises if this sadness or worry starts to leach into other parts of her life, or becomes all-consuming. As we've seen, treating mental health lightly and helping teenagers to see their feelings as signals and as shifting winds, rather than the foundation stones upon which their identities are built, are likely to be reasonable starting points. There may be other things your teenager can do, though, to bolster a faltering sense of mental health, as well as things you may be able to do to help them.

Researchers have divided coping strategies into two main types – 'engagement coping strategies', which means being proactive – and 'disengagement coping strategies' (effectively running away from the problem), which tend to be less constructive. Engagement coping strategies are linked to better mental health in teenagers. When a teenager has control over a situation, an appropriate coping strategy might be found by problem-solving – 'I'm worried about my maths exam, so I'm going to spend this weekend revising, and will postpone my plans to see my friends until the following weekend' – or by expressing their feelings about the situation ('This is bloody rubbish. I hate revising, and I was really looking forward to going out'). When a teenager has no control over a situation, they might reframe it ('I've failed this particular exam, but I've got plenty of time to revise and catch up ahead of my resits') or accept it.[25] Teenagers see more success in using these strategies for uncontrollable situations when they put them in place themselves – a suggestion from a parent may still be helpful here, but it works better if it comes from your teenager.[26]

So-called 'disengagement' coping strategies – when teenagers try to suppress their emotions, avoid them or deny them – are linked to worse mental health.[27] We have already seen the dangers of teenagers focusing too much on their mental health and ruminating about their problems – so this finding about the dangers of denial and suppression, which comes from a big review of studies, needs to be interpreted carefully.

My view is, again, that it's about nuance and balance. Standing on the North Pole, you have the teenager who evades all talk of feelings and desperately avoids thinking about them. Standing on the South Pole is the one who endlessly chews over their thoughts and feelings, and who labels themselves as being fundamentally anxious or depressed. Your role is to steer your teenager gently towards the Equator – you want them to take what they feel seriously and to use it to spur action where needed, but not to shroud themselves within their emotions or to imbue them with meanings of identity.

Supporting your child to manage or express their emotions appropriately is likely to be part of finding this balance.[28] Interest and curiosity are fundamental parts of this[29] – how is your teenager feeling about the hockey match on Thursday? How do they feel about their A level options? This curiosity can help teenagers to learn to trust their feelings and to use them as signals to make informed decisions. Light curiosity is the aim here. Too much questioning about teenagers' feelings risks them getting tangled up and starting to ruminate.

A sense of belonging is fundamental to your teenager's sense of well-being. They can find this at school, and they can hopefully develop it through their friendship groups and wider community. Things that may help teenagers to feel a sense of belonging within their families include having fun together (for us, this might be paddleboarding or testing who can behave the most outrageously in the card game Cheat), feeling understood and being at the receiving end of attention. A marker of belonging is teenagers wanting to spend time with the rest of the family. My own are quite clear that they'd prefer not to, thanks. If a teenager doesn't feel a sense of belonging in one or two of these areas, others may compensate – if they're short on friends, for example, giving teenagers a strong sense of belonging at home is likely to help make up for this lack.[30]

Some of the general Top-Class Parenting Solutions explored in Chapter 1 are likely to be useful to your child when it comes to mental health. These include being warm, offering autonomy and trying not to over-involve yourself in your teenager's life.[31] It means being careful not to criticise your child too much[32] or to invalidate their feelings,[33] and keeping unhealthy levels of anger away from your child, where possible.[34]

There's some interesting new practice in this area. Physiology First, for example, is an American not-for-profit training centre that simulates anxiety in teenagers by getting them – among other things – to hold their breath while they're pedalling at full tilt on stationary bikes, meaning their bodies build up a surfeit of carbon dioxide. The trainers then show the teenagers how to bring their heart rates back under control through breath work and cold immersion, for example. In theory, this will impart a sense of control, as well as a belief that symptoms of anxiety can be managed.[35] There haven't been any trials yet, that I'm aware of, but other evidence reviewed for this section implies potential for an intervention that supports teenagers to handle difficult feelings while managing not to identify with them. Equally, the recent studies on universal mental health interventions in schools teach us that we should be pretty wary of unintended consequences.

There are, of course, some areas of which we're probably already aware in terms of our own well-being that are likely to be equally useful tools in a teenager's arsenal. These include good sleep (see Chapter 6),[36] getting out into nature,[37] eating well,[38] decent levels of exercise[39] and making sure there are plenty of opportunities for positive social connection[40] – perhaps finding an out-of-school club in which they have an interest if they're not spending as much time with other people as they would like.

Encouraging a future orientation in teenagers also holds potential. This relates to their ability to plan for the future and to set goals.[41] One study of around 500 teenagers found that hopelessness – which is linked to various aspects of poor mental health – falls over the teenage years, and it falls faster in those who develop a future orientation more quickly.[42] Helping teenagers to develop a sense of purpose may help them to develop a future orientation.[43] This is easier said than done. (Me: 'What are you hoping to get out of whatever job you end up doing?' My teenager: 'Loads of money.')

If your teenager is going through a tough time, it's better to encourage realism than it is to make false promises that everything will be OK. Being a calm port that can provide relief from the turbulent waters on which their ship is sailing is another key attribute. If teenagers believe that you are panicked by their situation, they will place a similar lens on it. If you can show that it's part of the human condition to experience difficult feelings and that they will pass, your teenager will have absorbed some indispensable material.

Finally and importantly, it's worth keeping in mind that the adolescent mental health crisis is only part of the picture. Most teenagers are absolutely fine. We don't need to manufacture a catastrophe among the majority of teenagers for whom poor mental health is a fiction.

## Gender identity

Gender identity represents the belief that it's possible to feel a sense of gender that may vary from a person's physical sex. The number of teenagers who've been questioning their gender has risen exponentially over the last decade or so. In the ten years between 2012 and 2022, referrals to the NHS's former Gender Identity Development Service increased by almost 1,600%, from 210 to more than 3,500 per year.[44] An estimated 1% of sixteen- to twenty-four-year-olds in England and Wales identify as trans, according to the latest census (which is an imperfect guess, as the question used to get this data was poorly designed).[45] If we apply this percentage to the teenagers who aren't yet adults, and assuming it's the same across the UK, there are conceivably 150,000 sixteen- and seventeen-year-olds who identify as trans nationally.[46] The current generation of teenagers may have been taught from the earliest days of nursery school that they have an innate gender identity that doesn't necessarily match their sex.[47] A few years ago, a section on gender identity might have felt a little niche for a book about teenagers. Today, this concept affects all of them.

The battle lines have been drawn between those who believe that gender identity is a deep-seated inherent sense of being a man or boy, woman or girl, both, neither or something else, and those who believe that sex is real and – in some situations such as sport, rape crisis centres or child development – important. I used to be in the first group. A lot of reading, thinking and talking in the second half of the 2010s moved me into the second. This section is the first part of this book that I started to research, as I imagined it would be the most difficult to write fairly, given the strength of feeling among adherents and critics. I also wanted to start with the research and base my analysis on what it said, which I knew would be challenging, as it required me to put my beliefs to one side.

The proposition that I investigated is known as the 'gender affirmation' model, the risks of which were highlighted in the 2024 Cass Review of gender identity services for children and young people.[48] The gender affirmative model goes something like this. 'It is possible for a child to be born as a boy but to have a girl's mind or vice versa, or for a child to have a mind that isn't male or female, or that moves between different states. Social transition – where you change a child's name, pronouns and clothing to match the desired gender identity – has no risks and supports their mental health. Gender-affirming care – medicine to block puberty at its onset, followed by hormone treatment to mimic the secondary sex characteristics of the opposite sex – helps to resolve gender dysphoria and improves gender-questioning teenagers' mental health. Puberty blockers act as a pause button and give children space to work out what they really want. Transition is the right and only pathway for those who need it, and those who want it need it. Children who question their gender should be immediately affirmed in their chosen identity.'

Imagine a hypothetical twelve-year-old called Nellie. For months now, she has been wearing baggy clothes, and says one day that she would now like to be known as Noah and referred to using he/him pronouns. According to this gender-affirming model, Nellie's parents should immediately recognise that they have a son, not a daughter, and take all steps necessary – at school, with family and friends – to affirm their child in this male identity. They might, if they are living north of the English/Scottish border or elsewhere in the world, take urgent steps to get a referral to a doctor who can prescribe puberty blockers to arrest the development of female sex characteristics in Nellie/Noah's changing body.

Here are some things, based on the available evidence, that are likely to be true about this teenager (I will be referring to her as

Nellie and she, for reasons that I hope will become clear). She's probably got a pre-existing mental health condition like depression or anxiety. This may not have been diagnosed. She's almost certainly experiencing horrendous discomfort going through puberty and has seen the downsides of a developing female body – the male gaze, the misogynist porn shared through smartphone backchannels, or the impossible, glossy, slimline and high-maintenance stereotypes into which teenagers who are (truly, in her eyes) girls are expected to fit.

Nellie may well be autistic or have experienced some kind of past trauma – perhaps she's been bullied relentlessly or she's experienced sexual assault. She's almost certainly attracted to girls. She may well have spent countless hours on Tumblr, Reddit or TikTok, seeing other people's journeys of transition and absorbing the message that if she doesn't fit in or she's unhappy, a trans identity may be the solution she didn't know she was seeking.

Here are some things we suspect or know about Nellie's future if she gets immediately affirmed in her trans identity. We suspect that socially transitioning her will make her gender dysphoria more concrete – there's an increasing mismatch between the way she presents and the reality of her body, which causes her distress, and the fact that she is now publicly Noah means a humiliating volte-face if she changes her mind. We can be almost certain that if she starts puberty blockers, they won't act as a pause button and she'll go on to take cross-sex hormones – this happens in forty-nine cases out of fifty for those teenagers who are treated with blockers.[49] If she's taken puberty blockers and then cross-sex hormones, we know she'll be infertile. There is no way of having a baby if you haven't experienced the physical changes needed to do so. It's likely that she'll never have an orgasm.

Once her voice drops from taking testosterone, it will never go back to how it was, even if she stops the treatment. She'll probably be on medication for life, though. She's now more likely to suffer from heart complications, to have worse bone health and to experience painful vaginal atrophy. She can't physically change sex – no one can – and using medication to develop male-looking characteristics will take a severe toll on her body. Her mental health, after starting puberty blockers and cross-sex hormones, is likely to be no better than it was before she started taking them. It may even get worse. Something we don't know is how likely it will be, if she transitions, that she subsequently detransitions and returns – depending on the age at which she might do this – to identifying as a girl or woman. There is a growingly vocal population of detransitioners, but there's no reliable research on prevalence. There are some indications, though – a recent German study based on insurance data, for example, found that more than six in ten young people diagnosed with 'gender identity disorder' no longer had a diagnosis (this is not, necessarily, the same thing as desistance or detransition) five years later.[50]

Here are some related facts drawn from the limited evidence base on gender-questioning adolescents. Teenagers who identify as trans are ten times more likely than other teenagers to be attracted to their own sex.[51] They are at least eight times more likely than other teenagers to have autistic spectrum disorder.[52] They are more likely to feel anxious and depressed, to have a history of self-harm and feeling suicidal,[53] and to have an eating disorder.[54] These teenagers are eight times more likely to have been in care.[55] They are twice as likely as other teenagers to have experienced sexual abuse, and almost twice as likely to have experienced psychological or physical abuse.[56] If they go on to transition medically, their short-term mental health improvements are no better than they would be were they to take a placebo pill.[57] We don't know what the long-term mental health impacts are, as nobody has tracked cohorts of these teenagers to see what happens to them after a few years.

There's an alternative pathway for Nellie. Her parents could keep her options open. They could choose not to transition her socially and to avoid making the referral call to the doctor. They could support her with her underlying vulnerabilities. They could make clear to her that she can wear whatever she chooses and present herself however she likes, and that transition is a decision to be made – if she still wants it – in the future, once her mind and body have fully developed, and once she is able to consent to all these consequences as an adult. They could talk together about ideas and politics and philosophy. They could watch the docudrama *The Social Dilemma* with her. They could shift some of her focus from the inner world of her mind to her physicality and the world around her by introducing her to dancing, or new sports, or art, or photography, or films, or travel. They could validate her as an individual – showing that they embrace and accept the different aspects of her personality and interests.

How have we got into a situation in which the messages from campaigning groups and many parts of popular culture – and even many doctors – are so at odds with what the evidence shows us? Digging back through individual research reports, as I've done for this chapter and the series of research summaries that informed it, shows that so much of what is said about transition, mental health and outcomes is incorrect. Most of what's been reported – that taking gender medication improves mental health, say, or that you're putting your child at risk of suicide if you don't affirm them – isn't backed up. (Get professional help, of course, if you think your child is at risk – but vet the therapist first.) There's very little in the way of evidence in the first place – and the best-quality studies available, which follow teenagers over a period of time, do not show these things to be true when you pool their data together.[58]

## TEENAGERS: THE EVIDENCE BASE

Parts of individual studies have been cherry-picked and misreported, leading us to a situation in which vulnerable children are being medicalised and sterilised to fit a set of ideological beliefs that are entirely unverifiable and are dependent on reductive and regressive stereotypes about what it means to be a boy or a girl. There isn't space here for a detailed discussion about the evidence base, on which I have written extensively elsewhere. You can read the linked papers in the endnotes if you would like to know more. Five of the main diagnostic criteria relating to gender dysphoria in younger children are based purely on these stereotypes – for example, one of the criteria for natal boys is 'a strong rejection of typically masculine toys, games, and activities and a strong avoidance of rough-and-tumble play'. Does your younger son like playing with dolls and hate rugby? Perhaps he's really a girl.

Parents who question this affirmative model are swimming against the cultural tide. There are many external influences over which they have little control. By the time this book is published, it's possible that there will be tighter controls over what can be taught at school about ideas relating to gender identity – but the current generation of teenagers are likely to have absorbed messages about this since primary school or even earlier. They may have been taught about the 'genderbread person', which links being 'strong-willed, logical, athletic' to the identity of a man and 'empathetic, sensitive, caring' to that of a woman. The linked roles? For men, it's being a leader, a builder and a protector. For women, it's being a teacher, a caretaker and a supporter.[59] No wonder so many teenagers are fighting their way out of such constricting boxes.

Much-beloved books, too, may have shaped your child into believing it's possible for people to identify out of their biological realities. Perhaps, as a younger child, they read a book like *Introducing Teddy* by Jessica Walton, in which the title character, a boy teddy, signals that he is really a girl teddy by moving his bow tie onto his head to make it a hair adornment.[60] Or maybe they've read a book for teenagers by Lewis Hancox called *Welcome to St Hell: My Trans Teen Misadventure*, which describes breasts as 'fatty lumps that need to be gone', and taking puberty blockers as the 'best thing I ever did'.[61] In 2022, UK charity the Reading Agency placed Hancox's book on a well-being reading collection aimed at doctors, libraries and school nurses. These books are two examples of wide-ranging material being taught in nurseries and schools that support the idea that children can change their gender.

The internet, of course, is another source of information that forms part of a facilitating zeitgeist for this belief system. There are threads on Reddit with bingo cards for teenagers suggesting that if boys meets certain criteria – they like anime or manga, they're mocked for being sensitive, they're anxious or depressed, they don't lift weights – they're really girls.[62] There are trans influencers like Jeffrey Marsh, an adult 'non-binary' man with almost 700,000 followers on TikTok, who encourages estrangement from non-affirming families[63] and promises to be viewers' 'internet mom'.[64] There are whole communities in which vulnerable, isolated teenagers can find people who accept them, so long as they conform to trans norms.

These cultural tides are really hard for parents to counter – especially as teenagers are often looking for points of difference with their parents as a counterweight against which they can push as part of the normal process of separation. The intolerance of debate among many proponents of gender-identity beliefs means that very little, so far, has been written for parents who want to take an evidence-based perspective when it comes to this issue. From the work I have done in this area and the little that's been written on it to date, though, I would say there are a few things you can do (assuming you haven't closed this book in dismay at the suggestion that the current popular narrative has little, at least on current evidence, to recommend it).

The first is to be clear about biological reality, while not setting it up as a point of conflict. You can explain that you think X, your child thinks Y, and it's OK to think differently on these things. You can validate gender nonconformity and expose your child to nonconforming role models – the Princes and Arlo Parkses of this world. You can set clear limits on screens and devices. You can give your teenager plenty of opportunity to be present in their body through dance or sport. You can expose them to different ideas and ways of reasoning, and encourage them away from black-and-white thinking – the world is complicated, and there are few simple answers. You can validate the different aspects of your child's personality. You can help them to see identity as fluid and distress as something that can be managed, rather than an intrinsic part of them.

You can protect your child from things that pose clear safety risks – be wary of the skateboarding club that advertises all-age sessions for 'girls and minority genders', which can include males who don't identify as men or boys (your thirteen-year-old girl is not going to come out well from a crash with an adult male) or the summer school that organises sleeping accommodation by gender identity. Your teenager can't identify their way out of sexual assault, which is a risk of mixed-sex accommodation. If your teenager begins to question his or her gender, or if you want to know more about the research and evidence that sits behind this section, you can try reading *When Kids Say They're Trans*[65] or the three papers I wrote summarising the evidence base in this area, which are available on the Sex Matters website.[66]

This is a contested, heated area, in which the best way we can support our teenagers is – I believe – to grapple with the evidence, understand what it says and what we don't yet know, and move in these uncharted waters with as much knowledge as we can glean from the limited available data.

## Resilience and healthy stress

Not all pressure is bad. Resilience is forged in the fire of mild adversity – if teenagers reach adulthood having been protected from the experiences that might help them to cope more easily when they get there, we've done them a disservice. This doesn't mean sitting ourselves comfortably on the sofa and letting them get on with navigating the challenges of adolescence unmoored, but it does mean – perhaps – not swooping in to challenge every teacher who is giving them a hard time, and ensuring they have enough freedom to make the mistakes that permit them to learn.

It's a truism that every generation thinks the latest one is more fragile and entitled than the ones that preceded it. My friendships overflow with stories of Gen Z employees who struggle to manage a thirty-five-hour working week or who come off the clock at 5 p.m. rather than finish a piece of work that's due the next morning. These are the avocado toast eaters of the latest generation, according to the portraits painted of them. They look after themselves beautifully by doing yoga in their lunch hour and eschewing post-work boozing, but break down in tears if a manager points out something they got wrong.

We don't know if this is really true – perhaps it's yet another iteration of generational biases playing out. Our cultural horizons shift across time. We also lack a clear, consistent measure of resiliency that would allow us to test how it has changed across the decades. The pandemic has confused things, too, as we don't know if apparent falls in resilience are lockdown-related or part of a wider generational shift. We do know, though – as we've seen – that teenage mental health is getting worse, and greater resiliency helps to protect well-being by definition. It's something that's worth encouraging in our children.

Toxic stress, such as childhood trauma – being severely ill, for example, experiencing abuse or losing a parent – erodes resilience[67] and can have lifelong effects. One study took seventy-six new recruits to police academies across California and divided them into two groups according to whether they'd experienced trauma while they were growing up. These recruits watched a video that showed real-life police officers exposed to incredibly stressful events, including a suicide, a murder and an autopsy. The video also showed a car hitting one officer and another involved in an explosion. The researchers found that recruits who had experienced serious trauma in childhood showed significantly higher levels of a marker relating to the hormone norepinephrine, which is closely involved in the fight-or-flight response. In other words, the danger systems of those who'd previously been traumatised were on high alert as adults, even though their trauma was in the past.[68]

The plasticity of the teenage brain makes it particularly vulnerable to toxic stress, but also open to the influence of things that enhance its resilience. When teenagers experience mild stress, they can apply skills they already possess from other contexts while building new ones to make a stressful experience more manageable.[69] Growth derived from manageable stress may be particularly important in the early teenage years.[70]

We need, as parents, to let our teenagers experience healthy stress. There are exceptions – teenagers who've already experienced huge adversity are likely to need protecting from further stress, when possible and even if it's mild, as their ability to cope may already be overwhelmed.[71] And we need to help our teenagers to put systems in place that support this building of resiliency, of which more below. But for the average teenager, it seems clear that metaphorically letting them walk over hot coals on occasion will aid their ability to withstand heat in other circumstances.

There's probably an overlap between fragile teenagers who haven't been inoculated by healthy stress and those who have highly involved, overprotective parents (as these are the adults more likely to shield their children from unvarnished adversity). There doesn't seem to be much in the way of research weaving these ideas together, but there's certainly a link between 'helicopter parenting' and dented resilience. Researchers surveyed Irish university students, for example, to interrogate these connections, and found that depression was higher in those with helicopter parents due to their lower resilience levels.[72]

Humans aren't the only creatures who learn resilience through healthy stress. A team of scholars divided some very young squirrel monkeys into two groups. One group wasn't exposed to adversity. The other was exposed to what the scholars termed 'mild, intermittent' stress – each monkey was removed from its mother and its peers for an hour a week and placed next to monkeys who were strangers. Once they reached adolescence, the monkeys were tested for novelty-seeking behaviour by seeing whether they would explore an unfamiliar box that contained a mix of new and familiar objects. The monkeys who'd previously experienced mild stress were far more likely to explore the new area and to play with the unfamiliar objects, which – concluded the scholars – reflected 'mild early stress-induced adaptations that enhance curiosity and resilience'.[73]

Of course, it's not just stress that builds resilience. The environment in which children grow up is an important underlying factor – supportive and loving environments are, unsurprisingly, better for the development of resilience. Being catapulted too early into adult roles (as with teenage pregnancy, for example) may undermine longer-term resilience.[74] There are certain underlying personality traits and characteristics that make teenagers more or less resilient. Those who are agreeable, conscientious and open to experiences, while scoring low on neuroticism, are more likely to be resilient.[75] Other associated factors include having a strong social network, self-confidence, a positive outlook on life and a sense of humour. Having a religious faith is another factor, possibly because it gives adherents a sense of meaning.[76] Teenagers who can reframe difficult experiences and who can be flexible in their thinking are more likely to be resilient, as are those who are able to avoid ruminating about their problems.[77]

Teenagers find it easier to manage stress when they develop a deeper understanding of social relationships and other aspects of the world around them. This so-called 'social stress-related growth' includes learning to value other humans as they are, not how they would wish them to be (they may even, one day, recognise the value of those boundaries and limits you have so carefully put into place) and knowing how to ask for help from those around them when they need it. Another important aspect of this kind of growth is the appreciation of other people's perspectives, and recognition that their own way of seeing the world is not the only legitimate one.[78] This is particularly interesting to me – I've thought a lot about the idea that teenagers may be coalescing around an increasingly narrow set of socially acceptable ideas, and what this means for individual development as well as a pluralistic society. I talk about this a little more in Chapter 8.

It may also be helpful for teenagers to cultivate the ability to think about problems calmly, reflectively and with a decent dollop of optimism.[79] You might want to think about this point with your child as it relates to the coping strategies explored earlier in the chapter. Helpful strategies when it comes to adolescent adjustment include problem-solving, distraction and getting support from friends and family, and unhelpful ones include rumination and total avoidance of the issue at hand.[80] Engaging with whatever is causing them stress is generally more helpful than hiding from it,[81] as is learning to tolerate difficult feelings.[82]

Teenagers may also want to engage in a bit of trial and error when it comes to what helps them personally, and to develop awareness about what it is that they personally find really stressful – so that when these situations arise, they know how to help themselves. As a teenager, I found frightening films apparently much scarier than anyone else around me. (I still do. My daughters laugh at me when I need to leave the room because of something the people at the British Board of Film Classification have insanely found to be suitable for people aged twelve and over.) At teenage sleepovers, my friends went through a stage – after we'd got bored with reruns of *Dirty Dancing*, *Grease* and every early nineties film starring Julia Roberts – of getting pliant older siblings to rent horror films from the local video library. We'd sit watching them in the dark and, with an awareness of my propensity for nightmares, I'd keep my eyes shut during all the scariest parts (the soundtracks were bad enough). The absence of light kept my reputation intact.

As I touched on in an earlier chapter, another thing parents can do to help their teenagers to manage stress in a healthy way is to be available to listen to their problems but to try to avoid fixing them. Alternatively, you could ask your child how they might respond to a friend with a similar issue, which allows them to look at things from a slightly more objective perspective. If my daughter tells me she's feeling the pressure piling up at school, she'll probably be more reassured by my empathy and reassurance that it's normal to feel stressed in these circumstances than if I start talking to her about homework schedules or making better use of school planners. She'll also have a greater sense of control if she takes the lead on working some of these things out for herself.

On a similar note, it may be worth trying to drop some of the balls you may be carrying on your teenager's behalf. (I'm terrible at this. A common refrain of both my husband and my best friend is 'Drop the ball, Matilda!') Parents can foresee things their teenagers can't and often try to head these off. If I manage my daughter's homework schedule, she'll know when everything is due and be able to plan her work effectively. She won't, though, come up against the real-world consequences (detention) of not managing her own schedule effectively and, through this, develop the impetus she needs to learn to manage it on her own. As an extra bonus, leaving this in her hands also saves me time and stops us from locking horns too often about homework.

Self-esteem, which is one of the things that underpin resilience,[83] forms the last part of this chapter. There's evidence of a link between being self-compassionate and having self-esteem, though the latter probably drives the former – in other words, when teenagers believe themselves to be worthy, they are able to feel compassionate towards themselves.[84]

As with resilience more generally, some elements of your teenager's self-esteem may be tied into aspects of their personality that have already started to set like aspic, leaving them with limited wiggle room to evolve. Optimistic teenagers are more likely to have high levels of self-esteem, for example, while those who are neurotic are more likely to feel shame and to put themselves down.[85] Feeling empathy is another important area. Those who understand the emotions of others (while not feeling them deeply) are likely to have higher levels of long-term self-esteem.[86]

There's plenty that teenagers can do to boost the elements of self-esteem that aren't reliant on their characters, though. Feeling grateful for things, unlikely as it may sound, can boost self-esteem;[87] thinking about the nice things other people do for us makes us feel valued.[88] Happily, because this is probably relatively easy for parents who are invested enough to be reading a book about them, teenagers are more likely to feel grateful if they have plenty of emotional support from their parents.[89] They're also more likely to avoid unhealthy self-esteem – the type that hangs on the views of other people – if they feel loved and accepted unconditionally. This means being careful not to show your love only for individual achievements, as the deeper message they may receive from this is that your love is contingent.[90]

Teenagers can develop their self-esteem by doing things that help them to look outwards, rather than inwards.[91] Doing something meaningful – for example, volunteering in the community – can help to build self-esteem, as can things that help them to feel useful. This is an excellent reason why your teenager should be helping to take out the bins, clean the bathroom or do the Saturday lunchtime washing-up. (I shall be showing my teenagers this paragraph until they stop protesting.) Getting good at something they enjoy can also be a self-esteem boost – perhaps this is football, or graphic design, or making origami.

The most important point of this chapter, though, is that feeling things deeply is normal. If teenagers don't have their normal feelings pathologised by the trusted adults in their lives, they are more likely to feel able to manage them, and to cope with the turbulence and trickiness that are often an inherent part of being a teenager. Our teenagers need to hear the message that we believe they have the skills and knowledge to be able to handle challenging situations and feelings, and that we will be here to catch them on the rare occasion that they might fall.

# CHAPTER SUMMARY

## Anxiety and sadness

- **Prevalence of mental health issues.** Mental ill health was increasing in teenagers even before the most recent spike. It's important not to overstate the problem, though. Most teenagers are fine.
- **Reasons for mental ill health.** Screens and social media have a role to play, but it's not a simple one (see Chapter 2). Covid-19 and the resulting loneliness also contributed, but teenagers were on a worrying trajectory before it began. Wider contributing factors may include obesity, inequality, fears about the state of the world, loosening family ties and school pressure. Another explanation is that our well-meaning cultural focus on mental health conditions has backfired – there's evidence to suggest that when teenagers fixate upon and identify with labels like 'anxious' or 'depressed', their mental health takes a hit. This links to a common misconception that feeling worried or sad is a sign of mental ill health, rather than a normal, natural reaction to everyday occurrences that gives us useful information about what we should do in future. Rumination, which is more common in teenagers, can amplify these beliefs.
- **The need for balance.** It's useful to talk about feelings, but not to the point of repetition and obsession.
- **Engagement versus disengagement.** Coping strategies can be divided into those that are proactive – like trying to find solutions to a problem or talking about a feeling – and those that involve disengaging (or running away) from it. Engagement coping strategies are linked to better mental health. Reframing or acceptance works best in situations over which teenagers have no control – if they've been dumped, say, or they're sad about leaving school.

# Gender identity

- **The context.** Some people believe gender identity is an internal, immutable sense of being a man/boy or girl/woman, or something else, and that this can conflict with people's sex. Others believe that sex is real and matters in certain contexts, including child development and single-sex spaces. Despite a huge volume of research published by those who believe in the first statement, there's little evidence to back up the idea that it's good for children to transition socially or medically. Instead, doing so risks their long-term well-being – including their fertility and eventual sexual function, for those who medically transition – and there is clear evidence that identity shifts and reforms across adolescence and early adulthood, providing further challenge to the argument for making such a life-changing decision so early.

- **What we know from the research.** Most gender-questioning teenagers have underlying vulnerabilities, including mental health and neurodevelopmental conditions, experience of bullying and trauma. The majority are same-sex attracted. Gender dysphoria diagnosis is informed by stereotypes of what it means to be a boy or a girl. Taking puberty blockers followed by cross-sex hormones means that teenagers will never complete puberty. They will be infertile and will probably never experience orgasm. They'll be on medication for life and are more likely to suffer from a range of side effects including heart conditions and worse bone health. Some of the side effects are irreversible. Taking this medication is no better for mental health than taking a placebo. The proportion of teenagers experiencing gender dysphoria has grown exponentially in recent years. Before social transition was common, the vast majority of cases in younger children (we don't know if this was the case for teenagers, as there were so few of them

who started to question their gender during puberty) resolved themselves.
- ▶ **What's gone wrong.** Evidence has been cherry-picked and misreported, leading to widespread misunderstandings. Children have been taught that they have a gender identity across many educational settings, including nursery and pre-schools, over the last few years, and many of those who don't fit gender stereotypes are led to believe they need to present as the opposite sex. Television, social media and books have often propped up these messages. This issue affects all teenagers, not just those who are distressed about their gender.

## Resilience and healthy stress

- ▶ **Importance of healthy stress.** Teenagers need to experience manageable stress to become resilient (apart from those who have already experienced huge adversity, as they may become overwhelmed). Toxic stress, on the other hand, erodes resiliency.
- ▶ **Other things that build resilience.** Teenagers are more likely to be resilient if they've grown up in loving, supportive homes. Personality factors and traits play a role, including extraversion, self-confidence, having a positive outlook on life and a sense of humour. An ability to reframe experiences and to think flexibly is also important. Resilience is more likely in those who have a strong social network and among those who have a religious faith, possibly because they're imbued with a sense of meaning in their lives.
- ▶ **Self-esteem.** There are links between self-compassion and self-esteem, which, like resilience, can be tied into personality factors. Things that boost teenagers' self-esteem include practising gratitude, knowing they have parents who love them unconditionally, doing something meaningful (like community volunteering)

or useful (like taking out the bins), and getting good at something they enjoy.

## Ideas for parents

- **Treat mental health lightly.** Help your child to see their feelings as signals that shift and change, and move them away – if needed – from seeing mental health problems as part of their identity. Be curious about their feelings, which can help them to learn to trust what they feel and use it to help them make evidence-based decisions. If they're going through something difficult, be realistic rather than make false promises.
- **Cultivate a sense of belonging.** This can be done through activities that enable you to have fun together as a family, making your teenager feel understood, and paying them plenty of attention.
- **Try to make sure your teenager is ticking the boxes for things that support mental health.** They're more likely to feel OK in themselves if they're getting enough sleep and exercise, getting outside, eating well and connecting with other people. Foster a future orientation in them, if you can. Help them to open up to different perspectives on the world and the idea that there's no one right way of seeing most things.
- **Know when to worry.** Feeling sad or worried about something specific, like an upcoming test, is probably fine – but when it becomes more general, or takes over, it's more concerning. But it's important to show your teenager you're not panicking in the face of their anxiety or sadness. Instead, you can make clear that it's normal and human to experience difficult feelings, and they will pass. Help them to think calmly and optimistically about difficulties they're encountering.
- **Step in if your teenager is fixating on a problem to the extent that it's not likely to be good for them.** Get outside, go to the cinema,

play a board game, take a trip to see family – do what you can to get them out of their doom loop.
- **Help your child to understand biological reality and to be comfortable in their body.** Be clear that there are two sexes, while not setting it up as a point of conflict, and that it's OK to think differently to each other. Make sure your child has the opportunity to feel centred in their body through dance or sport. Open your child to different ideas and ways of thinking, and help them to understand that the world is complex. Validate different aspects of your child's personality. Be alert to safeguarding risks in schools and clubs. If you're doubtful about this position, as I expect many reading this will be, I invite you to read some of my more detailed analysis of the available data[92] – or even to go back to the original studies to draw your own conclusions about the evidence.
- **Encourage your child to ask for your help, or that of other people, when they need it.** Teenagers are better able to manage stress when they're able to ask for help as necessary. Suggest your child tries a few different approaches to managing problems, perhaps using some of the coping styles explored earlier in the chapter, to see what helps them most.
- **Don't fix your teenager's problems for them.** As explored in Chapter 2, listening to problems is generally better than trying to fix them or make suggestions, unless your child has asked you for your opinion. If they're struggling, you might ask how they would advise a friend who had a similar problem to open up their thinking. Give your teenager the message that you know that they can cope, and that you will be on hand to support them as they need.

# CHAPTER 6

# BODY

## General health during puberty

Puberty is a time during which the adult form starts to emerge from the child's body, though the mind is far from done in terms of its development. The onset of puberty shows itself through breast bud development in girls, which usually happens between the ages of eight and thirteen, and in testicular growth for boys. The male window for the start of puberty is a year later, on average, than the female one.[1] In one recent British study, girls started their periods – marking the formal end of puberty – at the age of 12.7, on average. The equivalent for boys is their voice breaking, which the same study showed to happen at an average age of 13.6.[2] There's wide variation here, so don't worry if your child is a bit ahead of or behind the curve.[3] Very early puberty can increase children's risk of mental health problems,[4] though, so those who experience it may need extra support. And each new generation experiences puberty a little earlier. Over the last 150 years, the age at which girls start their periods has fallen by four years.[5]

Before puberty, children grow an average of five or six centimetres a year. The puberty growth spurt increases this to around nine centimetres in a year for girls and ten for boys.[6] I've always been determined to remain taller than my children (rather optimistically, given that their father is over six foot). When my older daughter was finally observed to have overtaken me, the rest of my family enjoyed it greatly. 'You've just left the tallest half of the family. We'll be over here, talking about tall things.' UK growth charts are based on 1990 data, so it's likely that height has increased a little since they were developed, but they show that the typical thirteen-year-old girl is 155 centimetres tall, increasing to 164 centimetres by the time she reaches adulthood.[7]

Boys are the same height, on average, as girls at the age of thirteen. By adulthood, they are typically 13 centimetres taller, at 177 centimetres.[8] Boys develop more bone and muscle during puberty than girls do. Girls' muscle mass increases until around the age of fifteen, then stays static. In boys, muscle mass increases until the age of eighteen, with particularly rapid growth between twelve and fifteen, and they lose body fat between the ages of fourteen and sixteen.[9] By the end of this period, boys have three times as much muscle as they do fat, while girls have about 25% more muscle than fat.[10] These differences contribute to boys' advantage in sport.[11]

Going through puberty can be a mind bender. Bodies change shape, bones become longer, hair emerges in unfamiliar places, and outlandish moods and desires seemingly spring from nowhere. My partner, when he was a teenager, made several trips to A&E during a single year in which he grew fifteen centimetres. He no longer knew how to take a step safely, as his legs were an unfamiliar length – and a misjudgement of upper-body coordinates led to a chance meeting between a beaker of acid and his hand during one unfortunate chemistry lesson.

We know the basic recipe for health in teenagers. It's pretty similar to what we need in other stages of life. They need to exercise and to do a range of activities within this – things that get them out of breath and that strengthen their muscles and bones.[12] Team sport is particularly good.[13] Teenagers should, ideally, be a healthy weight.[14] Eating well is key. This means avoiding processed foods – the people making these recommendations clearly haven't met the average fifteen-year-old – and eating plenty of vegetables, fruit and healthy protein such as fish.[15] Like all of us, teenagers need social connection.[16] They need, of course, decent amounts of good-quality sleep.[17]

The teenage years are ones in which habits – both good and bad – can be formed, and in which our teenagers are exercising ever-greater independence over how they spend their time and what they choose to do with their bodies.[18] It's also a time during which well-meaning parental instructions and guidance can misfire. One study tested links between parents' behaviours and their teenagers' diets. It found a positive link between what parents eat and what their children eat. In other words, if you model healthy eating and have healthy food available in the house, your teenager's probably more likely to eat well. But the study found that having rules about junk food was linked to teenagers consuming more of it.[19] If you tell your teenager that something's forbidden, its illicit nature may encourage them to seek it out.

The research doesn't support a blanket 'no rules' approach when it comes to diet, though. A San Francisco experiment tested the link between having healthy food rules at home and the likelihood of teenagers selecting a healthy snack in a raffle (chances of my teenagers doing this: zero). Those who lived in households with rules relating to healthy eating were almost twice as likely as other teenagers to choose a healthy snack, and it made no difference to their choices to know whether or not their parent would need to approve the selection they'd made.[20]

These mixed findings mean the extent to which you choose to have rules probably depends on your instincts in this area (mine are that my children are probably old enough to decide these things for themselves, though I do question myself regularly on this when I see the food choices they make). The evidence on modelling and food availability is less equivocal. If you load your plate with vegetables, your children are more likely to do the same. And I know that if I fulfil my teenagers' requests to stock the cupboard with Super Noodles and pickled onion Monster Munch, they'll get eaten – and quickly. When I worry about their choices, I console myself with the fact that I eat pretty well as an adult, but I used to mainline instant noodles and Diet Coke in my mid-teenage years. I still have to bite back my inducements for my daughters to finish the vegetables on their plates, though.

One way to encourage health in teenagers is to have conversations at home about what it means to be healthy. Those living in families who have these kinds of chats are more likely to make healthy choices[21] and to believe in their ability to do so.[22] And having this belief means they are more likely to eat well whether they're with friends, at home and/or bored.[23]

The importance of good sleep can't be overstated. In one experiment, fifty teenagers spent three weeks trialling different sleep lengths. The first week was a baseline (business-as-usual) week. In the second week, they had six and a half hours in bed for five nights. In the final week, they had ten hours in bed for five nights. During the week of restricted sleep, teenagers assessed themselves as more tense, more angry and less vigorous (as well as, unsurprisingly, more tired) than they were when they were sleeping for longer. They were also more irritable during the restricted sleep period and found it harder to manage their emotions. The study authors pointed out that six and a half hours is a lot more sleep than the amount used in many adult studies, and yet the effects on teenagers were startling.[24]

It can be hard for teenagers to get enough sleep given that school days tend to start early, and teenagers' circadian rhythms – their daily cycles that dictate the time they want to sleep and eat, among other things – are later than for adults and younger children. One review of studies found that American teenagers get up on school days between 6 a.m. and 7 a.m. On weekends, when they have more choice about when to get up, ten- to thirteen-year-olds rouse themselves between ninety minutes and three hours later than this. The equivalent weekend delay for high school students – those between the ages of fourteen and eighteen – is between three and four hours.[25] This biological clock delay in teenagers is well known, and it affects their learning – it means they're less alert and less able to learn first thing in the morning.[26] When I first visited my older daughter's secondary school as a prospective parent, the then headteacher trumpeted the school's approach as being fully grounded in evidence. The first clue that this might be a smidgen overstated was the fact its school day begins at 8.30.

Of course, these are all just averages. One way of understanding differences between individuals and how they sleep is to divide them into whether they're larks (early risers who work better in the mornings) or owls (your average teenager).[27] If you were to take a group of ten teenagers, four would turn into owls or larks as adults, and six would be somewhere in between[28] (orks, perhaps). If you're not yet sure whether your child is going to end up flying with the breaking day or with the rising moon, you may be able to predict it from your own, assuming you are your child's biological parent – there's an element of heritability in this.[29] I'm a lark, my partner is an owl, and current evidence suggests we're going to end up with one of each in our children.

Many of the evidence-based recommendations on adolescent sleep are, frankly, statements of the bleeding obvious. (Tired? Try going to bed earlier.[30]) Others are more helpful – if your teenager's struggling to sleep, you can encourage them to be physically active during the day and to practise the off-puttingly named 'sleep hygiene'. A review of studies has found both these things to be linked to better sleep in teenagers.[31] According to the Sleep Foundation, sleep hygiene involves four main areas. The first is setting a sleep schedule, which involves trying to wake up at the same time each day, even at the weekend (good luck getting a teenager up at 6.45 on a Saturday), treating sleep as a priority and limiting naps. The second is following a routine at night. This might involve dimming lights, winding down by reading or listening to music for half an hour, and making sure there's a screen-free window before bed. The third involves cultivating healthy habits during the day – getting plenty of outdoors light, avoiding nicotine, being careful of post-lunch caffeine and making sure food isn't eaten too late. The final area is bedroom optimisation – making sure it's cool, that light and noise are minimised, and the bed is comfortable.[32]

The review of studies pointed to caffeine and nicotine, evening light, computer use and a negative environment at home as particular risk factors for poor sleep.[33] (It is possible, of course, that the causal links run the other way round for some of these, and that teenagers who are sleeping badly may turn to caffeine and nicotine to pep themselves up.[34]) Teenage sleep is negatively affected by using technology at bedtime. This includes listening to music: according to one study, teenagers who listen to music at bedtime are most likely of all technology users to experience problems falling asleep.[35] And the more time teenagers spend using electronic devices, the worse they slumber.[36]

Getting natural light in the morning is likely to be helpful. You could also try helping your teenager to reset their body clock, if it's affecting the amount of sleep they're able to get, by exposing them to bright light through a daylight bulb on weekend mornings. One study showed it's possible to move teenagers' body clocks by an hour over a single weekend through two and a half hours' exposure to a bright daylight bulb (at 6,000 lux, which is a measure of how much light is given out) each morning. This was timed to start between 5.15 a.m. and 8.45 a.m. on the Saturday morning, depending on the teenager's normal sleep patterns – with a two-hour nap in the afternoon to compensate for the early wake-up – and was done an hour earlier on the Sunday morning. The following week, 'dim light melatonin onset', a key measure of the circadian system, was a full hour earlier, on average (the study's researchers didn't track what happened beyond this point).[37]

When my daughters have been sleeping badly, I've wondered if the fact they can't see their bedroom floor beneath the piles of clothes and other detritus might be affecting their ability to sleep – but I have been told, firmly, that it isn't. A tip that's gone down slightly better is one that I've gleaned from my own lifelong tussles with insomnia, which is not to panic if you can't sleep on a given night – allowing yourself to rest is better than being up and active. Once your body knows it's safe to rest, sleep often follows. You can also try to provide a facilitating environment for your child's sleep – keeping noise down at night, making sure evening light in communal spaces isn't too bright and making sure everyone's personal devices (including yours) are kept out of bedrooms overnight.

## Appearance and body image

Over the course of puberty, teenagers have to come to terms with the fact that they look a certain way, and there's probably not a huge amount they can do to change it. Both sexes, of course, may struggle with issues relating to appearance and body image – though pressures are often greater for girls. There are particular looks that replicate across old and new media to the point that a new zeitgeist emerges. Teenagers then measure themselves against a supposed ideal, often finding themselves lacking.

When I was a teenager, the in-vogue body shape belonged to Kate Moss – long, lean lines and stark beauty. There are no diets or hacks that could have recast my physical structure into that of a Moss-like sylph. When I was rowing at university, my body fat got so low at one stage that my periods stopped, but my thighs still overlapped. My five-foot friend was never going to grow tall enough to hang off the ceiling straps of the number 88 bus into Colchester. Kevin from the boys' school was never going to win any boxing matches. We all – somehow – had to come to terms with our reality.

The new generation of teenagers has to do the same, but this time with a different set of physical standards and under the ever-present glare of social media. Negative emotions attached to appearance – embarrassment and shame, guilt and envy – increase over the teenage years.[38] Pressure isn't limited to body shape. It's also there in clothes and grooming. In Brighton, there's practically a uniform for teenage girls – joggers, tiny tops, hoodies, remarkable eyebrows. (My partner: 'What… What have you done to your eyebrows?' My teenager: 'I had to do it. I inherited my eyebrows from Mum.') My brother-in-law wanders round in a state of permanent bafflement that his son uses facial products, plucks stray hairs and talks casually of a 'tweakment' culture.

Social media replicates more traditional forms in its upholding of body ideals. Looking at #love on Instagram, which Google tells me is one of the most popular hashtags, includes no relationships in the top three images of people with which it presents me on the day I search. It shows, in order, a beautiful black man standing in a field of grass under blue skies, accessorised to the hilt; a white woman with long dark hair and a dress that carpets the floor, fully made up and with a hand suggestively pressed over her belly; and an AI-generated image of a girl with funky hair, tattoos, huge eyes and impossibly exquisite features. The images and the people within them are flawless. And how can a fourteen-year-old fully understand that red-blooded humanity is more meaningful, looks-wise, than what a computer imagines perfection to be? A focus on images and appearance is a feature of social media that may play into teenagers' body image worries – it tends to be very visual, and people get more engagement if they use attractive photos.[39]

I had imagined that ideals of body shape have become slightly more forgiving over the decades, but a 2016 literature review found that content across the internet still promoted thinness in girls.[40] Puberty moves girls away from the straight lines of the thin ideal as they start to fill out and their hips get wider.[41] Girls are more likely than boys to internalise a belief that they are responsible for how they look and that they can control their appearance, if they only put in enough effort.[42] But while girls can feel pressure to be thin, boys often feel an inducement to muscle up. The prevalence of so-called 'muscularity-oriented disordered eating' has been increasing in recent years.[43] Boys are more likely to have a poor body image if they're shorter than average and girls if they're heavier than average. Boys who go through puberty late and girls who go through puberty early are more likely to be unhappy with their bodies.[44]

The pandemic may have given a signal boost to body image issues, according to a group of Australian researchers. They point out that videoconferencing (like Zoom and FaceTime) has a well-documented link with poorer body image and a greater desire for both surgical and non-surgical treatments, and that teenagers spent much more time on these kinds of platforms during lockdowns.[45] Other research suggests that even brief exposure to certain idealised images can knock self-esteem and increase anxiety.[46] And it's not just media and culture that feed into our teenagers' conceptions of how they should look – their peers, of course, also play a role.[47] Those teenagers who feel the greatest shame about their bodies are most likely to try to control how they present themselves on social media, leading – in some cases – to problematic levels of social media use.[48]

It might seem as if the situation is hopeless. Barring a device ban and potential intra-household war, there's not much we can obviously do to protect our teenagers from the effects of social media. But there are buffers we can help them to put in place. There's some very early support in the research literature for the idea that social media literacy has a protective role when it comes to teenagers' body image and social media exposure.[49] In other words, talking to your teenager about the reality behind filters and photo selection may help to protect them from the potentially damaging effects of these images. Understanding the falseness of pictures, avoiding unhelpful content and feeling a sense of agency allow teenagers to internalise positive messages and reject negative ones.[50] It's no doubt of benefit to suspect that there are 100 discarded photos that didn't make it, and that the heavily filtered beautiful person on the screen still needs to take the bins out.

There's an important distinction to be made between destructive thoughts and behaviours as they relate to body image, and what researchers term 'adaptive appearance investment'. When teenagers invest in their appearance adaptively, they try to align it with their personality and preferred style – they might use facial treatments, wear jewellery or shave their chests, and do these things in a way that doesn't equate self-worth with appearance. Adaptive appearance investment is linked to a positive body image and is, arguably, healthier than either self-judgement or ignoring the body entirely. Someone with a positive body image might see a wide range of appearances as being beautiful, accept their body – even aspects with which they might feel slightly dissatisfied – and filter out messages that would otherwise harm their self-image.[51]

It's worth avoiding language focused on weight when speaking to your teenager, as they can see it as being critical even if it's not meant to be. Weight-focused language has also been linked to higher levels of distress and the development of unhealthy attitudes to food.[52] Girls tend to be at the receiving end of more negative parental comments than boys.[53] While conversations focused on weight are linked to high levels of disordered eating in teenagers, conversations about healthy eating are linked to the opposite.[54]

Thinking about what the body can do, not what it looks like, can help to promote a positive body image.[55] A piece of qualitative research in New South Wales, Australia, found that their upbringing, combined with the positive role models their parents had offered them, often left girls feeling able to handle unrealistic body images.[56] When parents have raised their children in a way that supports their autonomy, teenagers tend to have decent levels of self-esteem as well as a sense of security and well-being, all of which can help to protect them against feeling uneasy in their bodies.[57] A good relationship with mothers may help to protect teenagers from the influence of social media on body dissatisfaction.[58] (The same wasn't true for fathers – the research team didn't offer a convincing case as to why not.)

If your child's body image is poor, you could try encouraging them away from social media for a period. A study of sixty-five adolescent dancers found that a three-day social media fast reduced self-objectification in the form of body surveillance and body shame.[59] Assuming your child's poor body image isn't showing itself through a pre-existing gym fixation, encouraging physical activity may be another route – if you can do this in a way that doesn't pressure your child – as body image is better in those who exercise more.[60] This may be because embracing physicality gives people an appreciation of their bodies that they might otherwise lack. Alternatively, perhaps the changing shape that comes from exercise makes teenagers more likely to appreciate what they see in the mirror. (I'd like not to have this vanity, but it's present and correct. After I'd started rowing and lifting weights at eighteen, I remember flexing my newly emerging muscles when I thought nobody was looking.)

There are mixed findings on the long-term trajectories of poor body image in teenagers. One fifteen-year study found that body image is fairly stable from mid-adolescence, for example, suggesting that there's a window of opportunity to deal with any issues that slowly closes itself over the teenage years.[61] Other studies provide more comfort to parents who are worried about their teenagers' body image – they suggest that issues will resolve themselves with time, and negative influences will become less salient. A large review of studies found that being exposed to media showing thin or athletic ideals had a large effect on teenagers' body image, but the effect of similar exposure in emerging adults was only moderate – and for adults who've left this transition period, the effect wasn't significant.[62]

I talked about teenagers' identity development in Chapter 1. One theory is that those with a stronger sense of identity – which starts to crystallise when teenagers get older – see their bodies in a more favourable light.[63] This might be because they have a stronger sense of self, or perhaps having an identity as a medical student, an amateur photographer or a politics nerd takes older teenagers out of their heads, and makes any physical mismatches with societal ideals start to matter a little less.

## Girls and boys

Differences between girls and boys accelerate over the course of adolescence, driven by both social norms and the physical reality of teenagers' changing bodies. The effect of testosterone, for example – which is present at much higher levels in boys than it is in girls – is remarkable. It affects both social and emotional aspects of brain development.[64] As we've already seen, male puberty is linked to greater size and strength. Testosterone is also linked to boys being more aggressive than girls, though researchers aren't sure whether testosterone causes aggression directly, or whether becoming bigger and stronger allows boys (and, to a lesser extent, girls) an outlet for pre-existing aggressive tendencies.[65]

It's not just biology that drives differences between girls and boys over adolescence, though. Cultural pressures are also pervasive. Boys are influenced by ideas about what it is to be a man – through, for example, 'hegemonic masculinity', which is the insidious idea that men are superior. In this world view, they should be powerful, attractive, straight and physically dominant.[66] Girls experience different pressures – to be compliant, caring and beautiful, while being able to curb their hunger and any sexual appetites.[67] You don't need to look far to see these ideas – with few opposing visions of what our girls and boys might become – playing in kaleidoscopic technicolour all around them and insinuating themselves into their own world views.

Girls are more likely to experience stress than boys. A study of fourteen- to fifteen-year-olds living in Stockholm, for example, found that girls both report more stress and have higher morning levels of the stress hormone cortisol. In this study, the sources of stress were similar. Girls just had higher levels of it.[68] Other studies show that girls and boys have different sources of stress, though. Girls experience more stress as a result of other teenagers, whereas boys tend to experience more stress relating to school.[69] This latter point may relate to the fact that boys tend to develop more slowly than girls and have different interests that leave them lagging academically behind their female peers.[70] Boys are more likely than girls to suffer judgement for rupturing gender-related norms.[71]

Physical differences and social pressures combine to forge different pathways for girls and boys in a number of areas. Girls mature more quickly and are better able to understand other people's perspectives, on average.[72] More boys than girls report fighting with their parents about behaviour, while parents flag more friendship-related fights with daughters than with sons.[73] As mentioned in Chapter 3, friendships tend to be organised differently; boys' friendships coalesce around joint activities more than girls' do, for example.[74] Boys are more likely to be violent.[75] Sex drive, as measured by sexual desire and masturbation, is higher in boys than in girls – but girls are more likely to have a crush than boys are. (One researcher points out, slightly acidly, 'Crush is originally slang but a more technical term does not seem to be in contemporary usage.')[76]

We don't need to worry too much about a boy who is content with friendships built around gaming or a girl who enjoys emotional closeness with her inner circle. But averages make everything reductive. There are many teenagers who fall outside these patterns, and difficulties arise when they feel forced to align with sex-based norms and gender stereotypes or when they believe they're abnormal for falling outside them. Some teenagers, for example, may believe there is a mismatch between their minds and their bodies when they don't fulfil society's expectations of their sex (for more on this, see the section on gender identity in Chapter 5).

For boys, a casualty of society's rigid grasp of norms and stereotypes is often the availability of emotional support. Boys may start adolescence feeling emotionally close to their friends, and then see this closeness evaporate through the teenage years under the shadow of a masculine yardstick.[77] Some boys start to bully other teenagers to reinforce a masculine identity; others accept being victimised in the belief that doing anything about the bullying might paint them as vulnerable.[78] There is, of course, a negative impact on many girls, too, in a hyper-feminised ideal. Arguably, there's an impact on all girls when it comes to society valuing adherence to stereotypes and in risks of male violence – rape and other forms of abuse, whether or not they come to pass, jeopardise all girls and women. And this affects boys, too, in the knowledge they may be perceived to represent this threat.

## Sexual harassment

Almost nine in ten American young women report having experienced some kind of sexual harassment over their lifetimes – for example, when a man uses sexualised insults against them or when a stranger touches them without permission.[79] They are more likely to have experienced sexual harassment than they are willing to name it as such.[80] I remember a then-friend climbing uninvited into my bed after a party, putting his hand down my pyjama bottoms and not stopping when I said no. 'I just want to make you happy,' he whispered. It took me two decades to be able to name this, even to myself, as sexual assault. For girls who've experienced similar, it's likely that the distress is present even if the labels are not.

Why might teenage boys engage in this kind of behaviour or less serious versions of it? Being outmatched is one suggestion – girls' earlier development leaves boys feeling disadvantaged by this developmental unevenness. Age and experience are other factors – an American study showed both sexes getting more accepting of sexual harassment between grades 7 (aged twelve to thirteen) and 10 (aged fifteen to sixteen).[81] Potentially, teenagers become more tolerant of something they witness with ever-greater frequency or that they understand as being accepted by others.

Those who sexually harass others may also understand it differently to other teenagers. When asked why they do it, they give reasons like flirting or trying to be funny.[82] It may be, too, that there's a feedback loop between thinking sexual harassment isn't problematic and engaging in it – those who think it's acceptable are more likely to sexually harass other teenagers, and perpetrating this behaviour normalises it, thereby making it feel more acceptable.[83]

Culture inevitably feeds into sexual harassment and how normalised it is among teenagers. Porn is likely to have a huge role in this (see Chapter 7), but cultural influences can include school, television and film, online environments and even video games. One experimental study got fifty-seven teenagers to play a fifteen-minute video game. They were randomly assigned into two groups, one of which had a female game character who was, according to the study's researchers, depicted as sexualised – 'she wears tight, revealing clothes that emphasize her slim body,' they said. The character used by the other group wore loose clothing, and it was unclear if this version of the protagonist was male or female. At the end of the game, the teenagers answered questions that aimed to assess how much they accepted rape myths – measured, for example, by their agreement with the statement, 'Boys don't usually intend to force sex on a girl, but sometimes they get too sexually carried away' – and how tolerant they were towards sexual harassment. Those in the group with the sexualised female character were significantly more likely both to accept rape myths and to tolerate sexual harassment.[84]

Boys can, of course, be victims of sexual harassment, too. A Finnish study looked at more than 180,000 teenagers to assess the link between sexual harassment and depression, finding that while there's a link between these things for both sexes, it's stronger for boys. The researchers concluded that boys may find sexual harassment threatening to their masculinity, and they may have less support available to them.[85] An environment in which sexual harassment of girls is common can be bad for boys, too, even when they're not directly involved. This may be because a school that tacitly accepts sexual harassment is one that's fundamentally unsafe, and because it's upsetting to witness peers being harassed.[86]

What should adults do to reduce the likelihood of our teenagers experiencing sexual harassment or perpetrating it? We can take steps to help boys feel comfortable with a wider range of aspects that might constitute masculinity than the common norms – helping them to feel comfortable expressing their feelings, for example, and recognising their need to connect with other people.

We can also engage our children's critical thinking faculties. If teenagers are encouraged to question standard scripts, they'll be less likely to view stereotyped ideas as being ones with which they need to comply. We can educate our children about sex, with the aim of countering the messages coming from porn that men dominate and women serve their needs (see the next chapter). We can encourage our sons to form relationships with girls – to connect with them as humans, not objects. If we become aware of sexual harassment, we should intervene. Teenagers may understand a lack of action as tacit consent for the behaviours that are taking place.

There are some things, too, that require policy nudges. We can't effect these ourselves, but we can engage with our elected representatives who have power to do so, if it's something over which we feel strongly enough. Two key areas are a better-regulated porn industry, and testing out the idea that boys could participate in formal education a year later than girls (while ensuring there was some kind of play-based childcare cover for the missing year). This would allow them some time to catch up, and would help them not to lag behind their developmentally speedier female classmates. I've seen this suggested in a few places – it's an interesting idea.

# CHAPTER SUMMARY

## Puberty and general health

- **Puberty onset.** Puberty happens a little earlier in each new generation. It starts with breast bud development in girls (which generally happens between the ages of eight and thirteen) and concludes with periods. In boys, it starts with testicular growth (between nine and fourteen) and concludes with voices breaking. This happens on average, according to a recent British study, at 12.7 for girls and 13.6 for boys – though, of course, teenagers change and develop long after the formal end of puberty.
- **Sex differences.** Boys and girls tend to be about the same height at thirteen. By adulthood, boys are taller than girls, on average, by 13 centimetres, and develop more bone and muscle than girls do over and beyond puberty.
- **Foundations of health.** Physical and mental health habits are developed in the teenage years, and underpin many future life outcomes. Exercise over this time should include a range of activities, including things that get teenagers out of breath and build strength. They need good food, proper sleep and social connections.
- **Sleep delay.** Teenagers' body clocks tend to slip later during adolescence, which can affect their ability to learn – and getting enough sleep is vitally important at any age, but particularly so during this period of rapid development.

## Appearance and body image

- **Increased body-related unhappiness.** Teenagers tend to feel more embarrassment and shame, guilt and envy related to appearance over the course of their adolescence. Girls can feel pressure to be thin – and are more likely than boys to feel responsible for how they look and that their appearance is controllable, with enough work – while boys can feel pressure to gain muscle and to be tall. Girls are more likely to be unhappy with their bodies if they go through puberty early, while boys who go through puberty late feel similarly. Those with a strong sense of identity are likely to have a more positive body image.

- **Role of media and peers.** Exposure to idealised images can dent people's self-esteem and increase their anxiety, even if this exposure is brief. Other teenagers also play a role in how teenagers view themselves.
- **Understanding adaptive versus destructive thoughts.** There's a difference between negative thoughts and behaviours about appearance, and what's known as 'adaptive appearance investment' – mapping dress or grooming in a way that aligns with teenagers' personalities, and in a way that avoids coupling appearance with self-worth. This can be healthier than ignoring the body altogether. People tend to have a positive body image when they can see beauty in a wide range of appearances, accept their bodies (including perceived flaws) and have the ability to filter out harmful messages.
- **Things that help a poor body image.** Taking some time away from social media is likely to be useful, as is doing some physical activity (assuming the original issue doesn't relate to an unhealthy fixation with becoming muscly or similar). Many of the parenting practices covered in Chapter 1 are likely to be useful here.
- **Long-term trajectories.** Some evidence points to body image remaining stable from mid-adolescence; other research suggests that body image issues will probably resolve with time, and that teenagers will become more resilient to negative influences that include exposure to idealised images in new and traditional media.

## Girls and boys

- **Increasing differences.** Social norms and biological underpinnings both inform increasing differences between the sexes. Testosterone is a key differentiating factor that contributes to the differences in height, weight and strength we saw in the section on puberty and general health; it also influences social and emotional aspects of brain development. Boys tend to be more aggressive than girls, on average, and have a higher sex drive. Girls tend to mature more quickly and benefit more from social connections. Teenagers are also influenced by stereotypical and regressive ideas about what it means to be a man or a woman.
- **Impact of perceived and actual differences, and of pressures to conform to stereotypes.** If teenagers don't conform, they may believe they're not truly a girl or a boy. Boys may suffer from a lack of emotional support, and may begin to disconnect from themselves and other people to conform to societal expectations of what it means to be a man. Similar pressures lead them into bullying or acceptance of being bullied.

## Sexual harassment

- **Risks.** Girls are far more likely than boys to be sexually harassed and assaulted, and to be subject in other ways to male violence.
- **Normalisation.** Both sexes become more accepting of sexual harassment as they move through the teenage years. Culture is a heavy influence on perceptions and beliefs – for example, one study showed a link between playing a video game with a sexualised female character and later being more accepting of rape myths. This culture has negative impacts on both sexes.

## Ideas for parents

- **Model healthy eating habits and make healthy food available.** Be wary of setting rules relating to junk food, as they may misfire – though other research has shown rules relating to healthy eating to be linked to good outcomes. It probably depends on your teenager. It's worth having conversations, in either case, about what it means to be healthy.
- **Help your teenager to sleep better, if you suspect they're not getting enough of it.** Being physically active during the day is useful, as is practising sleep hygiene – for example, getting up and going to bed at the same time each day, following a nighttime routine, and ensuring bedrooms are cool, comfortable and dark. It's worth suggesting to a sleep-deprived teenager that they try to get into natural light as early in the day as possible, minimise caffeine (and nicotine, if they smoke or vape), reduce evening light and avoid technology at bedtime. If your teenager's body clock has shifted dramatically out of whack, you could try daylight bulb exposure, as explored on page 155.

    There are also things you can put into place as a family. These include keeping evening lights dim in communal areas (low-wattage lamps rather than overhead bulbs), keeping evening noise to a minimum and plugging in all devices in a communal space – the kitchen or living room – overnight to keep them out of bedrooms.
- **Avoid talking about people's weight, including your teenager's and your own.** It's been linked to the development of unhealthy attitudes to food, among other things. Talk about what bodies can do, not what they look like.
- **Help your teenager to feel comfortable in their skin.** Boys, in particular, may need help to feel comfortable expressing their feelings and to recognise their need to connect with other people.

If they're straight or bisexual, they also need to understand girls as people with whom they form relationships, not as sexual objects. Both sexes will need help to recognise that stereotypes are not a prescription of how they should be.

- **Intervene if you witness sexual harassment.** Anything else may be understood as tacit consent for the behaviour to continue.

# CHAPTER 7

# RISK AND REWARD

## Reasons for risk-taking

The psychoanalyst Dr Donald Winnicott, whose ideas informed much of our current thinking about the development of younger children and teenagers, wrote in 1965: 'Young people... do not know what they are going to become. They do not know where they are, and they are waiting. Because everything is in abeyance, they feel unreal, and this leads them to do certain things which feel real to them.'[1] These things include taking the kinds of risk that might induce a little retrospective shuddering in their future adult selves.

I entered my post-university years having done a number of things that I'd now file in the Really Bloody Stupid category, but having survived these experiences. By my early twenties, I'd blindly jumped off an eighty-foot rock into the sea. I'd drunk an obscene amount at a university sports society initiation having given blood the same day with some repercussions I'm not prepared to put down in writing. I'd got a motorbike lesson from a stranger when I was teaching English in South-East Asia – I had to fend off his advances in the middle of nowhere, and narrowly avoided several accidents once I started using the bike to commute to work. In another place and time, I smoked a joint with friends, having eaten 'special' brownies for the first time and without feeling any effect. I was unaware, until it was too late, that the results are delayed if you digest rather than inhale. I still have a scar on my eyebrow from hitting my head when I fainted the following morning.

There was lots else, besides. While it's often assumed that we take more risks in our teenage years than we do at other times of life, data shows that it's actually emerging adulthood – the decade after we hit eighteen – in which the most risks are taken.[2] If I think about the risks I just mentioned, they were all taken during the university years or just afterwards. The concentration of risk at this age may be because there's more opportunity to take it, rather than emerging adults being naturally more risk-taking than younger teenagers.[3]

Most of us come out of the other end relatively unscathed – though, of course, there are those who don't, and we have to hope our own children aren't among them. In England and Wales, the leading cause of death for five- to nineteen-year-olds is suicide, followed by congenital disorders and then road traffic accidents. While their absolute risk of dying is much lower than older age groups, the relative risk of dying due to a crash is higher than at any other age.[4] We overestimate risk-taking behaviour in teenagers. But teenagers do take risks, and risk varies by culture, suggesting that it's partly the act of pushing back that's so intoxicating to them. In Turkey, for example, the risks teenagers take are more likely to be wearing revealing clothes or pursuing political activism.[5]

Why do teenagers and young adults take risks? In many cases, of course, it's fun to do so.[6] The parts of the brain that make use of dopamine, which governs feelings of pleasure, are more active during the teenage years – and this seems to make teenagers more likely to seek out thrills, as well as more able to isolate the positives of taking risks from the potential downsides.[7] The perceived benefits of risky behaviour, including immediate gratification, seem to erase thoughts of danger.[8] Teenagers can feel bored if they're not taking part in something that helps them to feel alive. The uncomfortable truth is that for teenagers, in the moment, risk is fun.

While some have argued that more active dopamine pathways in adolescence make teenagers more vulnerable to addiction,[9] recent analysis suggests that dopamine activity relates more to the uncertainty inherent in this period than it does to simplified notions of risk and reward.[10] Either way, the peak of humans' sensitivity to reward is in the late teenage years.[11] Teenagers' bodies mature before their minds do. This 'maturity gap' is responsible, in part, for extreme behaviour – joyriding or passing out drunk gives teenagers access to what they see as the world of adults, at least for a moment.[12] Peer pressure is a major factor in adolescent risk. Teenagers are particularly sensitive to the fear of being rejected by peers, and this potential rejection outweighs health risks or other consequences of behaviour that might raise an adult eyebrow.[13] They are more likely to drink alcohol if their friends do.[14] The same is true for committing crime, smoking weed and nicotine addiction.[15]

To answer the question of whether just being in the company of others makes risk-taking more likely or whether a degree of pressure is needed, a group of researchers invited young people between the ages of eighteen and twenty to take part in a lab experiment. Those participating were asked to pump up a set of virtual balloons to earn money – the bigger the balloon, the more money they earned but the more likely it was to pop (at which point they lost the financial reward). There were three experimental conditions – no other young people in the room, young people present but not egging participants on to keep pumping, and young people present and putting on the pressure. It was only in this final condition that participants took more risks – in other words, just having others in the room didn't affect risk-taking behaviour.[16] It appears there's an element of inducement that explains the link between the presence of friends and risky behaviour.

Even adolescent mice drink more alcohol in the company of other mousey teenagers than when they're alone. This is under experimental conditions, unless there are some secret fermentation habits among wild mice of which we're unaware. The mouse study suggests an evolutionary underpinning to the adolescent drive to seek rewards in the company of their peers.[17] A group of Dutch researchers followed around 600 teenagers for three years to work out what drives them to take up smoking. They found that nicotine habits were predicted by the twin drivers of peer pressure and being impulsive.[18] My first cigarette followed this model. I was standing in a garden at a party aged sixteen, everyone around me was smoking, and I felt an overwhelming urge not to be left behind. (Fortunately for my teenage self, it tasted like inhaling an ashtray, and I didn't continue. Unluckily for my slightly older self, it tasted better the next time.)

Adolescents may also be using the rewards they get from drinking or taking drugs to help them to manage difficult internal feelings.[19] When I took caffeine tablets to help me stay awake to study, my conscious purpose was to get better marks – but, in reality, I was trying to manage worry (this experience taught me the retrospectively obvious life lesson that caffeine can stoke anxiety). Being depressed makes teenagers more likely to smoke, drink alcohol and take illegal drugs when they're a little older.[20] And, devastatingly, teenagers who've experienced physical and sexual abuse are more likely to take drugs and drink alcohol. The same is true, though to a lesser extent, for those who've been emotionally abused.[21]

An under-researched reason that teenagers take risks is to look 'cool' or 'tough' – though I suspect any self-respecting teenager might avoid those words, even if they agreed with the sentiment behind them. In one of the studies summarised to support this idea, words were translated from the original Dutch; in others, 'coolness' was described by adults and retrofitted into conclusions about teenagers. A more developmentally driven explanation is that flirting with new experiences helps us to develop the wisdom we need to become successful adults. This idea fits better with the data than the idea that risk results from teenage brain imbalances, as the latter would suggest a peak in risk-taking during adolescence, not emerging adulthood. Another theory is that being exposed to risk increases teenagers' curiosity and desire to act on it, and to see if doing so fits with their newly materialising identities.[22]

Most teenagers say they don't intend to take risks, but they often do so when presented with the opportunity.[23] There's also, naturally, a pull factor towards risk in terms of the psychoactive nature of alcohol and drugs – once teenagers have been exposed, this may tug them back for more.[24] On the other hand, those things that are especially risky may lose their appeal once initial curiosity has been satisfied and so long as the adventurers haven't become addicted along the way.[25] One teenager might try something, realise it's not brilliant and walk away, while another gets hooked.

Families can influence teenagers' risk-taking behaviour. For example, parents who drink alcohol and who make alcohol available to their teenagers are more likely to have children who drink themselves.[26] A well-stocked drinks cabinet to which teenagers have unmonitored access at a sleepover might be slightly less well stocked by the time parents next open it. Accessing such a bountiful supply as a fifteen-year-old put me off whisky for life. If teenagers have siblings, these siblings' drinking tendencies have an even stronger link to their own drinking habits than their parents' drinking does.[27] Poor-quality relationships with parents and parental psychological control are further risk factors, along with poor family communication and low levels of parental monitoring.[28]

Finding a balance is likely to be important – one study found the riskiest behaviour among teenagers whose parents were either very controlling or too light touch.[29] Those teenagers who have no limits are free to take whatever risks they please, whereas those who are tightly controlled may wish to cast off their shackles. Having authoritative parents (see Chapter 1) seems to make teenagers less likely to descend too far into problematic behaviour, probably because they're more satisfied with their lives.[30] Teenagers with permissive parents are five times more likely to have smoked than those with authoritative ones, and for those with authoritarian parents, the risk is almost double.[31] Culture, including media, has an impact too, of course.

Individual factors are also important, and drivers for teenage risk-taking can reveal themselves earlier than adolescence.[32] Those who find it hard to regulate their emotions are more likely to take risks,[33] as are children with limited attention spans.[34] So, too, are those who feel left out by other teenagers.[35] Conflict at home is another risk factor for risk.[36] A Dutch twin study tried to work out if teenagers having low self-control breeds family fights or if conflict erodes self-control. It found that the data fits the second explanation.[37] Teenagers who go through early puberty are more likely to drink alcohol and take up smoking, possibly because they have older friends.[38] Higher testosterone levels are linked to non-aggressive risk-taking, though there's no clear link with the aggressive form – for example, starting fights.[39]

Teenagers who've taken risks but had no consequences usually believe this behaviour is less dangerous than those for whom risk represents unmarked territory. This has led a group of scholars to warn that if a national health-promotion agency 'claims that smoking marijuana will transform your brain into a fried egg, and you nonetheless share a joint with friends on occasion and manage to maintain your [school achievement levels], then why trust what they say about cocaine and heroin?'[40] And risk may breed risk. Those who smoke weed, for example, are more likely to take sexual risks.[41]

It's important to bear in mind when we're thinking about teenage risk that it tends to be overstated for teenagers as a whole. Some of the most serious teenage risks – drunk driving and crime – involve only a fifth of teenagers, according to one study, meaning the rest are less obviously risk-taking.[42] (When an attempt was made to burn my daughter's school down, her response was, 'Wow. Someone got a bad test result.') Most of us therefore won't have teenagers in the very risky group. We are, though, likely to have teenagers who dip the odd toe into the tempting waters of risk and reward.

## Sex and porn

The world has changed since we were growing up, but one thing to remain true is that teenagers are mostly Very Interested In Sex. It combines the thrill of being part of the adult world to which so many adolescents are desperate to belong with some of the other things that are so intoxicating to teenagers – an area that's totally private from parents and that can make them feel present in their bodies. It's part of the wider sensation-seeking that marks this time of risk and reward – and it's doubly compelling as so few teenagers actually do it. Recent YouGov polling found that a quarter of adults between the ages of eighteen and twenty-nine had never had sex. The average age of first sex, for those who'd had it and were willing to say, was seventeen. Only a fifth were younger than sixteen.[43]

Writing in 2008, adolescent psychologists Professor Laurence Steinberg and Dr W. Andrew Collins termed a cultural shift towards greater acceptance of sex outside marriage and teenage girls having more sex as 'sexual evolution', marking the gentle pace of these changes.[44] Some ideas have not shifted, though. A district nurse came to talk about sex to my year 10 class back in the early 1990s. After demonstrating how to put a condom onto a plaster-of-Paris penis, she asked for a volunteer to do the same. Tanya French[45] immediately stuck up her hand. To the dismay of the nurse and the grudging awe of the rest of us, Tanya expertly rolled the condom down the counterfeit penis using only her mouth. Sexual evolutions aside, I suspect a health professional today would be equally horrified.

Evidence suggests there's good reason for the Tanya Frenches of this world to delay sex for rather longer. Waiting helps teenagers to fuse together physical aspects of sexuality with their attitudes, feelings and identities. Those who have sex young may do so because of pressure rather than desire, leading to later feelings of guilt and doubt.[46] They're also more likely to get sexually transmitted infections than those who have their first sexual experience when they're a bit older, and pregnancy becomes a more likely upshot.[47]

Health outcomes as adults are also likely to be worse for those who start having sex young, though we're not sure what, if any, the causal links are.[48] One long-term study of around 6,500 American teenagers suggests that the number of sexual partners may be more important to outcomes than the age at which teenagers first have sex.[49] And, of course, those who start having sex younger have more time for different partners. This research about the bad outcomes of teenage sex conflicts with my instincts on the issue, which probably arose from transitioning to adulthood at a time when peer respect was afforded to those girls who could drink hard, go clubbing until dawn and shag a selection of the least nerdy available boys. Culture is a hard thing to overcome when it comes to attitudes.

Fewer teenagers are having sex than is commonly believed by either adults or teenagers themselves. This fictitious belief that everyone else is getting laid can make teenagers think they're missing out and shame them into having sex before they're ready.[50] Other reasons contributing to teenagers' desire for sex, on top of those mentioned at the start of this section, include tacit consent of family and friends – they're more likely to have sex later and to have fewer sexual partners if their parents and friends disapprove of teenage sex.[51] Perceiving teenage pregnancy as normal is also linked to greater acceptance of and desire for sex in younger teenagers.[52] Following rumours of a pregnancy in my then fourteen-year-old's year group at school, this sliver of knowledge led me to say to her, 'We need to have the safe sex chat.' This was earlier than I thought it would be needed, as I was clearly massively naïve about her peers. 'Mum! We do not! We get that endlessly at school! Please don't,' she begged.

Other things that may influence teenagers to have sex at a younger age than average are online dating and chat rooms, cannabis and alcohol (*quelle surprise*).[53] Teenagers are also more likely to take risks with sex – for example, not using a condom – when they've been drinking.[54] Those who do a lot of music and drama are likely to have sex later.[55] Presumably, they're too busy for such shenanigans. For teenagers having sex, risk presents itself in at least two ways – the risk of having sex at all and the risk attached to *how* they have that sex. Unsafe sex is influenced, too, by teenagers' relative inability to control emotions arising in the heat of the moment – more sensible intentions to use a condom may be shot down by a naked body in front of them. This means that contraceptives that sit under the skin, or devices implanted in the uterus, are most effective at preventing unplanned teenage pregnancies.[56] They don't, of course, prevent sexually transmitted infections.

Part of teenagers' sexual development involves finding out about it. Research papers in this area have an astonishing ability to state the obvious. One paper tells us, 'Studies in this field have detected an increase in searching for information on sex among adolescents since the emergence of the Internet.'[57] I can imagine the tabloid headlines resulting from this insight: 'Teenagers Use Internet to Find Out About Sex'. The online world provides a more informative – and, of course, risky – medium than most parents of current teenagers had when they were growing up, unless they had their children young. My sex education was limited to the matter-of-fact and useless briefings we got at school, passing round tatty copies of *Just Seventeen* on the school bus and reading Jilly Cooper novels. To be fair to Cooper, she was very informative, though sex turned out to involve fewer jodhpurs and horny stablehands than she implied.

Sex can influence how much teenagers are accepted by those around them. A study of almost a thousand teenagers found that girls were accepted less by their peers once they'd had sex. Boys had the opposite experience. Girls' currency among their peers went up, though, if they'd snogged other people – so they were only hauled over the hot coals of other people's disapproval if they'd gone as far as to sleep with someone else.[58]

Teenagers' expectations about sex can be fractured by the sharp edges of its reality. In a 2019 study with young adults, two researchers asked participants to think back to what they had hoped for and expected before they first had sex. Many, as younger teenagers, had thought they'd first have sex with someone they trusted and liked, that the sex would be fully consensual and the experience would be meaningful. For the most part, these expectations hadn't been met. The same study cited earlier research showing that before they first have sex, teenagers' expectations about what it will be like are often shaped by what they have seen on television – leading, commonly, to a mismatch between expectation and reality.[59]

This seems perilously out of date, even though it's only a few years old – as we know how much information teenagers, and even younger children, are getting from exposure to pornography. A problem with research on porn is that the research world moves much more slowly than the internet and porn accessibility. Literature reviews about teenagers and their understanding of sex tend to include studies from early in the internet age – or even before it started – which are so far removed from the context of readily available porn as to be meaningless. The research literature on porn is also riven with controversy. Inconsistent ways of defining and measuring porn mean we can't be confident about findings,[60] and there's little agreement between different research camps on issues like whether internet porn can be addictive.[61]

These challenges make it hard for us to know just how prevalent watching porn is among teenagers. A recent review of studies found that boys have seen porn, on average, by the age of thirteen and girls by seventeen[62] – but I'm not sure these are really capturing current realities. A study of 1,500 fourteen- to eighteen-year-olds in Spain in 2020 found that just under half used porn,[63] and a 2017 Australian study of fifteen- to twenty-nine-year-olds found that porn had been seen by almost nine in ten of them.[64] But the research has not really caught up with the videos that get shared between teenagers on WhatsApp groups or shown to each other on the school bus, or the accidental TikTok exposure, or the easy access that teenagers have to brutal, theoretically age-restricted content through sites like Pornhub.

Teenagers who choose to access porn, as opposed to being exposed to it accidentally, are more likely to live in families where things aren't running smoothly – where they feel enmeshed with their parents or have a poor relationship with them, or where there's a lack of communication.[65] They're more likely to seek out new sensations and less likely to have self-control.[66] They're more likely to be boys. They're also more likely to suffer from poor mental health.[67] As we've seen, though, prevalence rates are sufficiently high that there are plenty of viewers breaking the moulds of these stereotypes. And there are reasons beyond curiosity and titillation that teenagers may seek out porn. Education is an important one – teenagers want to learn about sex, and to have a sense that they know what they're doing when the moment comes. They might, for example, want to learn how to initiate sex or to learn about different positions.[68]

I'm not going to put the porn industry under a spotlight here, though it has plenty of dark corners that would no doubt benefit from exposure of the non-explicit kind. I will, though, briefly cover some reasons why unfettered access to porn may be extremely detrimental for our kids. This is something about which the research is unequivocal.

Cognition is one such area. Teenagers' brains are still developing, and they may lack the impulse control needed to keep porn use within manageable margins. The images they see are remembered more indelibly than words. Teenagers can become preoccupied by thoughts of sex.[69]

There are mixed findings in the research about the extent to which porn influences the sexual risks that teenagers are willing to take. Some studies have found a link; others have not.[70] It is a fact, though, that porn normalises sex without a condom and with multiple partners.[71] Feelings of inadequacy are pervasive among teenagers who watch porn – a research review concluded that girls can feel inferior to the women they see onscreen, while boys can feel less able to perform (it seems feasible that the same is true in reverse, of course).[72]

Those who consume porn have worse relationships with their partners, on average.[73] Teenagers can also fail to understand that sex in pornography differs from sex in relationships. In other words, if they see depictions of violent or degrading acts like choking, they may understand them as normal. This can feed into their own relationships. One study looked at links between violent pornography and teenage dating violence. Even when accounting for other factors that might explain a link, including a history of being violent or a tolerance of rape myths (for example, agreeing with the statement, 'Sexual assault charges are often used as a way of getting back at guys'), researchers found boys who'd watched violent porn were at least three times more likely to commit sexual violence than those who had not.[74]

This is happening in the context of ever-more extreme content being uploaded to sites like Pornhub.[75] There's anecdotal evidence that the impact of this is leaching out into what's considered normal by younger generations, including those who may be approaching the age of having teenagers themselves. The journalist Marie Le Conte, who is in her early thirties at the time of writing, described in her book *Escape* a drunken discussion about choking that she'd had with female friends. She said, 'It felt like two alien species meeting each other for the first time. On one side, the older women discussed it as a niche BDSM act; something they had never done and would never want to do, and that felt on par with watersports or nipple clamps. On the other, my two friends and I explained, plainly, that we had all been choked numerous times by men our age, sometimes because we asked for it and sometimes with no warning.'[76] For her, it was unremarkable. It seems remarkable to me, however, that women might find something that threatens life to be this ordinary.[77]

And it's not just violent content that drives violence or abuse. One study found that boys who'd seen explicit content as young adolescents were more likely to be perpetrators of sexual harassment two years later.[78] Those who've been exposed to explicit material are more likely to be sexually aggressive, too – in other words, they engage in sexual behaviour despite absence of consent from the other party – as well as more likely to become victims of sexual aggression themselves.[79]

The aggression, violence and humiliation that saturate much contemporary porn links into regressive ideas about gender roles. Women are often objectified in porn, and both girls and boys exposed to explicit material are more likely to see women as sex objects.[80] Women in porn tend to be painted as submissive, passive vessels that contain male desires, while men are the literally thrusting subjects of the story and the custodians of sexual pleasure. Women, in porn, are the secretaries to the male bosses.[81] They exist for the use of men, who are depicted as lacking compassion or the ability to be intimate.[82] Both sexes are reduced to empty caricatures – ones without soul, and for which the model for an intimate, real-world sexual relationship turns into ashes.

Porn is part of the wider world of 'online sexual activity'. This is defined by researchers as internet-enabled activities related to humans' sexuality. It could involve sending graphic texts, pictures or videos, or seeking other people for sex, either online or in the real world.[83] Reasons for doing so include arousal and curiosity.[84] Online sexual activity can also help teenagers to develop sexual communication skills and to learn how to manage their sexual feelings. Teenagers who are insecure or shy may be particularly likely to prefer communicating this way with partners than talking face to face.[85]

Seeking out sexual activity online may be a normal part of healthy development – but, as you might expect, there are risks attached to it. Teenagers may lose inhibitions and develop intimacy more quickly than they would in real life. They may come across explicit material that makes them feel uncomfortable. They can become more likely to seek out online sexual activity again in future.[86]

Teenagers who sext – in other words, who share explicit texts in the form of messages, videos or photos via their devices – are more likely than others to be sexually active.[87] This doesn't seem particularly surprising, given that those in relationships are presumably more likely to sext than those who aren't. Teenagers who sext are also more likely to take sexual risks – to sleep with more people and to have sex with no protection – and to take other risks, such as taking drugs and smoking.[88] They're more likely to experience sexual abuse and violence from sexual partners.[89] They are more likely to have mental health problems.[90] We don't know what the causal links are for these factors, or indeed whether there are any; it could be that a teenager with poor mental health is more likely to look for external validation through sending sexts, for example.

But we do know there are risks attached where we can be more certain of cause and effect. These include sexts being shared without consent, bullying, and a sexual partner taking a sext as a sign of consent to other activities, when it's anything but.[91] Double standards mean that sexting damages girls' reputations in a way it doesn't for boys.[92] The stereotype of the private image of a girl that then catches light across the mobile phones of a school community like wildfire is, unfortunately, all too real.

A review of studies that analysed the habits of over 100,000 teenagers found that between 15% and 27% of teenagers have sent and received sexts, with the proportion increasing both as teenagers get older and over time. In other words, rates were higher in more recent studies. This review was published in 2018, so rates are likely to be even higher now. According to the same review, 12% of teenagers had forwarded a sext without having the permission of the person involved to do so, and 8% had sent a sext that was then forwarded without their consent.[93]

Consent is paramount, so this high prevalence is concerning and something to discuss with teenagers. Other hazardous sexting behaviour includes coercion – in other words, pressuring others into sexting when they don't want to. A Spanish study found nearly one in six teenagers said they'd been coerced into sharing sexual content online.[94] And adults may become involved with minors through this medium.[95] Analysis of data on around 3,000 teenagers and young adults found that one in eight had experienced grooming.[96] Receiving unsolicited sexts is another hazard that many teenagers are likely to experience.

For those teenagers who want to engage in consensual sexting with others of the same age, it may be better to promote being safe than it is to advise they don't do it.[97] Online child safety expert Karl Hopwood advises having conversations with teenagers about what safe sexting means. If they're sharing images, for example, it means keeping their heads out of the picture, ensuring there are no identifying pieces of jewellery or tattoos, and taking any other steps needed to make sure an image isn't clearly identifiable. He also advises that teenagers increasingly need to be aware of deepfakes.[98] An image or video presented as being of them, or of another teenager, may be a sophisticated hoax.

How should parents and educators manage sex, porn, sexting

and other types of online sexual activity? We can't erase porn from our teenagers' lives, much as we might want to – even the tightest parental controls aren't going to affect what gets shared at a sleepover. Education is, instead, likely to provide the key. According to Dr Mandy Sanchez of the campaigning organisation Culture Reframed, 'If we don't talk to kids about porn as parents or as trusted adults, then we're leaving it up to the porn industry to have that conversation.'[99] A small study that looked at the effects of a porn education programme found that, by the end of it, teenagers were less likely to think that working in porn is a good way to make money, that porn is realistic and that calling someone nasty or a slut during sex is something done by everybody. This education programme covered topics such as porn addiction, different types of intimacy, healthy flirting and how to set boundaries, commercial sexual exploitation and how to talk with other teenagers about porn.[100]

Part of this education, whether it's something formal that happens at school or informal chats that take place at home, is about developing media literacy. Being able to think critically about explicit online material is likely to be useful.[101] If teenagers understand the reasons the porn industry presents material in a particular way and the profit motives driving moves towards ever-more extreme material, they're more likely to understand it as they might see their reflection in a hall of mirrors – manipulated and distorted, not a truthful depiction of the world.

Professor Emily Rothman of Boston University has a number of recommendations when talking to teenagers about porn. One is to be as open and non-judgemental as you can, which helps to preserve trust and to ensure your teenager feels comfortable to have this kind of chat in future. Another is to accept the inevitable awkwardness and the likely brevity of the conversation. She recommends preparing what you're going to say in advance, following a statement (for example, that porn doesn't reflect real life in areas such as consent) with a question (for example, what your teenager has learned about consent at school).[102]

If the idea of talking to your teenager about porn is as appealing to you as walking barefoot through a slug-infested field after the rain – and I'd honestly prefer to take my chances with the slugs – I'm sorry to say that conversations about awkward topics don't end there. Broader conversations about sex are needed, too. Parents believe they talk about sex more than their teenagers perceive them to – suggesting, perhaps, a deep teenage squeamishness prevents them absorbing the messages their parents are so reluctantly determined to impart. This means that one-off conversations aren't enough. Regular communication about sex is linked to later safer sex practices.[103]

Necessary topics include consent, desire – for example, the importance of only having sex if *they* genuinely want to, and not feeling pressured to take part in any practices that cause them discomfort – and the importance of mutual respect. Parents tend to focus on warnings and negative aspects of sex to the exclusion of the good side of it – love, pleasure and intimacy, for example.[104] One study found that the choice of partner for teenagers' first experience of sex was the most important factor in shaping whether the reality of sex met their expectations of it, suggesting that this is an area parents and teachers should highlight as being something teenagers ought to consider.[105]

You might also want to cover puberty, masturbation (highlighting that it's normal, healthy and private), contraception and sexual orientation. Same-sex-attracted teenagers may find their parents have previously assumed they're straight, and – for boys and men – later conversations about sex may centre around stereotypical ideas about negative health outcomes.[106] Sexual risk – for example, having sex without protection – is another area in which teenagers can lack parental input.[107] But caution is needed here. Talking to teenagers about the benefits of using contraception have, counter-intuitively, been linked to them placing less value on having sex within a meaningful relationship. Perhaps this kind of conversation implies that parents are open to them having casual sex; alternatively, perhaps parents only bring up contraception when they think casual sex is on their child's horizon.[108]

How you talk to your child about sex may be as important as what you talk about. Most research in this area has looked at whether parents and teenagers have talked about certain topics, not how they have talked about them. Conversations may go better when parents follow their teenagers' lead in terms of how the conversation flows, take on board their children's perspectives where possible, ask open-ended questions and keep pressure to a minimum. It's worth trying to anticipate how your teenager may react and where the conversation may end up, and trying to avoid lectures or interruptions. If you want to avoid a formal talk, you could pick up on cues from what's happening around you – news coverage of sexual abuse, for example, or unrealistic body ideals on social media. You could also try being open about how you feel – perhaps saying that you feel uncomfortable about having the conversation, but it's important as you want to keep your teenager safe.

One paper written for doctors, which covers how to talk to parents about their teenagers' sexuality, outlines potential worries for both parents and adolescents. A parent might fear not knowing the answers, giving their child too much information about their own sexual histories, finding out something they don't want to know about their child – that they're already having sex, for example – or that their child will shut down, or think they're out of touch. A teenager might fear being wrong about what they say, getting criticised, getting asked awkward questions or making their parent angry. Either may feel embarrassed, afraid or ashamed.[109]

Other than talking to your child about sex, porn and related issues, there are some things you may want to do. One is keeping an eye on what is being taught to your child at school about sex, and whether it's accurate and age-appropriate – some of the 'sex-positive' material, in particular, risks inappropriately eroding your teenager's boundaries. Another step you can take is to communicate norms of love and respect with your teenager. A study of around 500 Dutch adolescents between the ages of thirteen and sixteen found that parents who communicated these norms had teenagers who had a slower path towards sexual maturity. Their attitudes towards sex were less permissive than those of other teenagers, and boys were less likely to take sexual risks. To measure these norms, teenagers were asked things like whether their parents ever said they shouldn't have sex without being in love, or that they shouldn't do anything sexual the other person doesn't want to do.[110]

You'll probably want to monitor your child's social media, at least in the younger teenage years (see Chapter 3). Parental controls on devices for under-eighteens can help stem the tide of inappropriate porn flowing past the barriers you have constructed (though see Chapter 3 for a minor caveat here on potential unforeseen consequences of parental controls).[111] Assuming your teenager is still young enough for you to put this kind of rule in place without turning your home into a theatre of war, you could try restricting internet-enabled devices to public areas – the kitchen or front room, say, and not bedrooms. This needs to be balanced against the risk that teenagers will become more secretive if your rules are too restrictive.[112] You may also want to rope in a friendly adult you trust who can be there to answer questions if your child doesn't feel comfortable talking to you – an older nephew or niece, for example.[113]

You can also take solace from the fact that porn is a public health matter. It's not a question of shame or moral failure if your child has accessed it. But if they have – and, on the basis of the statistics, we can be reasonably sure, at least with older teenagers, that they have – knowing it's a public health matter isn't going to help them to manage it. And that's where your support and guidance come in, along with those horrendously awkward but essential conversations.

## Drink and drugs

When I was sixteen, a local teenager died after taking ecstasy. It was a moment that crystallised the intangible warnings we'd been given by the adults around us and made me more careful than I might have been otherwise. Drugs aren't just a risk to the teenagers who take them, though. Others can get caught up in county lines, through which teenagers and younger children – who are less likely than adults to attract suspicion, are easily controlled and cost less – are exploited into shifting drugs locally or regionally.

Teenagers between the ages of fourteen and seventeen are most likely to be targeted by county lines gangs.[114] They're often caught in criminal webs through coercion and threatened or actual violence, and they're more likely to be targeted if they attend alternative education or special educational needs settings.[115] Those who've been singled out often have poor mental health or are themselves addicted to substances. You might want to watch out for your teenager being able to afford expensive clothes or jewellery, disappearing for long periods of time, missing school, or having a significant change in mood or injuries they're not able to explain away.[116] The campaign group Ivison Trust, formerly Pace (Parents Against Child Exploitation), offers resources and suggested avenues for concerned parents.[117]

The teenage drug scene has gone through significant change since most parents of today's teenagers were growing up. Monitoring the Future is an annual survey on drug use in the United States, which it's been tracking among teenagers since 1975. Street drugs have declined since the 1990s, replaced in the 2000s by so-called psychotherapeutic drugs – in other words, those that have a medicinal purpose when not being abused – such as amphetamines, tranquillisers and sedatives.[118] Since 2006, the use of psychotherapeutic drugs has also been falling.[119]

The most recent data showed an accelerated fall in drug use over the pandemic, though the proportion of teenagers taking cocaine, heroin, hallucinogens and prescription opioids is now back to pre-pandemic levels. The fraction taking ecstasy, crack and tranquillisers, though, isn't as high as it was before 2020. One area showing a rapid rise is the use of gym-centric drugs such as anabolic steroids, accompanied by an increase in food supplements used to enhance performance. The study authors suggest this represents a growing interest in fitness, including lifting weights, among some teenagers, with an accompanying need to protect them from the harm that can accompany unsupervised use.[120]

Teenage use of alcohol also fell over the pandemic, but it's also now back to where it was.[121] The effects of alcohol and other substances can be wide-ranging – they can affect mental health, relationships and school outcomes.[122] Other potential impacts include sexually transmitted infections, road accidents and physical health.[123] These, though, aren't universal. Some teenagers emerge unharmed, while a small amount of experimentation can have devastating consequences for others.[124] A night doing shots in the local park may lead to a sore morning head for one teenager and to stomach pumping (or worse) for another. I suspect I was saved from the worst consequences of my first proper underage drinking session – pubs in Colchester weren't strong on ID checks in the 1990s – by throwing up most of what I'd consumed before it had the chance to cause me much harm.

If your teenager's had a lot to drink and you're worried about alcohol poisoning, things to look out for include confusion, vomiting, skin that's pale or tinged blue, seizures and fits, not being able to talk, soiling themselves and losing consciousness. If you're concerned, you should call emergency services. You should also stay with them to prevent them choking on their vomit or stopping breathing, sit them up if conscious (or put them in the recovery position if not), get them to sip water if they can swallow it and keep them warm.[125]

Vaping is an increasing concern to parents of teenagers. Corner shops sell candy-coloured vapes in tactile shapes, and vaping is a much easier habit to hide from parents and teachers than smoking used to be. A teenager can vape in their bedroom or the school loos with little fear of detection, unless there's a sharp-nosed adult in the vicinity. There's no need to mess around with the changes of clothes, hand-washing, minty mouth sprays or orange eating that went hand-in-hand with more traditional teenage smoking. I tend to think of vaping in the context of nicotine, though many teenagers vape cannabis-derived compounds or substance-free liquids.

Teenage vaping has also been encouraged through marketing campaigns and the message that vaping is safer than smoking. It's reversed decades of declines in nicotine use among teenagers.[126] The Millennium Cohort Study follows around 19,000 babies who were born in the UK between 2000 and 2002. Researchers assessed vape use among half of these at different time points, finding that around one in seven fourteen-year-olds had tried vaping, rising to almost one in two seventeen-year-olds.[127] There's a time lag between researchers measuring prevalence and peer-reviewed studies being published, and vaping is a rapidly moving beast. These figures may therefore be much higher today.

The preponderance of flavours available has a clear link to teenage vaping. Teenagers who vape non-traditional flavours (blueberry or biscuit flavour, say, rather than tobacco, mint or flavourless) are much more likely to get hooked.[128] And the market is set up for this – as far back as 2014, there were almost 8,000 unique flavours of vape available.[129] A move from clunky models that needed charging and refilling towards disposable vapes has also smoothed the path for teenagers. Between January 2021 and April 2022 in Great Britain, for example, one study found the proportion of eighteen-year-old vapers using single-use vapes had increased from less than half a per cent to more than 50%. This was – on paper, but possibly not reflecting reality – more than five times the rate of forty-five-year-old vapers.[130]

One argument for promoting vapes has been that they're better for health than smoking. As an adult, I manifested this justification by using vaping to ditch cigarettes. I gradually decreased the level of nicotine in my vape until it was zero, then used it as a crutch for more than a year before stopping altogether. (A sample comment from my brother-in-law: 'Cor, I bet it was *really* hard to give up your nicotine-free vaping habit, Matilda.') But it seems that while this argument may work for adult former smokers, it's less useful when thinking about teenagers who have never smoked tobacco. One study found, for example, that every increase in nicotine concentration level (from none to low to medium to high) for teenage vapers roughly doubles the chances of being a frequent cigarette smoker six months later.[131]

Vaping is such a recent phenomenon that long-term outcomes are largely unknown. The limited evidence we have, though, suggests that it's linked to poorer heart and lung health, as well as inflammation caused by the multiple chemical compounds that get inhaled, lower immunity to infection and oxidative stress.[132] Teenagers who vape are more likely than other teenagers to have a chronic cough, congestion or phlegm, and to get bronchitis.[133] Vaping-induced oxidative stress may also influence teenagers' developing brains, with damaging effects on memory, academic performance, sleep, behaviour and mental health.[134] Early evidence of damaging outcomes has led the European Academy of Paediatrics to deem vapes to be 'very dangerous' and to caution that they are more acutely toxic than smoking.[135] Health risks seem to be higher in those who vape cannabis-based products.[136] We can safely say that vaping isn't the harmless pastel-hued diversion that's been implied by its marketers.

## Managing risky behaviour

When thinking about risks, we need to be mindful of which are real and which are overstated. Kidnap risk is amplified beyond its reality. Risk of sexual assault probably isn't. We also need to keep in mind that risk profiles have changed since we were teenagers. A shared joint may not have been seen as a particularly dangerous thing in the past, but it's a different prospect today – a review of studies published between 1970 and 2017 has shown the psychoactive part of marijuana, THC, has increased by an annual average of 0.29% in weed and 0.57% in hash.[137] Friends who smoke weed tell me this greater intensity is well recognised, and that they yearn wistfully for the (weaker) 'bushweed we got back in the day'.

Teenagers and their parents, unsurprisingly, understand risk in different ways, meaning they have distinct ideas about how best to manage it. In a study of the varying ways in which parents and their teenagers understand adolescent risk, researchers found that parents were more likely to see risks attached to anxiety, insufficient exercise and poor diet, while teenagers were more likely to see risks attached to poor sleep, too much screen time and drugs.[138] I might think my teenager is risking her health when she regularly ignores the fruit bowl in favour of the energy bars and the prawn-cocktail-flavoured crisps. I started to write the words, 'She might think she's taking a risk when…' and realised there are precisely zero scenarios in which she might think she's taking a risk while I blithely perceive no threat.

Parents don't affect their teenagers' risky behaviour – either positively or negatively – in a vacuum. The risks teenagers take are affected by what's seen as normal around them. A case in point is the research I referenced earlier in the chapter showing that teenagers tend to have sex younger when teenage pregnancy is normalised. Another study of around 11,000 twelve- to thirteen-year-olds in England and Wales showed that shifting social norms can change teenagers' risky behaviour. Researchers divided the adolescents' schools into two groups. One group saw influential students trained in smoking prevention, while schools in the other group carried on as normal. In the first group, social norms were successfully shifted and students became less likely to take up smoking.[139]

We can't, as parents, mould ourselves into the position of an influential peer. We're far too annoying for that. But there are plenty of things we can do to minimise future risk-taking. (Minimising being the operative word; teenagers will take risks.) Parenting, as with so many other areas, is critical here. Various other parenting strategies to adopt and behaviours to avoid are set out in the initial part of this chapter on links with risk. And it seems that it's parenting approaches rather than inherited traits that are the important factor. One study tried to isolate the effect of genes by comparing adopted teenagers with those who lived with their biological parents. It found that having more involved parents in the early teenage years was linked to lower levels of substance abuse later in adolescence. Findings were consistent for both groups of teenagers, suggesting this link is driven by the family environment, not by genes.[140]

Another way to set the scene for healthy risk-taking is to provide a framework that enables teenagers to do risky things we know they can manage. I might put my thirteen-year-old on a train from Brighton, knowing her grandmother will be in London to meet her. Or I might trust her to research and source someone to come out to fix the boiler. Another is to build your teenager's self-esteem (see Chapter 5), which seems to be protective against the non-healthy variety of risk.[141] One study found a link between living in an unsafe area and teenagers' substance use, with an indirect pathway in the form of self-esteem. In other words, if teenagers' self-esteem was dented by a constant sense of threat, they were more likely to take risks. The study found that the more support these teenagers had, the less neighbourhood safety was able to influence their risk-related decisions.[142]

As implied earlier in this chapter, keeping a check on your own risky behaviour is also worthwhile. Teenagers are more likely to drink alcohol when they see their parents doing the same,[143] and they're more likely to smoke if cigarette use is normalised by their parents.[144] Vaping has a similar effect.[145] Opportunity may be equally important. One of the PE options at a friend's secondary school, about which I have benefited from more than two decades of teasing him, was golf. He and his mates used to hide in the copse behind the second hole and smoke spliffs, before emerging and trundling off for forty-five minutes of ineffectual hacking. I'm not sure the health outcomes were the ones intended by his school.

Building media literacy is another preventative strategy you can try. This links back to research we've already covered about minimising the negative impacts of porn. A review of studies has found that building media literacy skills can help to make teenagers less attracted to risky health behaviours and to make better choices.[146] If a teenager understands how advertising influences choices, and sees an ad full of beautiful people eating a gallon bucket of triple-chocolate-crunch ice cream laden with marshmallows and slivers of almond brittle, they may recognise how they're being manipulated into buying it and will choose to give it a wide berth when they're next in the supermarket.

If your teenager learns to drive, it's worth agreeing expectations before they start.[147] (I'm not sure if this would have deterred one set of friends in their teen years, who seem to have spent a lot of time driving around in whatever car they could lay their hands on, regardless of ownership, insurance or valid driving licences. Incredibly, one of them is now a lawyer.) It's also worth having some rules in place once they've passed their test. A few months after getting my licence, I borrowed my parents' car to drive to a holiday job working in a Colchester travel agent and clipped a parked car's wing mirror on my way through – without noticing, I hasten to add, though I realise this sounds fishy. The first I knew of it was when the post arrived one Saturday morning while I was still in bed, at which point my mum came up to demand – reasonably – why she'd just had a letter saying that her car had been involved in a hit-and-run.

Driving-related rules can be gradually relaxed – research shows that any accidents tend to happen very soon after learning to drive. A team of researchers surveyed hundreds of teenagers twice a year to assess the likelihood of them crashing their cars during their first 3,500 miles of driving. They found that teenagers are much more likely to crash in the first month after receiving their licence and during the first 500 miles of post-licence driving. They are also more likely to crash if their parents don't set rules, like not being allowed to drive at night.[148] It may be worth ensuring your teenager doesn't drive with friends or at nighttime until they've got some miles under their wheels.

When talking about risk, finding a positive reason not to engage is better than a negative one – valuing health or getting one over on the advertising companies, say. According to Professor Daniel Siegel, 'The most effective strategy to get adolescents to avoid smoking was not offering teens medical information or trying to frighten them with images of graveyards... The strategy that worked was to inform them about how the adults who owned the cigarette companies were brainwashing them to smoke so that they could get their money. Rather than getting teens to say no to smoking because some adult was frightening them into it, this strategy focused on the positive value of being strong in the face of manipulative adults out to get rich.'[149]

Similarly, conversations with teenagers about risk may be more successful when framed around the things teenagers want for themselves, like a clean school record or decent grades, than what we want for them. Clear expectations are good; instructing or bribing is bad. Therapist and parent coach Alicia Drummond tells a story about her dad saying he'd give her £100 if she made it to the age of twenty-one without smoking. She says, 'I thought, God, if he's going to pay me that much, it must be really amazing. I... took to it with great gusto at fifteen.'[150]

It's worth being careful about the messages you're passing on during conversations that touch on risk, making sure that risk-taking is seen as a behaviour rather than an intrinsic character trait. As mentioned in Chapter 1, labelling teenagers as risk-takers may cause them to adopt a risk-taking mentality as part of their identity. Another message to be careful about passing on is the idea that lots of other teenagers are taking risks – if a certain behaviour is seen as normal or even popular, its attractiveness increases.[151] When I thought that everyone else in my year group was drinking cider, it made me want to drink it, too. (This can also inoculate teenagers. Memories of the hours at dawn following an evening guzzling Strongbow – which I spent hanging over a fence to ensure that any vomit landed in a field, not my friend's garden – have ensured fermented apples have been safe in my presence ever since.)

One way to approach these conversations is to focus on your child's friends. 'If you're at that party on Saturday and Steve's taken something dodgy, this is what you need to know,' or, 'Hopefully there won't be too much messiness at the festival, but if Helen drinks too much, this might help.' Fiona Spargo-Mabbs is the mother of a teenager who died from taking ecstasy at a rave, and who founded a drugs education charity in his name. She recommends being pragmatic in your advice if your teenager is going somewhere there might be drugs. This might include sticking together, trying a tiny amount of any substance (knowing that if they take it, they'll be testing it on their own bodies) to see its effects before deciding whether to take more, not mixing drugs with alcohol, and stepping up and getting help from emergency services if a friend is in trouble.[152] Many clubs and festivals now offer drug-testing facilities – and use of these can also be normalised by conversations with your teenager.

You can also help your teenager to plan how to manage a difficult situation if they're determined not to drink or take drugs, but there's a chance their friends will be doing those things. It's harder to say no in the moment, so having strategies to stay safe is likely to be useful. Your teenager might say they can't drink, for example, because you're picking them up and you have a nose like a bloodhound. Or perhaps they quietly order a soda water with lemon to look like gin and tonic. Or perhaps they just say they don't want to – but pre-planning it will make it easier to stick to.

You may also want to look out for signs your teenager is using drugs. Some of the signs are indistinguishable from normal teenage behaviour – moodiness, rudeness or changes in appetite – but others will be more telling. These can include unfamiliar smells, things going missing, dilated pupils and self-harm. Spargo-Mabbs recommends approaching it gently if you're worried – perhaps asking an open-ended question about well-being in place of asking more directly, at least initially. She also recommends accessing the resources offered by the charity Addiction Family Support (formerly DrugFAM).[153]

A final point, reiterating one I've already made, is to be a safe port when your child is sailing on stormy seas. This means providing help, not blame, if your child asks for your assistance – and letting them know this is what they can expect. They need to understand that mistakes can happen, and you'll drop everything to help them if they get into trouble at a party or need your help navigating risks in other ways. My mother's boyfriend told me that he'd always made it clear to his daughter that if she got herself into a scary situation – for whatever reason, anywhere and at any time – she should call him and he would help. 'I reserved the right never to stop moaning about it afterwards,' he said, 'but I'd never let her down.'

# CHAPTER SUMMARY

## Risk-taking

- **The context.** Teenagers take fewer risks, overall, than we think they do. The type of risk taken varies by culture – so at least part of the appeal probably lies in the pushing of cultural limits. The early years of adulthood are the time for most risk-taking, possibly because there's more opportunity for it. Teenagers often don't intend to take risks, but may end up doing so when the opportunity arises.
- **Brain development.** Pleasure-seeking parts of the brain are more active in adolescence; teenagers also seek to alleviate boredom. Sensitivity to reward peaks in the late teenage years.
- **Other reasons.** It's fun to take risks. Peer pressure is a key factor, possibly underpinned by teenagers' sensitivity to rejection – they're more likely to drink alcohol, smoke weed, become addicted to nicotine and commit crime if their friends do the same. Taking risks may help teenagers to manage depression, anxiety or the feelings that arise following abuse.
- **Those most likely to take risks.** Teenagers are more likely to take risks if they have low levels of self-control, or if they have parents and siblings who take risks themselves. Early puberty is another potential contributor, as are poor emotional regulation, high testosterone levels and having been bullied. There are a number of underlying family factors that make risk-taking more likely, including having psychologically controlling parents, poor relationships with parents and family conflict. Underlying factors include cultural influences and the environment in which teenagers grow up.
- **Danger of no adverse consequences.** Teenagers believe there's less danger attached to risk if they've taken a risky decision before

but not suffered any consequences than if they've never tried something before. And taking risks in one area can lead to risk-taking in others.

## Sex and porn

- **The context.** One UK estimate is that teenagers have sex for the first time at seventeen, on average – but this misses wide variation, including the quarter of adults between eighteen and twenty-nine who've never had sex. Fewer teenagers are having sex than they or their parents believe.
- **Outcomes for those who have sex young.** Health outcomes as adults are worse, although this may be related to the number of sexual partners (those who have sex young have more time to sleep with more people) than the actual fact of having early sex. But those who have sex young may do so due to pressure, not desire, which has its own impacts.
- **Risk factors for having early sex.** Teenagers are more likely to have sex early if they believe their peers are having sex, if there's no parental disapproval of it and if teenage pregnancy has been normalised. Online dating and alcohol are also linked – alcohol is linked to early and unsafe sex.
- **Sex education and expectations.** Teenagers may turn to the internet and/or porn to find out about sex. Teenagers' expectations of sex, including that it will be fully consensual and that the experience will be meaningful, are often not met.
- **Sexual double standards.** Boys tend to be more accepted by those around them when they've had sex, while girls experience the opposite.
- **Pornography.** One estimate is that boys have seen porn by the age of thirteen, on average, and girls by seventeen – but this is probably far younger now. Teenagers are more likely to access porn if

they have difficult family relationships or other problems at home. There are a number of dangers attached to porn. These include a potential inability to keep porn use within reasonable limits, due to brains that are still developing, and a preoccupation with sex. Feelings of inadequacy among users are rife, and unsafe sex is normalised. Teenagers may not understand that porn sex differs from relationship sex in important ways – they may see violent acts like choking as normal and transfer them into their own relationships. In boys, there are links between violent porn and dating violence, and between early porn exposure and sexual harassment perpetration. Much of porn drives damaging and regressive stereotypes about both men and women.
- **Sexting.** Sexting may be part of healthy development, but it carries risks – those who sext place intimate material in the hands of other people. They're more likely to take risks in other areas, and to be victims of sexual abuse and violence. Forwarding sexts without consent is widespread among teenagers – one estimate suggests that more than one in ten teenagers have done this. Coercion may drive some teenagers to sext.

## Drink and drugs

- **Shifting preferences.** Street drugs were superseded by psychotherapeutic drugs in the 2000s, including amphetamines, tranquillisers and sedatives. Performance-enhancing drugs are being used more than they were previously, perhaps linked to an increasing interest in fitness (but with potentially harmful consequences).
- **Impacts.** Substance use can negatively affect mental health, relationships and teenagers' ability to do well at school. Their physical health can suffer, and they're more likely to contract sexually transmitted infections and to be involved in road accidents. Effects vary hugely, though – one teenager may be fine taking

drugs frequently, whereas a one-off experiment can have devastating consequences for another.
- **Vaping.** Vapes are marketed in a way that appeals to teenagers, and there are fewer barriers to entry than there are with smoking. The chances of taking up smoking are higher in those who vape, and this chance increases in line with their chosen nicotine concentration level. Long-term outcomes are uncertain due to a lack of data. Early evidence points towards impacts on both heart and lung health, higher inflammation levels and compromised immunity, and potential impacts on brain development in teenagers. Short-term effects are better known – vaping teenagers are more likely to have a chronic cough and to develop bronchitis, for example. Health risks are greater in those who vape cannabis-related products.

## Ideas for parents

- **Be careful what you model and what you offer.** Teenagers are more likely to drink alcohol if their parents drink themselves, and if they make alcohol available.
- **Don't overinflate the issue in your mind.** Most teenagers don't take the most serious risks.
- **Discuss porn, however awkward that seems.** The alternative is that they learn about porn from the industry itself. It's worth being open and non-judgemental (to build trust) in any conversations about porn; preparing what you want to say in advance; and working out linked statements and questions on, for example, consent. Consider device rules.
- **And discuss sex, regularly.** Topics should include consent, desire, mutual respect and the positive elements such as love, pleasure and intimacy. Choice of first partner seems to be particularly important in informing teenagers' first experiences of sex. Other potential topics include puberty, masturbation, sexual risk,

contraception and sexual orientation. (Though be careful when talking about contraception, as it's been linked to teenagers placing less value on having sex within a meaningful relationship.) Conversations may go better when you follow your child's lead, consider their perspectives, ask open-ended questions and try not to exert any pressure. You could also use what you see on TV or read in the paper as prompts for discussions. Communicate norms of love and respect.

▶ **Discuss the risks of sexting.** You may also want to talk about how to be safe if they do sext – for example, making sure their faces and identifying features aren't shown in any photos. Deepfakes are worth discussing, too.

▶ **Talk about how the media – including porn and advertising – works.** If teenagers know the commercial benefits of presenting information in a particular way and driving content towards more extreme material, they're more likely to understand that it doesn't represent the real world. Similarly, understanding the way advertising works may help your teenager to make choices that are less risky.

▶ **Check what your teenager's being taught at school when it comes to sex and relationships.** Be cautious, in particular, about 'sex-positive' material that might risk your teenager not being able to set appropriate boundaries within a relationship.

▶ **Consider asking a trusted friend or relative, whom your teenager also trusts, to act as an information source.** This can be useful for any questions your child doesn't feel comfortable asking you.

▶ **Look out for signs of drug use.** These can include dilated pupils, missing items and unfamiliar smells. And look out for danger signs of county lines or other involvement in drug supply. These might include the purchase of seemingly unaffordable clothes or jewellery, injuries they can't explain and disappearing for long periods.

- **Watch out for signs of alcohol poisoning in your teenager, and take action if you suspect it.** Signs of it include confusion, vomiting, skin that's pale or tinged blue, seizures or fits, slurring words or not being able to talk, a lack of coordination, soiling themselves and losing consciousness. Call emergency services, stay with your teenager to prevent them choking on vomit and keep them warm.
- **Support your child to take healthy risks.** Find plenty of opportunities for them to take such risks and experience positive events.
- **Articulate positive reasons to avoid risky behaviours – if possible, framing discussions around what your child might want for themselves.** Don't lecture or bribe. Make sure risk-taking is framed as a behaviour, not a character trait. Try framing conversations about risk around your child's friends – 'If you're at a party and someone takes a pill, this is what you need to know.' Help your child to develop strategies to stay safe in situations in which it might be hard, in the moment, to say no to something.
- **If your teenager plans to learn to drive, get in place some early rules and expectations.** These could include rules designed to minimise crash risks in the early months – such as not driving at night or with friends until they have some experience.
- **Let your teenager know that you'll always help them if they get into trouble.** Make it clear that they won't be sorry for doing so – you will provide their safety net.

# CHAPTER 8

# EQUIPPING A FUTURE ADULT

## Building a well-rounded person

Through the mellow lens of hindsight, there are things I'd have found it useful to have been told as a teenager – or more likely things I *was* told, to which paying a little attention would have been helpful. Flossing is more important than you think it is. Hyaluronic acid won't burn your face off, and it will stop you looking reptilian. The people who matter will still like you if you set clear boundaries – but you can't make everyone like you, and nor should you try. Fat is not the enemy. Archers and lemonade is horrible. It's OK to relax sometimes. Being strong is excellent.

It's worth bearing in mind that our education system rewards certain attributes that aren't necessarily the ones that will benefit your teenager in the long term. If your child is someone who functions well in the mornings, the system's likely to reward them – and if they aren't, they may suffer for it now in terms of grades, but could end up becoming someone who ends up writing code overnight. Sleep specialist Dr Chris Winter has commented, 'Are we actually artificially creating doubt in some kids' minds as to their academic readiness simply because we're making them take a class when they're not ready to take it? It's like evaluating runners by waking everybody up at three o'clock in the morning and having them run a 5K... It's one of the things that I think about a lot in terms of super-brilliant business people that I know who completely failed at academic work."[1]

This may be a conversation you want to have with your teenager. Another point to bear in mind when thinking about your child as a future adult is that it's easy to slip into a pattern of thinking about weaknesses rather than strengths. On the flip side of the coin, it may be easy, as adults, to forget what teenagers may not yet know or be able to do. I was taken aback one day to realise that my daughter didn't know what a pair of compasses was – I'd assumed this would be covered at school, although perhaps its weapons-grade sharpness now makes it inappropriate for classroom use. It can be easy to forget that we can learn from our children, too. A friend was reminded by his daughter, now in her late forties, that she still listens to the music he used to play loudly during her teenage years – the Kinks, Jimi Hendrix and Natalie Merchant – just as he still listens to the music she chose on long car journeys – Madonna, Morcheeba and Ocean Colour Scene. They taught each other to appreciate a wider range of music styles.

Lots of the skills required to thrive in adulthood will be learned at school. I think I learned more about cooking from experimenting at home with random ingredients, though, than I did from my stunningly unimaginative home economics teacher. I can only remember a few fragments of learning from her – they include the need to conform mercilessly to the recipe's instructions (untrue) and that liver must be eaten with oranges to maximise vitamin C (grim). It's also a little unfair, not to mention highly unrealistic, to expect schools to confer the full range of life skills in addition to maths, science, English, humanities, arts and sports – there's not enough time within the school day nor sufficient flexibility within the curriculum. Expecting teenagers to absorb these skills by osmosis from the school environment also leads to scenarios like the one created by my university friend Dan, who offered to make a few of us dinner a week or so into our first term. He asked for help when he couldn't work out why the dried spaghetti, which he was dry-frying in a saucepan, wasn't cooking.

A sense of responsibility is something that many adults are keen to see their teenagers acquire. This responsibility can be personal – with obvious benefits including those relating to education and work – or social, developing through relationships and communities. A study of responsibility development through the lens of organised youth programmes found that there are four main elements to it. Teenagers become more responsible when they choose to take on roles and duties, when they get challenged by these, when they're motivated to fulfil what they've taken on, and when they develop a belief that they'll be responsible in other circumstances.[2]

Responsibility can also be fostered by taking on obligations that increase in scale and challenge as teenagers move towards adulthood, the theory being that doing so improves skills and helps teenagers to see themselves as responsible.[3] When I was thirteen, my main non-school-related tasks were to do the lunchtime washing-up at weekends and holidays (my parents had a principled and wholly erroneous objection to getting a dishwasher – 'We don't need a dishwasher! We have a human who fulfils the same function!') and to clean the bathroom, badly and resentfully. I also had the occasional money-earning activity in the form of serving pints – no doubt entirely illegally – to literal drunken sailors at the occasional post-sailing race party that took place in an island barn.

By the time I was seventeen, my web of responsibility had extended into all sorts of other areas, including managing other staff in my waitressing job and giving post-orchestra lifts home to younger pupils. (I'm self-reflective enough to know, with age and hindsight, that my sense of responsibility gets in the way of being able to relax, so there may be more of a happy medium here.) Self-control is closely linked to responsibility and is also important to outcomes. One study in Germany tracked individuals between their teenage years and the age of thirty-five to see how teenage development of self-control was linked to longer-term outcomes. The researchers found that self-control levels increase between the ages of twelve and sixteen (so if your early adolescent isn't yet demonstrating any propensity for delayed gratification, don't despair).

They also found that self-control was linked to what happened later in people's love lives and work. Developing greater self-control over the teenage years was linked to better-quality relationships as adults, with more relationship satisfaction, less conflict and better communication skills. It also linked to feeling competent at work, being motivated at work, and being open to further training and development.[4] Another study found that teachers believe the difference between girls and boys in their academic achievement – girls do better, on average, than boys – is explained by higher motivation levels as well as higher self-control, but this wasn't borne out by the data. Instead, girls having higher levels of self-control than boys appeared to be the crucial factor.[5]

Parenting is an excellent predictor of the development of self-control, so following some of the ideas set out in Chapter 1 is likely to support its development in your teenager. The effects run both ways. If your teenager has self-control, you're likely to be a more effective parent. On the other hand, low teenage self-control can lead parents to be less warm and supportive, and to use more punishment. It seems that parenting and teenage self-control can spin into positive or negative cycles.[6] General Good Parenting can, unsurprisingly, support teenagers in other life skills and qualities, too. Those who have a good relationship with their parents, for example, are more likely to develop empathy and are less likely to behave antisocially.[7]

Social responsibility, according to one study, can be cultivated through modelling and expressing concern for other people. Your child is more likely to be socially responsible if they see you exhibiting similar behaviours. Opportunities to practise civic skills can also be useful – for example, getting into politics or fulfilling a role within a club or community.[8]

Critical thinking skills may be one of the most important areas in which parents can support their children. We've seen in earlier parts of the book how a degree of media literacy or deeper critical thinking can help to ward off the spectre of unquestioning absorption of online information. Even critical family discussions, though, may not be sufficient to help fully protect your child. One mum told me about her young adult son who reports 'news' items he's seen on TikTok and other platforms as fact, as do his friends. She prompts him regularly to think about who is feeding him the information and why, but it's not enough to keep his information filters functioning fully. A future society in which everyone swallows the algorithmically driven polarities they are fed is probably not going to be one that operates optimally. We need nuance and shades of grey between the black and white.

One theory is that there's an increasing lack of critical thinking skills among teenagers, and that normal developmental processes – which see the development of theoretical and abstract reasoning in early adolescence – have been interrupted, resulting in a generation of teenagers and young adults who are more likely to challenge the validity of perspectives that do not perfectly align with their own.[9] In the United States, for example, the proportion of high school students agreeing with the statement 'A person should be allowed to say what they want on social media without government censorship' fell from 66% in 2016 to 59% in 2022.[10] You might argue that there should be limits on social media – I certainly would, in confined areas such as incitement to violence – but it's an interesting signal that support for opposing positions might be waning.

Being able to think critically isn't exactly the same thing as being open-minded, but there's an overlap. Teenagers who can think critically are more likely to recognise that their own positions may be informed by bias or incomplete information, leaving them more open to the ideas of other people. Potential ways to encourage critical thinking at home are to debate ideas with your teenager, to challenge what you watch and read as a family (is that news report really capturing the nuance of a given conflict, or is it taking one side?), to ask for evidence to support opinions and to engage with a wide range of material. You might, for example, watch a film on cults to see how groupthink gets spread. It's also worth being overtly – or even aggressively – open to subtlety, challenge and other people's ideas yourself. 'That's an interesting perspective – I hadn't thought about that angle,' or 'I think people who think differently than me on this might argue…'. Listening is, perhaps, an underdeveloped teenage skill that's closely related to critical thinking. Those who are able to listen may be more likely to take on board other people's perspectives and to be able to consider issues in the round.

Chores are one way to develop certain knowledge and skills in your teenager. Your child's future life partner will be grateful if you see these through in the face of inevitable and overwhelming opposition. It can feel, in the moment, like an uphill struggle. As the authors of *Get Out of My Life…* point out, 'With most teenagers, parents do have to expend an enormous amount of energy in order to produce a small amount of teenage labour.'[11] But if you let your child remain idle, you risk spending your life picking up after them, they'll think it's acceptable to change their sheets once every eight weeks and – if they ever get married – they risk early divorce (personal opinion). Parents believe that chores contribute to teenagers' sense of autonomy, as well as to their personal development.[12] The process of fulfilling tasks and obligations also helps to cultivate a sense of responsibility.[13]

There is, however, a possible link with feelings of depression when there's a lot of conflict over chores.[14] And there's some evidence to suggest that it may be better for you to steer clear of joint chores – doing household tasks with parents has been linked to lower levels of well-being in teenagers.[15] I wonder if this might be due to the propensity of parents to pick up on the quality of their children's work. If my daughter is clearing plates while I'm wiping down surfaces, I'm likely to call her out if she leaves the sink full of food dregs, whereas if I'm not with her, I'll notice when it's too late to pick her up on it (which is really annoying for me, and much less annoying for her). If you have girls, it's worth checking if you're being fair over chore allocation – girls tend to be given more chores than boys, especially when their mums are working longer hours than usual.[16]

If you have friends or family members who get on well with your teenager, and who have something to offer them in the way of life experience and insight, they may provide a useful mentoring role. A study of more than 2,000 older teenagers and young adults found that relationships with mentors who weren't in their immediate families were linked to a number of positive outcomes relating to education, work and physical health. These mentoring relationships were particularly useful when teenagers and mentors felt close to each other.[17] I had an evening waitressing job between the ages of sixteen and eighteen, and saw my wonderful boss, Ann, as a mentor. She had a beautiful way of guiding behaviour with warmth, like the day I turned up to work in a sleeveless shirt – 'Darling, you've got lovely pits, but our guests don't need to see them.'

People outside the family may inadvertently drive teenage creativity or other attributes. When my girls were younger, we employed the teenage daughter of some acquaintances – I'll call her Lottie – as a babysitter. At the end of the first summer of Covid, we returned from a camping holiday in France to new rules that we had to self-isolate at home, and paid Lottie to walk our greyhound during our housebound fortnight. On the first day of her new duties, she returned him to us looking slightly green around the gills – she'd never before had to pick up dog shit and was, quite reasonably, horrified by the reality of it. The second day, she came prepared. She was dressed exquisitely, accessorised with a pair of elbow-length yellow Marigolds. On the third day, she sent her dad.

A short-term way of supporting your teenager's development of skills and knowledge is to get involved with your child's homework; parental involvement has been linked to higher levels of academic achievement.[18] The research doesn't suggest what to do when the level of understanding needed to support your child with their homework has long since floated away from your grasp. It's also very likely that the foundations laid for your child's school engagement have already started to harden, so your input – while it had its place back in the mists of your child's younger days – may no longer have much traction. Motivation to learn for the satisfaction of doing so ossifies as children get older.[19]

You may, more feasibly, be able to support your child with exam stress. I remember my mum baking me endless rounds of chocolate cake to persuade me to revise when I'd decided there was no point, as I was going to fail everything anyway. I made the temporary decision that the hard work of revision was worth it for the sugar reward. You can also be clear about the links between education and future success – doing so is linked to better grades and fewer so-called problem behaviours in teenagers.[20] Being relatively relaxed about video games may also be worth a shot, as those that involve strategy can support the development of problem-solving skills in teenagers. These skills have a positive knock-on impact on academic achievement.[21] The section on resilience and healthy stress in Chapter 5 is likely to be helpful here, too.

Extracurricular activities can, of course, help your teenager to build knowledge and skills – or at least to develop an understanding of their own limits. You may be familiar with The Duke of Edinburgh's Award scheme (DofE), through which teenagers learn a skill, volunteer, do a physical activity and go on an expedition. My daughter's expedition was character-building. They walked for two days through the South Downs in a heatwave. They got very lost, she fainted due to heat exhaustion and had to be revived by teachers, and they were chased by a herd of cows (or two herds, depending on the story's retelling). Her cousin's group, who did their DofE practice expedition earlier that year, ran out of dry footwear and forgot to bring food for the second day. My partner fell neck-high into a bog on Snowdon during his DofE Gold expedition and got hypothermia. (I'm sure there are some positive stories out there, and they are all stronger people for it – or possibly just more realistic ones who now avoid the Great Outdoors in favour of warm, cosy cities.)

Parental enthusiasm for extracurricular activities may also be contingent, of course. My mother's boyfriend, when he was of an age to have a teenager, spent winter weekends shivering as he watched his daughter running cross-country races. 'One day she very sheepishly asked whether it would be OK for her not to compete any more,' he told me. 'We hid our euphoria very well.' Involvement in extracurricular activities is affected by family circumstances and national policy – schools in the poorest areas are least likely to offer certain activities to their students, and within those schools that do, disadvantaged students are under-represented by a third. If your child attends a school with a low proportion of pupils eligible for free school meals – in other words, a school that's in a relatively wealthy catchment area – it's twice as likely as a school at the opposite end of the wealth spectrum to offer debating as an option.[22]

One study tried to predict adult voting and volunteering from teenagers' participation in extracurricular activities. It collected five waves of data over twelve years across every US state. The study's authors found that those who took part in these activities as teenagers were more likely both to vote and to volunteer as adults. The same study found adult voting and volunteering was also linked to taking part in community service as teenagers, even when this was mandatory – a fact that gets my dictatorial muscles flexing. This is probably because community service involvement shapes identity ('I am the kind of person who does community service, therefore I get involved in community-minded activity').[23]

My dad once persuaded me to do a touch-typing course, which has helped me enormously in my adult study and work. I borrowed his Mac the summer I was sixteen and used it to do 'Mavis Beacon Teaches Typing'. As I remember it, the typing was linked to being on a racetrack and the typing speed was linked to the car's speedometer, which played beautifully into my competitive nature. As well as being able to type quickly, it meant I developed the spectacularly pointless ability to type with my eyes closed (useful, perhaps, if I ever find myself with a typewriter in a power cut at nighttime).

I encouraged my own children to do some touch-typing when they were much younger, with limited success – they're speedy now, but without the elegant use of specific digits that I think Ms Beacon and her ilk would recommend.

Teenagers obviously get a level of careers guidance at school, but often rely on their families to learn about the world of work. This may be wildly unrealistic – my daughters see me dictating the terms of my engagement with research projects and what I choose to write, and have watched me disappear to conduct research in Thailand, Zanzibar and St Lucia. (My partner: 'It's an amazing coincidence just how many of your research destinations happen to be among the most beautiful places on earth.') I know just how lucky I am, but I'm not sure they do. They also haven't seen the years of less optimal working conditions that preceded it, without which there's no way I'd be able to do what I do now. They didn't see the fifty-five-hour weeks, the raging egos, the constructive criticism or the general graft. They weren't aware of the newspaper editor who offered to file my story so I could leave early, then passed off the resulting front page under his name – I never made a similar mistake again. So much of what's good now was forged in some fairly uncomfortable fires, alongside a healthy dose of good fortune. This is a hard message both to impart and to understand.

According to an interview-based study with young adults, parents and grandparents, there are three main ways families help their children to learn about work. One is through household chores and pocket money or an allowance. Another is through helping their children to find paid employment, and the final one is encouraging their children to be entrepreneurial – through, for example, mowing lawns, babysitting or selling cakes. During peak demand for the energy drink Prime, some Scottish teen entrepreneurs were selling it to their peers for £20 a pop, according to friends of mine.

Entrepreneurship seems equally, or possibly more, effective than the other areas in teaching work skills and developing teenagers' understanding of finances.[24] My teenage side-hustle was teaching an adult neighbour to play the oboe. I also took part in a sixth-form business scheme called Young Enterprise. We weren't allowed to keep any of the profit we made, but it was a great way of finding out how many parents were willing to buy teenage-produced tat. I suspect there are now dozens upon dozens of Essex attics filled with hubcap clocks and tie-dye dungarees. This will be a nice little puzzle for future archaeologists.

The research is mixed on the benefits of paid employment. Perceived upsides can include the fostering of independence, new skills and a work ethic, alongside having more money to pay for things. Risks include tiredness and a lack of time for schoolwork and other interests. Your own experience is likely to colour your views on this. I found myself nodding away to a line that read, 'Most parents like the idea of their children working, as they think that employment instills a whole array of positive traits,' catching myself uncomfortably at the follow-up: 'Parents believe that the jobs that they themselves held during adolescence helped them to acquire these very same attributes.'[25]

To underscore this point about untested theories and bias, I have an idea that crumbling levels of paid employment among teenagers have at least some link to the declining resilience levels and poor mental health we saw in Chapter 5. Paid employment for British sixteen- to seventeen-year-olds fell over twenty years from 48% to just 25%, according to a 2020 think tank analysis; while some of the fall is explained by increased participation in education and training, two thirds of it relates to fewer young people working while in full-time study.[26] There's some research that backs up the link between working as a teenager and longer-term resilience – including the inoculation effect of a little bit of hard graft (I can hear my grandparents' voices in my words here). For example, while stressful jobs can have negative effects in the short term, including depression and dented self-esteem, work stress seems to build resilience over the longer term and leave teenagers better able to handle similar situations in future.[27] They can also, anecdotally, build gratitude – I once did a summer job that involved factory work in thirty-five-degree heat, and I regularly think how glad I am that my experience was only a temporary one. It may be that our teenagers are paying for the short-term comfort of swerving the shifts in McDonald's with a more fragile future. I only have correlations and opinion to back this up, though, so don't take it too seriously.

In the shorter term, jobs that pay well and involve training can make teenagers feel competent.[28] They may benefit from jobs that have a mixed-age workforce – if they're surrounded by adults, as opposed to being surrounded mainly by other teenagers, they have the opportunity to learn more and to develop important mentoring relationships. A good job also means being able to balance work with other commitments, and to gain knowledge and skills. Good jobs can be those that pay well and that involve relatively few hours – lifeguards, coaches, tutors or those in offices, for example – set against those that involve long hours and low pay – shop assistants or those serving food.[29] Blue-collar jobs fall into the poor-quality jobs category, according to the researchers that have proposed this metric, though obviously this depends on the job. My nephew was employed during his A levels as a plumber's assistant, working the odd Saturday and taking home a decent wedge each time.

Quality tends to change with age and experience – a teenager working in a restaurant may need to start with the washing-up, gradually moving up to clearing tables and, later, taking orders and serving food. The same job in different places can also be of hugely different quality. I worked in one pub with gleaming surfaces and a lovely clientele, and another where my feet stuck to the floor and the punters would ask, leeringly, for the pub's speciality cocktail. 'Two of your Slippery Nipples, please, love.'

Work's likely to be better for teenagers when it's not too time-intensive, so it's worth encouraging your child to take on something that allows them enough time to do schoolwork and to enjoy sport, music, time with friends or whatever else it is that interests them.[30] The more thinly teenagers are spread in terms of their commitments outside school, the higher their sense of anxiety.[31] Finding a balance seems to be good for families, as well as for teenagers – one study of 725 teenagers found that family relationships were strongest when teenagers worked at low intensity, which was defined by working up to twenty hours per week. They were worst when they worked for twenty hours or more, with non-workers falling somewhere in the middle.[32]

There's a link between teenagers working and being involved in other activities, and having a sense of optimism.[33] Having hope for the future helps teenagers to thrive.[34] There are lots of reasons for today's generation of teenagers having a more muted view of future possibilities than their parents did – stories of climate catastrophe and AI-generated destruction dominate news cycles, house prices spiral ever further out of reach and human progress no longer seems inevitable. Hope becomes possible, though, when teenagers can think realistically about what they want from life, have the motivation to seek this out and know how to achieve it.[35]

You will be helping your teenager to be well equipped for the future if you can help them to see the possibilities and to be excited about them. If I was seeing my future in fragments from the vantage point of my eighteen-year-old self, I might glimpse spending dusk until dawn in a meadow with twenty friends, with a campfire, beer and someone strumming a guitar; swimming in the middle of a deserted lake, watching the colours of sunset blaze on one side while the full moon rises on the other; living in North London with friends, amidst Greek and Turkish shops selling buckets of olives and slabs of fresh halloumi; caterwauling karaoke at the top of my lungs in a Soho booth; arriving at my wedding by boat and nearly falling into the sea before joining the festivities; having my daughters pressed against my skin for the first time; and cycling along a pine-shaded beach in France, surrounded by my family.

There's so much to be positive about in reaching adulthood, even if the world around us isn't quite where we might wish it to be for our teenagers. With some luck, their future will hold love affairs, deep friendships and riveting passing acquaintances, new experiences, fun jobs and employment so awful that it provides a lifetime of anecdotes. One day, they might see their football team win the league, or eat some astonishing food they remember forever, or form unbreakable bonds with fascinating, deeply kind humans. There's plenty to feel excited about. They just might need a little help to see it.

## Permission to fail

The consequences of mistakes ratchet up in the teenage years. Poor exam results, taking a tablet laced with an unknown substance, unplanned pregnancy or nicotine addiction have long-term effects. Parents have to walk a tightrope, balancing the twin weights of our teenagers' growing independence and the knowledge of where thoughtless decisions can lead. As my teenagers get older, I can advise them and provide safe harbour when things go wrong. I am progressively less able to control the situations that might get them into trouble, though – and it's increasingly less appropriate for me to do so.

Mistakes of minor consequence contain lessons. My thespian credentials leave much to be desired, so taking GCSE Drama was a slightly absurd decision. Discovering this and switching to German after half a term taught me that it was possible to rectify mistakes and that working hard helped me catch up, despite bafflement in the face of what I felt to be unnecessary linguistic complexity. Taking diazepam on a friend's recommendation to help me sleep through an overnight bus journey taught me that my body doesn't respond well to tranquillisers and kept me safely away from hard drugs. Leaving my well-stocked-but-later-empty purse in my bag during an end-of-term assembly taught me to keep things of value on my person. There's value in piecemeal trial and error – in not having a parent shadowing every decision and unwittingly heading off an opportunity to learn.

Teenagers will make mistakes, just as we did and do. And when they err, they need our steady presence to help them to pick up any necessary pieces, and our permission that they can falter and fail again next time. They need to see us making our own mistakes and learning from them. And they need to understand that human perfection only exists in imperfection. Through this, they will come to understand that curiosity and connection – like the gold lacquer used in the Japanese art of kintsugi – will transform these errors and rough edges into an adult who is perfectly, deeply human.

# CHAPTER SUMMARY

## Building a well-rounded person

- **Narrow rewards of education.** Future success comes in different forms — some teenagers may be less suited to an education system that rewards being able to function well in the mornings, but there's an increasing choice of careers that allow flexible and evening working.
- **Rightful limits of school.** There's not enough room within the curriculum to cover the development of all the skills and traits that teenagers will need to thrive. Some of these must come from home.
- **Useful traits and skills.** A sense of responsibility (fostered by taking on obligations that gradually increase in scale and challenge) can have positive benefits for both education and work. Self-control in adolescence predicts better-quality romantic relationships in adulthood, as well as work competence and motivation. Empathy is also a handy trait. Critical thinking skills are vitally important, but there are concerns that teenagers are increasingly moving towards a one-dimensional view of the world in which other positions are written off as invalid. Listening skills are related, and perhaps underdeveloped in many teenagers.
- **Chores.** Doing household tasks, while often detested by teenagers, helps to contribute to their personal development and a sense of autonomy and responsibility. It also helps them to learn about the world of work.
- **Extracurricular activities.** These help to build knowledge and skills. They can even go some way to predicting whether your child votes or volunteers in adulthood.
- **Paid work.** There's mixed evidence on outcomes linked to paid work — but, on balance, it seems to be good for teenagers when

it's not too onerous in terms of hours or intensity. High-paid jobs that offer training can be good – though low-quality jobs may offer longer-term resilience (while being tough in the short term).

## Permission to fail

- **The importance of failure.** Teenagers will need a steer to avoid the big mistakes that could change their lives – but parents can't fully protect them from these. There's also value in making less consequential mistakes in terms of what they teach our teenagers, and value in having the freedom to do so. There is a point at which parents need to step back.

## Ideas for parents

- **Focus on your child's strengths.** This can be more useful than thinking about their weaknesses.
- **Build skills at home that may not be covered – or at least not sufficiently – at school.** You can encourage critical thinking skills by debating ideas with your child, questioning and challenging information that comes through TV or books, asking for evidence to support opinions, and engaging with a wide range of material. Be open yourself to nuance, challenge and other people's ideas.
- **Keep a semi-watchful eye on your child's homework.** You may not be able to get as involved as you once were, but parental involvement with homework in the teenage years is linked to better academic outcomes. You can also be clear about links between education and future success, and support your child with exam-related stress.
- **Get your teenager to do chores.** This is important in the face of their opposition and the disproportionate amount of energy it may take to get them to see these through. If you can do this while

minimising conflict (perhaps by stating your expectation and then leaving the room to minimise the potential for arguments), it's likely to be better for your child's well-being. Don't try to tackle chores together. Ensure that chore allocations are fairly divided, and that female members of the household aren't being given more to do than male ones, as is common.

- **Prompt your child to take part in available extracurricular activities.** Those focused on community service can be particularly useful for teenagers' development.
- **Steer your teenager towards a mentor.** Hopefully, a mentoring relationship with someone outside the immediate family – a friend of yours, perhaps, or a favoured uncle – will develop organically, but you could try some gentle facilitation. These kinds of connections are linked to positive teenage outcomes, especially when teenagers and mentors have a close relationship.
- **Encourage your child to find good part-time work, if you can.** This means work that doesn't take so much of their time that it distracts them from schoolwork or makes them overly tired. Jobs that offer training and that have a mixed-age workforce (offering them the ability to learn from people with experience) can be particularly valuable. You might also want to steer your child in the direction of more entrepreneurial activity, like babysitting or lawn-mowing.
- **With these things in mind, advise your child not to spread themselves too thinly.** Having too many paid, unpaid and study commitments can make teenagers feel anxious.
- **Foster a sense of optimism about the future.** There's much to look forward to in adulthood. Hope for the future is good for our teenagers – and we can help to paint a picture of the many exciting experiences and opportunities that will, with luck, come their way.
- **Give your child your permission to fail.** Teenagers need to experience the consequences of their decisions, while knowing we will be there to hold them through any distressing reverberations.

They need to understand that they can survive – and even thrive – after having made a judgement call they later regret. Doing so will help them avoid similar errors in future, but will also help them to understand that the world doesn't end when we get things wrong. Understanding the fallibility of the human condition will brilliantly equip them to live a life that's inevitably and beautifully imperfect.

**For a free PDF with a Q&A on teenage mental health, and for regular reviews of the latest research on teenage mental health and well-being, please sign up at**

**matildagosling.com/teenagers**

# ACKNOWLEDGEMENTS

Thank you to the past, present and future teenagers for changing the way I see the world through their eyes and, of course, for giving me an important subject to research. My own two wise, funny, formidable girls, Lola and Ivy, are at the heart of this group. The others include (but are definitely not limited to) Albert, Alice B., Alice W., Amoli, Arla, Arthur, Barney, Cam, Charlie, Connie, Daisy, Elsa, Farah, Hal, Hamish, Ihor, Isla, Laura, Leo, Lily, Max, Nina, Nora, Oscar, Rory, Rosa, Sasha, Sophia, Tomas, Vera and Zac.

Mark Richards and Diana Broccardo have built a fearless, original publishing house in Swift Press. It's an honour to be published by them. I'm grateful to the Tetragon team for production, Ian Howe for copy-editing, Rachel Nobilo for publicity and, of course, to my agent, Rufus Purdy.

My thanks go, too, to Dr Natalie Cheatle, a clinical psychologist and parenting expert, for her feedback and wise notes on the manuscript. Thank you to Jules Mercy and Chris Hollis for giving me a warm, human lens through which to view the psychological research.

Thank you to Maya Forstater, Helen Joyce and their brave, brilliant colleagues at Sex Matters for publishing the linked papers on teenagers and gender identity. These would have been far too long for this book and were written at a time, before the Cass Review was published, when there was little available for parents who wanted to understand the evidence base in this area.

My friends Natalie Orringe and Rakhee Rajani have patiently and perceptively talked me through publicity ideas. I'm lucky to have a wealth of other friends who have provided support, too, including Adam Conduct, Ben Stevens, Camille Gatin, Dora Napolitano, Gemma Dunn, Geoff Braterman, Gregor MacLennan, Janet Graham, Jo Blackman, John Willan, Jung-ui Sul, Kate McSweeney, Maryna Tkachenko, Mel Dowding, Rachel Cashman, Rowan Diamond, Simon Fanshawe, Simon Gallagher and Suvra Jans.

I'm particularly grateful to Sara Fakhro, one of the best humans I know, for both her incredible friendship and her detailed vocabulary feedback.

Thank you to my mum and much-missed dad for seeing me through my teenage years with the necessary humour and fortitude, and for being so pragmatic about the more reckless of my early adult intentions ('Darling, can we talk things through over a glass of wine before you make a decision?'). Sorry for the grumpier periods. Thanks, too, to my inspirational half-sisters, Amanda Gosling and Catherine Gosling Fuller; their partners, Andy Wroe and Ben Gosling Fuller; my mum's partner, Peter Goonery; and my parents-in-law, Mary and John Daly.

Last and most, thank you to Pete Daly for being my partner in life and parenting, and for his love, levity and wisdom.

# ENDNOTES

## A recap and an introduction to teenagers

1 E.g. Moroń, M. et al. (2023). Parental and pandemic burnout, internalizing symptoms, and parent-adolescent relationships: a network analysis. *Journal of Psychopathology and Behavioral Assessment* 45(2), 428–443.

2 Ran, G. et al. (2021). The association between interparental conflict and youth anxiety: a three-level meta-analysis. *Journal of Youth and Adolescence* 50, 599–612.

3 Roddy, M. K. et al. (2020). Meta-analysis of couple therapy: effects across outcomes, designs, timeframes, and other moderators. *Journal of Consulting and Clinical Psychology* 88(7), 583.

4 https://www.youtube.com/@TheGottmanInstitute

5 Markman, H. J. et al. (2022). Helping couples achieve relationship success: a decade of progress in couple relationship education research and practice, 2010–2019. *Journal of Marital and Family Therapy* 48(1), 251–282.

6 Research shows that emotional dysregulation in parents is linked to emotional dysregulation in adolescents, and these are linked to emotional and behavioural problems: Buckholdt, K. E., Parra, G. R. and Jobe-Shields, L. (2014). Intergenerational transmission of emotion dysregulation through parental invalidation of emotions: implications for adolescent internalizing and externalizing behaviors. *Journal of Child and Family Studies* 23, 324–332.

7 Gottman, J. M. et al. (1997), cited in Klimes-Dougan, B. et al. (2007). Parental emotion socialization in adolescence: differences in sex, age and problem status. *Social Development*, 16(2), 326–342.

**8** Matias, M. and Recharte, J. (2021). Links between work–family conflict, enrichment, and adolescent well-being: parents' and children's perspectives. *Family Relations* 70(3), 840–858.

**9** Kelly, A. B. et al. (2016). Depressed mood during early to middle adolescence: a bi-national longitudinal study of the unique impact of family conflict. *Journal of Youth and Adolescence* 45, 1604–1613.

**10** Tucker, C. J. et al. (2018). Household chaos, hostile parenting, and adolescents' well-being two years later. *Journal of Child and Family Studies* 27, 3701–3708.

**11** Larsen, S. A. et al. (2022). Measuring CHAOS? Evaluating the short-form Confusion, Hubbub and Order Scale. *Journal of Applied Developmental Psychology* 16(3), 429–444.

**12** Human, L. J. et al. (2016). Congruence and incongruence in adolescents' and parents' perceptions of the family: using response surface analysis to examine links with adolescents' psychological adjustment. *Journal of Youth and Adolescence* 45, 2022–2035.

**13** Hoskins, D. H. (2014). Consequences of parenting on adolescent outcomes. *Societies* 4(3), 506–531.

**14** Pinquart, M. (2017). Associations of parenting dimensions and styles with internalizing symptoms in children and adolescents: a meta-analysis. *Marriage & Family Review* 53(7), 613–640.

**15** Soenens, B. and Vansteenkiste, M. (2010). A theoretical upgrade of the concept of parental psychological control: proposing new insights on the basis of self-determination theory. *Developmental Review* 30(1), 74–99.

**16** Pinquart (2017).

**17** Kivisto, K. L. et al. (2015). Family enmeshment, adolescent emotional dysregulation, and the moderating role of gender. *Journal of Family Psychology* 29(4), 604.

**18** Adapted from Collins, W. A. and Steinberg, L. (2008). Adolescent development in interpersonal context. In W. Damon and R. M. Lerner (eds), *Child and Adolescent Development: An Advanced Course*. John Wiley & Sons, pp. 551–590.

**19** Bornstein, M. H. and Putnick, D. L. (2018). Parent–adolescent relationships in global perspective. In J. E. Lansford and P. Banati (eds),

*Handbook of Adolescent Development Research and its Impact on Global Policy.* Oxford University Press, pp. 107–129

20  Kobak, R. et al. (2017). Adapting to the changing needs of adolescents: parenting practices and challenges to sensitive attunement. *Current Opinion in Psychology* 15, 137–142.

21  Izzo, F., Baiocco, R. and Pistella, J. (2022). Children's and adolescents' happiness and family functioning: a systematic literature review. *International Journal of Environmental Research and Public Health* 19(24), 16593.

22  Hancock Hoskins, D. (2014). Consequences of parenting on adolescent outcomes. *Societies* 4(3), 506–531.

23  Izzo, Baiocco and Pistella (2022).

24  Babskie, E., Powell, D. N. and Metzger, A. (2017). Variability in parenting self-efficacy across prudential adolescent behaviors. *Parenting* 17(4), 242–261.

25  Hou, Y., et al. (2019). Discordance in parents' and adolescents' reports of parenting: a meta-analysis and qualitative review. *American Psychologist* 75(3), 329.

26  Buchanan, C. M. et al. (2023). Adolescent storm and stress: a 21st century evaluation. *Frontiers in Psychology* 14, 1257641.

27  Collins and Steinberg (2008).

28  Casey, B. J. et al. (2019). Development of the emotional brain. *Neuroscience Letters* 693, 29–34.

29  Elkins, R. K. et al. (2017). The stability of personality traits in adolescence and young adulthood. *Journal of Economic Psychology* 60, 37–52.

30  Buchanan, C. M. et al. (2023). Typicality and trajectories of problematic and positive behaviors over adolescence in eight countries. *Frontiers in Psychology* 13, 991727.

31  Jacobs, J. E., Chhin, C. S. and Shaver, K. (2005). Longitudinal links between perceptions of adolescence and the social beliefs of adolescents: are parents' stereotypes related to beliefs held about and by their children? *Journal of Youth and Adolescence* 34, 61–72.

32  Buchanan et al. (2023).

33  Hall, G. S. (1904). *Adolescence: Its Psychology and Its Relations to*

*Physiology, Anthropology, Sociology, Sex, Crime, Religion and Education.* Read Books Ltd.

**34** Crone, E. A. and Dahl, R. E. (2012). Understanding adolescence as a period of social–affective engagement and goal flexibility. *Nature Reviews Neuroscience* 13(9), 636–650.

**35** Giedd, J. (2016). The amazing teen brain. *Scientific American*, 1 May. Available at: https://www.scientificamerican.com/article/the-amazing-teen-brain/ (accessed 15 October 2023).

**36** Blakemore, S. J. and Choudhury, S. (2006). Development of the adolescent brain: implications for executive function and social cognition. *Journal of Child Psychology and Psychiatry* 47(3–4), 296–312.

**37** Crone and Dahl (2012).

**38** Siegel, D. J. (2014). *Brainstorm: The Power and Purpose of the Teenage Brain* [Kindle edn]. Scribe.

**39** E.g. Sawyer, S. M. et al. (2018). The age of adolescence. *The Lancet Child & Adolescent Health* 2(3), 223–228.

**40** Tervo-Clemmens, B. et al. (2023). A canonical trajectory of executive function maturation from adolescence to adulthood. *Nature Communications* 14, 6922.

**41** Kobak et al. (2017).

**42** Hadiwijaya, H. et al. (2017). On the development of harmony, turbulence, and independence in parent–adolescent relationships: a five-wave longitudinal study. *Journal of Youth and Adolescence* 46, 1772–1788.

**43** Klimstra, T. A. et al. (2009). Maturation of personality in adolescence. *Journal of Personality and Social Psychology* 96(4), 898.

**44** Siegel (2014).

**45** Wolf, T. and Franks, S. (2020). *Get Out of My Life: But First Take Me and Alex into Town* [Kindle edn]. Profile Books, 4th Edition.

**46** Lee, K. H. et al. (2015). Neural responses to maternal criticism in healthy youth. *Social Cognitive and Affective Neuroscience* 10(7), 902–912.

**47** Feelings shifting: Guyer, A. E., Silk, J. S. and Nelson, E. E. (2016). The neurobiology of the emotional adolescent: from the inside out. *Neuroscience & Biobehavioral Reviews* 70, 74–85.

**48** Wolf and Franks (2020).

**49** Perry, P. (2019). *The Book You Wish Your Parents Had Read (and Your Children Will Be Glad That You Did)*. Penguin UK.

**50** Sillars, A., Koerner, A. and Fitzpatrick, M. A. (2005). Communication and understanding in parent–adolescent relationships. *Human Communication Research* 31(1), 102–128.

**51** Transmission of emotions: Mancini, K. J., Luebbe, A. M. and Bell, D. J. (2016). Valence-specific emotion transmission: potential influences on parent–adolescent emotion coregulation. *Emotion* 16(5), 567.

**52** Vandenkerckhove, B. et al. (2021). Daily ups and downs in adolescents' depressive symptoms: the role of daily self-criticism, dependency and basic psychological needs. *Journal of Adolescence* 91, 97–109.

**53** Milkie, M. A., Wray, D. and Boeckmann, I. (2021). Creating versus negating togetherness: perceptual and emotional differences in parent-teenager reported time. *Journal of Marriage and Family* 83(4), 1154–1175.

**54** Guyer, Silk and Nelson (2016).

**55** Human et al. (2016).

**56** Murty, V. P., Calabro, F. and Luna, B. (2016). The role of experience in adolescent cognitive development: integration of executive, memory, and mesolimbic systems. *Neuroscience & Biobehavioral Reviews* 70, 46–58.

**57** Schwarz, B. et al. (2012). Does the importance of parent and peer relationships for adolescents' life satisfaction vary across cultures? *The Journal of Early Adolescence* 32(1), 55–80.

**58** Noller, P. and Callan, V. (2015). *The Adolescent in the Family*. Routledge.

**59** Freud, A. (1961). *The Ego and the Mechanisms of Defence*. The Hogarth Press.

**60** Keep Laughing Comedy TV. Kevin & Perry – *Harry Enfield & Chums* [video]. YouTube. https://www.youtube.com/watch?v=Q50w5BriSNE.

**61** Sznitman, G. A., Zimmermann, G. and Van Petegem, S. (2019). Further insight into adolescent personal identity statuses: differences based on self-esteem, family climate, and family communication. *Journal of Adolescence* 71, 99–109.

**62** Berzonsky, M. D. (1990), cited in Luyckx, K. et al. (2016). Intergenerational associations linking identity styles and processes in adolescents and their parents. *European Journal of Developmental Psychology* 13(1), 67–83.

**63** Berzonsky, M. D., Branje, S. J. and Meeus, W. (2007). Identity-processing style, psychosocial resources, and adolescents' perceptions of parent-adolescent relations. *The Journal of Early Adolescence* 27(3), 324–345.

**64** Laursen, B. and Hartl, A. C. (2013). Understanding loneliness during adolescence: developmental changes that increase the risk of perceived social isolation. *Journal of Adolescence* 36(6), 1261–1268.

**65** Morita, H., Griffioen, N. and Granic, I. (2022). Digital media and the dual aspect of adolescent identity development: the effects of digital media use on adolescents' commitments and self-stories. In J. Nesi, E. H. Telzer and M. J. Prinstein (eds), *Handbook of Adolescent Digital Media Use and Mental Health*. Cambridge University Press, pp. 63–84.

**66** Luyckx, K. et al. (2016). Intergenerational associations linking identity styles and processes in adolescents and their parents. *European Journal of Developmental Psychology* 13(1), 67–83.

**67** Arnold, M. E. (2017). Supporting adolescent exploration and commitment: identity formation, thriving, and positive youth development. *Journal of Youth Development* 12(4), 1–15.

**68** Branje, S. (2022). Adolescent identity development in context. *Current Opinion in Psychology* 45, 101286.

**69** Nurmi, J. E. (2004), cited in Collins and Steinberg (2008).

**70** Kroger, J., Martinussen, M. and Marcia, J. E. (2010). Identity status change during adolescence and young adulthood: a meta-analysis. *Journal of Adolescence* 33(5), 683–698.

**71** Defoe, I. N., Rap, S. E. and Romer, D. (2022). Adolescents' own views on their risk behaviors, and the potential effects of being labeled as risk-takers: a commentary and review. *Frontiers in Psychology* 13, 945775.

## Your relationship with each other

**1** Harris-McKoy, D. (2016). Adolescent delinquency: is too much or too little parental control a problem? *Journal of Child and Family Studies* 25, 2079–2088.

**2** Ebbert, A. M., Infurna, F. J. and Luthar, S. S. (2019). Mapping developmental changes in perceived parent–adolescent relationship quality throughout middle school and high school. *Development and Psychopathology* 31(4), 1541–1556.

**3** Hadiwijaya, H. et al. (2017). On the development of harmony, turbulence, and independence in parent–adolescent relationships: A five-wave longitudinal study. *Journal of Youth and Adolescence* 46, 1772–1788.

**4** Hostinar, C. E., Johnson, A. E. and Gunnar, M. R. (2015). Parent support is less effective in buffering cortisol stress reactivity for adolescents compared to children. *Developmental Science* 18(2), 281–297.

**5** Ebbert, Infurna and Luthar (2019).

**6** Jorgensen-Wells, M. A. et al. (2023). Best friends forever and family ties: continuity and change in closeness with parents and friends among Australian adolescents. *Journal of Family Studies* 29(5), 2046–2067.

**7** Moore, K. A. et al. (2004). Parent-teen relationships and interactions: far more positive than not. *Child Trends* 25(1), 1–8.

**8** Hadiwijaya et al. (2017).

**9** Collins, W. A. et al. (2000), cited in Branje, S., Laursen, B. and Collins, W. A. (2012). Parent–child communication during adolescence. In A. L. Vangelisti (ed.), *The Routledge Handbook of Family Communication*. Routledge, 2nd Edition, pp. 283–298.

**10** E.g. Kågesten, A. et al. (2016). Understanding factors that shape gender attitudes in early adolescence globally: a mixed-methods systematic review. *PLOS One* 11(6), e0157805.

**11** Collins, W. A. and Steinberg, L. (2008). Adolescent development in interpersonal context. In W. Damon and R. M. Lerner (eds), *Child and Adolescent Development: An Advanced Course*. John Wiley & Sons, pp. 551–590.

**12** Siegel, D. J. (2014). *Brainstorm: The Power and Purpose of the Teenage Brain* [Kindle edn]. Scribe.

**13** Kapetanovic, S. and Skoog, T. (2021). The role of the family's emotional climate in the links between parent-adolescent communication and adolescent psychosocial functioning. *Research on Child and Adolescent Psychopathology* 49, 141–154.

**14** Sorkhabi, N. and Middaugh, E. (2014). How variations in parents' use of confrontive and coercive control relate to variations in parent–adolescent conflict, adolescent disclosure, and parental knowledge: adolescents' perspective. *Journal of Child and Family Studies* 23, 1227–1241.

**15** Perry, P. (2019). *The Book You Wish Your Parents Had Read (and Your Children Will Be Glad That You Did)*. Penguin UK, p. 230.

**16** Laursen, B., DeLay, D. and Adams, R. E. (2010). Trajectories of perceived support in mother–adolescent relationships: the poor (quality) get poorer. *Developmental Psychology* 46(6), 1792.

**17** Main, A., Paxton, A. and Dale, R. (2016). An exploratory analysis of emotion dynamics between mothers and adolescents during conflict discussions. *Emotion* 16(6), 913–928.

**18** Juang, L. P. and Syed, M. (2014). Sharing stories of discrimination with parents. *Journal of Adolescence* 37(3), 303–312.

**19** Damour, L. (2023). *The Emotional Lives of Teenagers* [Kindle edn]. Allen & Unwin.

**20** Wolf, T. and Franks, S. (2020). *Get Out of My Life: But First Take Me and Alex into Town* [Kindle edn]. Profile Books, 4th Edition.

**21** Richardson, R. A. (2004). Early adolescence talking points: questions that middle school students want to ask their parents. *Family Relations* 53(1), 87–94.

**22** Silva, K. et al. (2021). Stereotyped beliefs about adolescents and parent and teen well-being: the role of parent-teen communication. [Abstract.] *The Journal of Early Adolescence* 41(6), 886–904.

**23** Siegel (2014).

**24** Damour (2023).

**25** Crocetti, E. et al. (2016). The dynamic interplay among maternal empathy, quality of mother-adolescent relationship, and adolescent antisocial behaviors: new insights from a six-wave longitudinal multi-informant study. *PLOS One* 11(3), e0150009.

**26** Manczak, E. M., DeLongis, A. and Chen, E. (2016). Does empathy have a cost? Diverging psychological and physiological effects within families. *Health Psychology* 35(3), 211.

**27** Hanson, R. on Earle, A. (Host) (2023, 12 March.) Ep 232: Solving Conflict and Building Connection [Audio podcast episode]. In *Talking to Teens: Expert Tips for Parents of Teenagers*. https://podcasts.apple.

com/gb/podcast/talking-to-teens-expert-tips-for-parenting-teenagers/id1330031134?i=1000603808292.

28 Bornstein, M. H. and Putnick, D. L. (2018). Parent-adolescent relationships in global perspective. In J. E. Lansford and P. Banati (eds), *Handbook of Adolescent Development Research and its Impact on Global Policy*. Oxford University Press, pp. 107–129.

29 Ehrenreich, S. E. et al. (2020). How adolescents use text messaging through their high school years. *Journal of Research on Adolescence* 30(2), 521–540.

30 Coyne, S. M. et al. (2014). 'Media Time = Family Time': Positive media use in families with adolescents. *Journal of Adolescent Research* 29(5), 663–688.

31 Elgar, F. J., Craig, W. and Trites, S. J. (2013). Family dinners, communication, and mental health in Canadian adolescents. *Journal of Adolescent Health* 52(4), 433–438.

32 Holmes, E. K. et al. (2013). Mother knows best? Inhibitory maternal gatekeeping, psychological control, and the mother–adolescent relationship. *Journal of Adolescence* 36(1), 91–101.

33 Niehaus, C. E. et al. (2019). Maternal emotional and physiological reactivity: implications for parenting and the parenting–adolescent relationship. *Journal of Child and Family Studies* 28, 872–883.

34 E.g. Beyers, W. and Goossens, L. (1999), cited in Soenens, B., Vansteenkiste, M. and Beyers, W. (2019). Parenting adolescents. In M. H. Bornstein (ed.), *Handbook of Parenting: Vol. 1: Children and Parenting*. Routledge, pp. 101–167.

35 Branje, S., Laursen, B. and Collins, W. A. (2012). Parent–child communication during adolescence. In A. L. Vangelisti (ed.), *The Routledge Handbook of Family Communication*. Routledge, pp. 283–298.

36 Branje, S. (2018). Development of parent–adolescent relationships: conflict interactions as a mechanism of change. *Child Development Perspectives* 12(3), 171–176.

37 Holmbeck, G. N. (2016). A model of family relational transformations during the transition to adolescence: parent-adolescent conflict and adaptation. In J. A. Graber, J. Brooks-Gunn and A. C. Petersen (eds),

*Transitions Through Adolescence: Interpersonal Domains and Context.* Psychology Press, pp. 167–200.

**38** Laursen, B., Coy, K. C. and Collins, W. A. (1998). Reconsidering changes in parent-child conflict across adolescence: a meta-analysis. *Child Development* 69(3), 817–832.

**39** Collins, W. A. and Steinberg, L. (2007). Adolescent development in interpersonal context. In N. Eisenberg (vol. ed.), W. Damon and R. Lerner (eds), *Handbook of Child Psychology. Volume III: Social, Emotional, and Personality Development.* Wiley, pp. 1003–1067.

**40** Buist, K. L. et al. (2002), cited in Jaramillo-Sierra, A. L., Kaestle, C. E. and Allen, K. R. (2016). Daughters' anger towards mothers and fathers in emerging adulthood. *Sex Roles* 75, 28–42.

**41** Shanahan, L. et al. (2007), cited in Soenens, Vansteenkiste and Beyers (2019).

**42** Hadiwijaya et al. (2017).

**43** Privacy invasions: Hawk, S. T. et al. (2009). Mind your own business! Longitudinal relations between perceived privacy invasion and adolescent-parent conflict. *Journal of Family Psychology* 23(4), 511. Intrusiveness: Weymouth, B. B. and Buehler, C. (2016). Adolescent and parental contributions to parent–adolescent hostility across early adolescence. *Journal of Youth and Adolescence* 45, 713–729.

**44** E.g. Missotten, L. C. et al. (2018). Adolescents' conflict management styles with mothers: longitudinal associations with parenting and reactance. *Journal of Youth and Adolescence* 47, 260–274.

**45** Sorkhabi and Middaugh (2014).

**46** Soenens, Vansteenkiste and Beyers (2019).

**47** Huey, M. et al. (2017). Mother–adolescent conflict types and adolescent adjustment: a person-oriented analysis. *Journal of Family Psychology* 31(4), 504.

**48** Alaie, I. et al. (2020). Parent–youth conflict as a predictor of depression in adulthood: a 15-year follow-up of a community-based cohort. *European Child & Adolescent Psychiatry* 29, 527–536.

**49** Eisenberg, N. et al. (2008). Understanding mother-adolescent conflict discussions: concurrent and across-time prediction from youths' dispositions and parenting. *Monographs of the Society for Research in Child Development* 73(2), vii–viii.

50  Laursen, B. et al. (2016). Youth negative affect attenuates associations between compromise and mother–adolescent conflict outcomes. *Journal of Child and Family Studies* 25, 1110–1118.

51  Van Lissa, C. J. et al. (2017). The cost of empathy: parent–adolescent conflict predicts emotion dysregulation for highly empathic youth. *Developmental Psychology* 53(9), 1722.

52  Missotten, L. C. et al. (2016). Adolescents' conflict resolution styles toward mothers: the role of parenting and personality. *Journal of Child and Family Studies* 25, 2480–2497.

53  Silva, K., Ford, C. A. and Miller, V. A. (2020). Daily parent–teen conflict and parent and adolescent well-being: the moderating role of daily and person-level warmth. *Journal of Youth and Adolescence* 49, 1601–1616.

54  Laursen et al. (2016).

55  LoBraico, E. J. et al. (2020). Exploring processes in day-to-day parent–adolescent conflict and angry mood: evidence for circular causality. *Family Process* 59(4), 1706–1721.

56  Steinberg, L. (2001). We know some things: parent–adolescent relationships in retrospect and prospect. *Journal of Research on Adolescence* 11(1), 1–19.

57  Laursen et al. (2016).

58  Donohue, E. et al. (2022). Parent–child recurring conflict: a mediator between parental anger management and adolescent behavior. *Family and Consumer Sciences Research Journal* 51(1), 6–19. For examples of anger management strategies, see American Psychological Association (2022). Control anger before it controls you, 3 March. Available at: https://www.apa.org/topics/anger/control (accessed 22 November 2023).

59  Wolf and Franks (2020).

60  Asli, S. and Richards, R. (Hosts) (2023, 10 May.) 41: Conflict resolution skills can deepen your relationship with your teen; here's how [Audio podcast episode]. In *Teenagers Untangled*. https://podcasts.apple.com/gb/podcast/teenagers-untangled-parenting-teenagers-in-an-audio-hug/id1601611493?i=1000612433404.

61 Personal correspondence, with permission to share, from Simon Fanshawe OBE, 22 November 2023.

62 Moed, A. et al. (2015). Parent–adolescent conflict as sequences of reciprocal negative emotion: links with conflict resolution and adolescents' behavior problems. *Journal of Youth and Adolescence* 44, 1607–1622.

63 Missotten, L. C. et al. (2017). Examining the longitudinal relations among adolescents' conflict management with parents and conflict frequency. *Personality and Individual Differences* 117, 37–41.

64 Marceau, K. et al. (2015). Adolescents', mothers', and fathers' gendered coping strategies during conflict: youth and parent influences on conflict resolution and psychopathology. *Development and Psychopathology*, 27(4pt1), 1025–1044.

65 Laursen et al. (2016).

66 Branje, S. J. et al. (2009). Parent–adolescent conflicts, conflict resolution types, and adolescent adjustment. *Journal of Applied Developmental Psychology* 30(2), 195–204.

67 Meter, D. J. et al. (2019). Relations between parent psychological control and parent and adolescent social aggression. *Journal of Child and Family Studies* 28, 140–151.

68 LoBraico et al. (2020).

69 Ferrar, S. J. et al. (2022). Conflict resolution and emotional expression in sibling and mother-adolescent dyads: within-family and across-context similarities. *The Journal of Early Adolescence* 42(2), 227–261.

70 Moed et al. (2015).

71 Wolf and Franks (2020).

72 Moed et al. (2015).

73 Hanson on Earle (Host) (2023).

74 Soenens, Vansteenkiste and Beyers (2019).

75 Powdthavee, N. and Vignoles, A. (2008). Mental health of parents and life satisfaction of children: a within-family analysis of intergenerational transmission of well-being. *Social Indicators Research* 88, 397–422.

76 Soenens, Vansteenkiste and Beyers (2019).

77 Manczak, DeLongis and Chen (2016).

78 Zimmermann, G. et al. (2022). Parents' storm and stress beliefs about

adolescence: relations with parental overprotection and parental burnout. *Swiss Psychology Open* 2(1).

## Other connections

1 Orben, A., Tomova, L. and Blakemore, S. J. (2020). The effects of social deprivation on adolescent development and mental health. *The Lancet Child & Adolescent Health* 4(8), 634–640.

2 Loades, M. E. et al. (2020). Rapid systematic review: the impact of social isolation and loneliness on the mental health of children and adolescents in the context of COVID-19. *Journal of the American Academy of Child & Adolescent Psychiatry* 59(11), 1218–1239.

3 Van Harmelen, A. L. et al. (2017). Adolescent friendships predict later resilient functioning across psychosocial domains in a healthy community cohort. *Psychological Medicine* 47(13), 2312–2322.

4 Mitic, M. et al. (2021). Toward an integrated model of supportive peer relationships in early adolescence: a systematic review and exploratory meta-analysis. *Frontiers in Psychology* 12, 589403.

5 Foulkes, L. and Blakemore, S. J. (2018). Studying individual differences in human adolescent brain development. *Nature Neuroscience* 21(3), 315–323.

6 Andrews, J. L., Ahmed, S. P. and Blakemore, S. J. (2021). Navigating the social environment in adolescence: the role of social brain development. *Biological Psychiatry* 89(2), 109–118.

7 You, S. (2011). Peer influence and adolescents' school engagement. *Procedia – Social and Behavioral Sciences* 29(2), 829–835.

8 Laursen, B. and Veenstra, R. (2021). Toward understanding the functions of peer influence: a summary and synthesis of recent empirical research. *Journal of Research on Adolescence* 31(4), 889–907.

9 Bingham, C. R. et al. (2016). Peer passenger norms and pressure: experimental effects on simulated driving among teenage males. *Transportation Research Part F* 41, 124–137.

10 Allison, S., Warin, M. and Bastiampillai, T. (2014). Anorexia nervosa and social contagion: clinical implications. *Australian & New Zealand Journal of Psychiatry* 48(2), 116–120.

**11** O'Sullivan, S. (2021). *The Sleeping Beauties: And Other Stories of Mystery Illness.* Picador [Kindle edn].

**12** Gosling, M. (2022). Part 1: Why might teenagers question their gender? *Teenagers and Gender Identity: The Evidence Base.* Sex Matters.

**13** Telzer, E. H. et al. (2018). Social influence on positive youth development: a developmental neuroscience perspective. *Advances in Child Development and Behavior* 54, 215–258.

**14** Von Salisch, M. (2018). Emotional competence and friendship involvement: spiral effects in adolescence. *European Journal of Developmental Psychology* 15(6), 678–693.

**15** Huntley, J. and Owens, L. (2013). Collaborative conversations: adolescent girls' own strategies for managing conflict within their friendship groups. *International Journal of Adolescence and Youth* 18(4), 236–247.

**16** Flynn, H. K. (2018). Friendships of adolescence. In G. Ritzer and C. Rojek (eds), *The Blackwell Encyclopedia of Sociology.* John Wiley & Sons. doi: 0.1002/9781405165518.wbeosf073.

**17** Way, N. (2013). Boys' friendships during adolescence: intimacy, desire, and loss. *Journal of Research on Adolescence* 23(2), 201–213.

**18** Rose, A. J. (2002). Co–rumination in the friendships of girls and boys. *Child Development* 73(6), 1830–1843.

**19** Spendelow, J. S., Simonds, L. M. and Avery, R. E. (2017). The relationship between co-rumination and internalizing problems: a systematic review and meta-analysis. *Clinical Psychology & Psychotherapy* 24(2), 512–527.

**20** Schwartz-Mette, R. A. and Rose, A. J. (2012). Co-rumination mediates contagion of internalizing symptoms within youths' friendships. *Developmental Psychology* 48(5), 1355.

**21** Stone, L. B. et al. (2022). Adolescent girls' intrapersonal and interpersonal parasympathetic regulation during peer support is moderated by trait and state co-rumination. *Developmental Psychobiology* 64(1), e22232.

**22** Lam, C. B., McHale, S. M. and Crouter, A. C. (2014). Time with peers from middle childhood to late adolescence: developmental course and adjustment correlates. *Child Development* 85(4), 1677–1693.

23 Rueger, S. Y. et al. (2016). A meta-analytic review of the association between perceived social support and depression in childhood and adolescence. *Psychological Bulletin* 142(10), 1017.

24 Telzer, E. H. et al. (2018). Social influence on positive youth development: a developmental neuroscience perspective. *Advances in Child Development and Behavior* 54, 215–258.

25 Various, cited in Collins, W. A and Steinberg, L. (2008). Adolescent development in interpersonal context. In W. Damon and R. M. Lerner (eds), *Child and Adolescent Development: An Advanced Course*. John Wiley & Sons, pp. 551–590.

26 Laursen, B and Hafen, C. A. (2010). Future directions in the study of close relationships: conflict is bad (except when it's not). *Social Development* 19(4), 858–872.

27 Huntley and Owens (2013).

28 Soenens, B., Vansteenkiste, M. and Beyers, W. (2019). Parenting adolescents. In M. H. Bornstein (ed.), *Handbook of Parenting: Vol. 1: Children and Parenting*. Routledge, pp. 101–167.

29 Siegel, D. J. (2014). *Brainstorm: The Power and Purpose of the Teenage Brain* [Kindle edn]. Scribe.

30 Stitt, E. on Sargeant, D. (Host) (2022, 21 October.) Elisabeth Stitt: Managing Parent and Teen Conflicts. In *Raising Parents: The Parenting Science Insights Podcast*. https://podcasts.apple.com/gb/podcast/raising-parents-the-parenting-science-insights-podcast/id1648316813?i=1000583391155.

31 Keijsers, L. et al. (2012). Forbidden friends as forbidden fruit: parental supervision of friendships, contact with deviant peers, and adolescent delinquency. *Child Development* 83(2), 651–666.

32 Soenens, Vansteenkiste and Beyers (2019).

33 Noller, P. and Callan, V. (2015). *The Adolescent in the Family*. Routledge.

34 Tilton-Weaver, L. C. et al. (2013). Can parental monitoring and peer management reduce the selection or influence of delinquent peers? Testing the question using a dynamic social network approach. *Developmental Psychology* 49(11), 2057–2070.

35 Collins and Steinberg (2008).

36 Ashcraft, A. M. and Murray, P. J. (2017). Talking to parents about adolescent sexuality. *Pediatric Clinics* 64(2), 305–320.

37 Fisher, H. E. (2015). Broken hearts: the nature and risks of romantic rejection. In A. Booth, A. C. Crouter and A. Snyder (eds), *Romance and Sex in Adolescence and Emerging Adulthood: Risks and Opportunities*. Routledge, pp. 3–28.

38 Shakespeare, W. (1597). *Romeo and Juliet*.

39 Takahashi, K. et al. (2015). Imaging the passionate stage of romantic love by dopamine dynamics. *Frontiers in Human Neuroscience* 9, 191.

40 Fortenberry, J. D. (2013). Puberty and adolescent sexuality. *Hormones and Behavior* 64(2), 280–287.

41 Van Goozen, S. H. et al. (1997), cited in Fisher (2015).

42 Daniels, E. A., Zurbriggen, E. L. and Ward, L. M. (2020). Becoming an object: a review of self-objectification in girls. *Body Image* 33, 278–299.

43 Fisher (2015).

44 Furman, W. and Shaffer, L. (2003). The role of romantic relationships in adolescent development. *Adolescent Romantic Relations and Sexual Behavior: Theory, Research, and Practical Implications*, 3–22.

45 Connolly, J. and Goldberg, A. (1999). Romantic relationships in adolescence: the role of friends and peers in their emergence and development. In W. Furman, B. B. Brown and C. Feiring (eds), *The Development of Romantic Relationships in Adolescence*. Cambridge University Press, pp. 266–290.

46 Giordano, P. C., Manning, W. D. and Longmore, M. A. (2015). Adolescent romantic relationships: an emerging portrait of their nature and developmental significance. In A. Booth, A. C. Crouter and A. Snyder (eds), *Romance and Sex in Adolescence and Emerging Adulthood: Risks and Opportunities*. Routledge, pp. 127–150.

47 Furman, W. and Shomaker, L. B. (2008). Patterns of interaction in adolescent romantic relationships: distinct features and links to other close relationships. *Journal of Adolescence* 31(6), 771–788.

48 Collins, W. A. and Steinberg, L. (2007). Adolescent development in interpersonal context. In N. Eisenberg (vol. ed.), W. Damon and R. Lerner (eds.), Social, emotional, and personality development. *Handbook of Child*

*Psychology. Volume III: Social, Emotional, and Personality Development.* Wiley, pp. 1003–1067.

49 Fisher (2015).

50 Giordano, Manning and Longmore (2015).

51 Booth, A., Crouter, A. C. and Snyder, A. (eds) (2015). *Romance and Sex in Adolescence and Emerging Adulthood: Risks and Opportunities.* Routledge, p. 19.

52 Fisher (2015).

53 Suleiman, A. B. and Deardorff, J. (2015). Multiple dimensions of peer influence in adolescent romantic and sexual relationships: a descriptive, qualitative perspective. *Archives of Sexual Behavior* 44, 765–775.

54 Stonard, K. E. et al. (2017). 'They'll always find a way to get to you': technology use in adolescent romantic relationships and its role in dating violence and abuse. *Journal of Interpersonal Violence* 32(14), 2083–2117.

55 De Meyer, S. et al. (2017). 'Boys should have the courage to ask a girl out': gender norms in early adolescent romantic relationships. *Journal of Adolescent Health* 61(4), S42–S47.

56 Ha, T., Kim, H. and McGill, S. (2019). When conflict escalates into intimate partner violence: the delicate nature of observed coercion in adolescent romantic relationships. *Development and Psychopathology* 31(5), 1729–1739.

57 Brar, P., Boat, A. A. and Brady, S. S. (2023). But he loves me: teens' comments about healthy and unhealthy romantic relationships. *Journal of Adolescent Research* 38(4), 632–665.

58 Weisz, A. N. et al. (2007). Informal helpers' responses when adolescents tell them about dating violence or romantic relationship problems. *Journal of Adolescence* 30(5), 853–868.

59 Fisher (2015).

60 Fisher (2015).

61 Fisher (2015).

62 Widman, L. et al. (2016). Parent-adolescent sexual communication and adolescent safer sex behavior: A meta-analysis. *JAMA Pediatrics* 170(1), 52–61.

**63** Deptula, D. P., Henry, D. B. and Schoeny, M. E. (2010). How can parents make a difference? Longitudinal associations with adolescent sexual behavior. *Journal of Family Psychology*, 24(6), 731.

**64** Weissbourd, R. et al. (2017). *The Talk: How Adults Can Promote Young People's Healthy Relationships and Prevent Misogyny and Sexual Harassment.* Making Caring Common Project and Harvard Graduate School of Education.

**65** Ashcraft and Murray (2017).

**66** Weissbourd et al. (2017).

**67** Giordano, Manning and Longmore (2015).

**68** Gómez-López, M., Viejo, C. and Ortega-Ruiz, R. (2019). Well-being and romantic relationships: a systematic review in adolescence and emerging adulthood. *International Journal of Environmental Research and Public Health* 16(13), 2415.

**69** Masarik, A. S. et al. (2013). Romantic relationships in early adulthood: influences of family, personality, and relationship cognitions. *Personal Relationships* 20(2), 356–373.

**70** Ewing, J. et al. (2020). Working out relationships: research, education, and the quest for lasting love. *Child and Family Law Quarterly* 32(4), 331–354.

**71** Spies Shapiro, L. A. and Margolin, G. (2014). Growing up wired: social networking sites and adolescent psychosocial development. *Clinical Child and Family Psychology Review* 17, 1–18.

**72** Uhls, Y. T., Ellison, N. B. and Subrahmanyam, K. (2017). Benefits and costs of social media in adolescence. *Pediatrics* 140 (Suppl. 2), S67–S70.

**73** Davis, K. (2012). Friendship 2.0: adolescents' experiences of belonging and self-disclosure online. *Journal of Adolescence* 35(6), 1527–1536.

**74** Lenhart, A. et al. (2010). Teens and mobile phones: text messaging explodes as teens embrace it as the centerpiece of their communication strategies with friends. Pew Internet and American Life Project.

**75** Rideout, V. et al. (2022). *The Common Sense Census: Media Use by Tweens and Teens, 2021.* Common Sense Media.

**76** Blair, B. L. and Fletcher, A. C. (2011). 'The only 13-year-old on planet Earth without a cell phone': meanings of cell phones in early adolescents' everyday lives. *Journal of Adolescent Research* 26(2), 155–177.

# ENDNOTES

77 Best, P., Manktelow, R. and Taylor, B. (2014). Online communication, social media and adolescent wellbeing: a systematic narrative review. *Children and Youth Services Review* 41, 27–36.

78 Yau, J. C. and Reich, S. M. (2017), cited in Odgers, C. L. and Jensen, M. R. (2020). Annual research review: adolescent mental health in the digital age: facts, fears, and future directions. *Journal of Child Psychology and Psychiatry* 61(3), 336–348.

79 Uhls, Ellison and Subrahmanyam (2017).

80 Chan, T. K. H. (2021). Does self-disclosure on social networking sites enhance well-being? The role of social anxiety, online disinhibition, and psychological stress. In Z. Lee, T. Chan and C. Cheung (eds), *Information Technology in Organisations and Societies: Multidisciplinary Perspectives from AI to Technostress*. Emerald, pp. 175– 202.

81 Ruppel, E. K. et al. (2017). Reflecting on connecting: meta-analysis of differences between computer-mediated and face-to-face self-disclosure. *Journal of Computer-Mediated Communication* 22(1), 18–34.

82 Posner, G. (2021) This family foundation is quietly going to war with Facebook over how it affects kids' brains. *Forbes Daily Cover*, 14 October. Available at: https://www.forbes.com/sites/magteam/2021/10/14/this-family-foundation-is-quietly-going-to-war-with-facebook-over-how-it-affects-kids-brains/ (accessed 26 October 2023).

83 Ra, C. K. et al. (2018). Association of digital media use with subsequent symptoms of attention-deficit/hyperactivity disorder among adolescents. *JAMA* 320(3), 255–263.

84 Chiu, M. and Chein, J. (2022). Digital media and the developing brain. In J. Nesi, E. H. Telzer and M. J. Prinstein (eds), *Handbook of Adolescent Digital Media Use and Mental Health*. Cambridge University Press, pp. 104–134.

85 Hale, L. and Guan, S. (2015). Screen time and sleep among school-aged children and adolescents: a systematic literature review. *Sleep Medicine Reviews* 21, 50–58.

86 Centers for Disease Control and Prevention (2021). *Youth Risk Behavior Survey: Data Summary & Trends Report, 2011–2021*. CDC.

87 E.g. Haidt, J. (2023). Social media is a major cause of the mental illness epidemic in teen girls. Here's the evidence. After Babel, 22 February.

Available at: https://www.afterbabel.com/p/social-media-mental-illness-epidemic (accessed 30 November 2023).

88  Moreno, M. A. and Jolliff, A. F. (2022). Depression and anxiety in the context of digital media. In J. Nesi, E. H. Telzer and M. J. Prinstein (eds), *Handbook of Adolescent Digital Media Use and Mental Health*. Cambridge University Press, pp. 217–241.

89  Patton, G. C. et al. (2016). Our future: a Lancet commission on adolescent health and wellbeing. *The Lancet* 387(10036), 2423–2478.

90  Kelly, Y. et al. (2018). Social media use and adolescent mental health: findings from the UK Millennium Cohort Study. *EClinicalMedicine* 6, 59–68.

91  George, M. J., et al. (2020). Young adolescents' digital technology use, perceived impairments, and well-being in a representative sample. *Journal of Pediatrics* 219, 180–187.

92  Orben, A. and Przybylski, A. K. (2019). The association between adolescent well-being and digital technology use. *Nature Human Behaviour* 3(2), 173–182.

93  McCrae, N., Gettings, S. and Purssell, E. (2017). Social media and depressive symptoms in childhood and adolescence: a systematic review. *Adolescent Research Review* 2, 315–330.

94  Moreno and Jolliff (2022).

95  Beyens, I. et al. (2020). The effect of social media on well-being differs from adolescent to adolescent. *Scientific Reports* 10(1), 10763.

96  Choukas-Bradley, S. et al. (2022). The perfect storm: a developmental-sociocultural framework for the role of social media in adolescent girls' body image concerns and mental health. *Clinical Child and Family Psychology Review* 25(4), 681–701.

97  Bissonette Mink, D. and Szymanski, D. M. (2022). TikTok use and body dissatisfaction: examining direct, indirect, and moderated relations. *Body Image* 43, 205–216.

98  Giedinghagen, A. (2023). The TIC in TikTok and (where) all systems go: mass social media induced illness and Munchausen's by internet as explanatory models for social media associated abnormal illness behavior. *Clinical Child Psychology and Psychiatry* 28(1), 270–278.

**99** Logrieco, G. et al. (2021). The paradox of Tik Tok anti-pro-anorexia videos: how social media can promote non-suicidal self-injury and anorexia. *International Journal of Environmental Research and Public Health* 18(3), 1041.

**100** Gosling, M. (2022). Part 1: Why might teenagers question their gender? *Teenagers and Gender Identity: The Evidence Base.* Sex Matters.

**101** Giedinghagen (2023).

**102** Gámez-Guadix, M. et al. (2013). Longitudinal and reciprocal relations of cyberbullying with depression, substance use, and problematic internet use among adolescents. *Journal of Adolescent Health* 53(4), 446–452.

**103** Spies Shapiro and Margolin (2014).

**104** Burnette, C. B., Kwitowski, M. A. and Mazzeo, S. E. (2017). 'I don't need people to tell me I'm pretty on social media': a qualitative study of social media and body image in early adolescent girls. *Body Image* 23, 114–125.

**105** Khurana, A. et al. (2015). The protective effects of parental monitoring and internet restriction on adolescents' risk of online harassment. *Journal of Youth and Adolescence* 44, 1039–1047.

**106** Hiniker, A., Schoenebeck, S. Y. and Kientz, J. A. (2016, February). Not at the dinner table: parents' and children's perspectives on family technology rules. In *Proceedings of the 19th ACM Conference on Computer-Supported Cooperative Work & Social Computing* (pp. 1376–1389).

**107** Internet Matters (2023). Online safety tips for parents of 11–13 year olds. Available at: https://www.internetmatters.org/wp-content/uploads/2023/01/Internet-Matters-Age-Guide-11-13-Jan23.pdf (accessed 30 November 2023).

**108** Stoilova, M., Bulger, M. and Livingstone, S. (2023). Do parental control tools fulfil family expectations for child protection? A rapid evidence review of the contexts and outcomes of use. *Journal of Children and Media*, 1–21.

**109** Internet Matters (2023). Online safety tips for parents of 11–13 year olds.

**110** Internet Matters (2023). Online safety tips for parents of teenagers: 14+ year olds. Available at: https://www.internetmatters.org/wp-content/uploads/2023/01/Internet-Matters-Age-Guide-14plus-Jan23.pdf (accessed 30 November 2023).

111 Internet Matters (2023). How to create an environment for kids to talk. Available at: https://www.internetmatters.org/wp-content/uploads/2023/01/Internet-Matters-Create-Environment-for-Kids-to-Talk-Jan-2023–2.pdf (accessed 30 November 2023).
112 Milovidov, E. on Wills, H. (Host) (2020, 6 October.) Understanding what's happening online and trusting your teen anyway… [podcast episode]. In *Teenage Kicks Podcast*. https://podcasts.apple.com/gb/podcast/teenage-kicks-podcast/id1501488455?i=1000493750004.
113 Hopwood, K. on Shone, J. and Sertin, J. (Hosts) (2020, 24 January.) Talking Teenagers – Season 1: Technology & Teens with Karl Hopwood [podcast episode]. In *Talking Teenagers*. https://podcasts.apple.com/gb/podcast/talking-teenagers/id1500452887?i=1000466954355.
114 @parentingteenagersuntangled (2023, 15 November.) How to: Talk to your kids about porn, with Dr Mandy Sanchez of Culture Reframed [video]. YouTube. https://www.youtube.com/watch?v=UwYRIzWUihA.
115 Lauricella, A. R. and Cingel, D. P. (2020). Parental influence on youth media use. *Journal of Child and Family Studies* 29, 1927–1937.
116 Hopwood on Shone and Sertin (Hosts) (2020).
117 Hiniker, Schoenebeck and Kientz (2016, February).

## Mind, Part 1: Mood and maturity

1 Burnett et al. (2011). The social brain in adolescence: evidence from functional magnetic resonance imaging and behavioural studies. *Neuroscience & Biobehavioral Reviews* 35(8), 1654–1664.
2 Crone, E. A. and van Duijvenvoorde, A. C. (2021). Multiple pathways of risk taking in adolescence. *Developmental Review* 62, 100996.
3 Vannucci, A. et al. (2019). Protective factors associated with daily affective reactivity and instability during adolescence. *Journal of Youth and Adolescence* 48, 771–787.
4 Mayfield, K. T. and Fosco, G. M. (2021). Links between school and home: associations between adolescent school day experiences and maternal perceptions of family relations. *Journal of Child and Family Studies* 30, 121–133.

**5** Vannucci et al. (2019).

**6** Silk, J. S., Steinberg, L. and Morris, A. S. (2003). Adolescents' emotion regulation in daily life: links to depressive symptoms and problem behavior. *Child Development* 74(6), 1869–1880.

**7** Somerville, L. H. (2013). The teenage brain: sensitivity to social evaluation. *Current Directions in Psychological Science* 22(2), 121–127.

**8** Forbes, E. E. et al. (2011). Neural systems of threat processing in adolescents: role of pubertal maturation and relation to measures of negative affect. *Developmental Neuropsychology* 36(4), 429–452.

**9** Siegel, D. J. (2014). *Brainstorm: The Power and Purpose of the Teenage Brain* [Kindle edn]. Scribe.

**10** Ladouceur, C. D. (2012). Neural systems supporting cognitive-affective interactions in adolescence: the role of puberty and implications for affective disorders. *Frontiers in Integrative Neuroscience* 6, 65.

**11** Vannucci et al. (2019).

**12** E.g. Sebastião, R., Neto, D. D. and da Silva, A. N. (2023). Recalled parental emotion socialisation and psychological distress: the role of emotional schemas. *Psychological Reports*, 00332941231204304.

**13** E.g. Reece, H. (2013). The pitfalls of positive parenting. *Ethics and Education* 8(1), 42–54.

**14** Buckholdt, K. E., Parra, G. R. and Jobe-Shields, L. (2014). Intergenerational transmission of emotion dysregulation through parental invalidation of emotions: implications for adolescent internalizing and externalizing behaviors. *Journal of Child and Family Studies* 23, 324–332.

**15** Damour, L. (2023). *The Emotional Lives of Teenagers* [Kindle edn]. Allen & Unwin.

**16** Boelema, S. R. et al. (2014). Executive functioning shows differential maturation from early to late adolescence: longitudinal findings from a TRAILS study. *Neuropsychology* 28(2), 177.

**17** Reeves, R. (2022). *Of Boys and Men* [Kindle edn]. Swift Press.

**18** Collins, W. A. and Steinberg, L. (2008). Adolescent development in interpersonal context. In W. Damon and R. M. Lerner (eds), *Child and Adolescent Development: An Advanced Course*. Wiley, pp. 551–590.

**19** Wuyts, D. et al. (2018). The role of observed autonomy support, reciprocity, and need satisfaction in adolescent disclosure about friends. *Journal of Adolescence* 65, 141–154.

**20** Walker, L. J. and Hennig, K. H. (1999). Parenting style and the development of moral reasoning. *Journal of Moral Education* 28(3), 359–374.

**21** Patrick, R. B. and Gibbs, J. C. (2012). Inductive discipline, parental expression of disappointed expectations, and moral identity in adolescence. *Journal of Youth and Adolescence* 41, 973–983.

**22** Hou, M. (2023). The impact of parents on adolescent moral development. *Journal of Education, Humanities and Social Sciences* 8, 1177–1182.

**23** Hardy, S. A., Padilla-Walker, L. M. and Carlo, G. (2008). Parenting dimensions and adolescents' internalisation of moral values. *Journal of Moral Education* 37(2), 205–223.

**24** Dornbusch, S. M. et al. (1985) and Lamborn, S. D., Dornbusch, S. M. and Steinberg, L. (1996), cited in Soenens, B., Vansteenkiste, M. and Beyers, W. (2019). Parenting adolescents. In M. H. Bornstein (ed.), *Handbook of Parenting: Vol. 1: Children and Parenting*. Routledge, pp. 101–167.

**25** Hasebe, Y., Nucci, L. and Nucci, M. S. (2004), Qin, L. L., Pomerantz, E. M. and Wang, Q. (2009) and Smetana J. G., Campione-Barr, N. and Metzger, A. (2004), cited in Alonso-Stuyck, P., Zacarés, J. J. and Ferreres, A. (2018). Emotional separation, autonomy in decision-making, and psychosocial adjustment in adolescence: a proposed typology. *Journal of Child and Family Studies* 27, 1373–1383.

**26** Soenens, B., Vansteenkiste, M., and Beyers, W. (2019). Parenting adolescents. In M. H. Bornstein (ed.), *Handbook of Parenting: Vol. 1: Children and Parenting*. Routledge, pp. 101–167.

**27** Daddis, C. (2011). Desire for increased autonomy and adolescents' perceptions of peer autonomy: 'Everyone else can; why can't I?' *Child Development* 82(4), 1310–1326.

**28** Kuhn, E. S., Phan, J. M. and Laird, R. D. (2014). Compliance with parents' rules: between-person and within-person predictions. *Journal of Youth and Adolescence* 43, 245–256.

**29** Collins, W. A. and Steinberg, L. (2007). Adolescent development in interpersonal context. In N. Eisenberg (vol. ed.), W. Damon and R. Lerner (eds), Social, emotional, and personality development. *Handbook of Child Psychology. Volume III: Social, Emotional, and Personality Development.* Wiley, pp. 1003–1067.

30 Soenens, Vansteenkiste and Beyers (2019).

31 Remaining friends: Soenens, B., Vansteenkiste, M. and Niemiec, C. P. (2009). Should parental prohibition of adolescents' peer relationships be prohibited? *Personal Relationships* 16(4), 507–530.

32 Sufficient freedom: Siegel (2014).

33 Ravindran, N. et al. (2020). Dynamics of mother–adolescent and father–adolescent autonomy and control during a conflict discussion task. *Journal of Family Psychology* 34(3), 312.

34 Zhang, J. et al. (2024). Coercive parent-adolescent interactions predict substance use and antisocial behaviors through early adulthood: a dynamic systems perspective. *Research on Child and Adolescent Psychopathology* 52(1), 141–154.

35 *The Sopranos.* Season 2, Episode 3: Toodle-Fucking-Oo [TV programme].

36 Alonso-Stuyck, P., Zacarés, J. J. and Ferreres, A. (2018). Emotional separation, autonomy in decision-making, and psychosocial adjustment in adolescence: a proposed typology. *Journal of Child and Family Studies* 27, 1373–1383.

37 Keijsers, L. et al. (2016). What drives developmental change in adolescent disclosure and maternal knowledge? Heterogeneity in within-family processes. *Developmental Psychology* 52(12), 2057.

38 Garthe, R. C., Sullivan, T. N. and Kliewer, W. (2018). Longitudinal associations between maternal solicitation, perceived maternal acceptance, adolescent self-disclosure, and adolescent externalizing behaviors. *Youth & Society* 50(2), 274–295.

39 Kapetanovic, S. and Boson, K. (2022). Discrepancies in parents' and adolescents' reports on parent-adolescent communication and associations to adolescents' psychological health. *Current Psychology* 41(7), 4259–4270.

40 Baudat, S. et al. (2022). How do adolescents manage information in the relationship with their parents? A latent class analysis of disclosure, keeping secrets, and lying. *Journal of Youth and Adolescence* 51(6), 1134–1152.

41  Frijns, T. et al. (2005). Keeping secrets from parents: longitudinal associations of secrecy in adolescence. *Journal of Youth and Adolescence* 34(2), 137–148; Frijns, T. et al. (2010). What parents don't know and how it may affect their children: qualifying the disclosure-adjustment link. *Journal of Adolescence* 33, 261–270.

42  Laird, R. D. et al. (2013). Information management strategies in early adolescence: developmental change in use and transactional associations with psychological adjustment. *Developmental Psychology* 49(5), 928–937.

43  Nowell, C. et al. (2023). Value of self-disclosure to parents and peers during adolescence. *Journal of Research on Adolescence* 33(1), 289–301.

44  Garthe, Sullivan and Kliewer (2018).

45  Weinstein, N., Huo, A. and Itzchakov, G. (2021). Parental listening when adolescents self-disclose: a preregistered experimental study. *Journal of Experimental Child Psychology* 209, 105178.

46  Tilton-Weaver, L. et al. (2010). Open up or close down: how do parental reactions affect youth information management? *Journal of Adolescence* 33, 333–346.

47  Smetana, J. G. et al. (2009). Early and middle adolescents' disclosure to parents about their activities in different domains. *Journal of Adolescence* 32, 619–713.

48  Rodríguez-Meirinhos, A. et al. (2020). When is parental monitoring effective? A person-centered analysis of the role of autonomy-supportive and psychologically controlling parenting in referred and non-referred adolescents. *Journal of Youth and Adolescence* 49, 352–368.

49  Smetana, J. G. (2008). 'It's 10 o'clock: do you know where your children are?' Recent advances in understanding parental monitoring and adolescents' information management. *Child Development Perspectives* 2(1), 19–25.

50  Solís, M. V., Smetana, J. G. and Comer, J. (2015). Associations among solicitation, relationship quality, and adolescents' disclosure and secrecy with mothers and best friends. *Journal of Adolescence* 43, 193–205.

51  Baudat et al. (2022).

52  Perkins, S. A. and Turiel, E. (2007), cited in Rote, W. M. and Smetana, J. G. (2015). Acceptability of information management strategies: adolescents'

and parents' judgments and links with adjustment and relationships. *Journal of Research on Adolescence* 25(3), 490–505.

53 Bureau, J. S. and Mageau, G. A. (2014). Parental autonomy support and honesty: the mediating role of identification with the honesty value and perceived costs and benefits of honesty. *Journal of Adolescence* 37(3), 225–236.

## Mind, Part 2: Mental health and resilience

1 See various older citations in Bodner, N. et al. (2018). Affective family interactions and their associations with adolescent depression: a dynamic network approach. *Development and Psychopathology* 30(4), 1459–1473.

2 Panchal, U. et al. (2023). The impact of COVID-19 lockdown on child and adolescent mental health: systematic review. *European Child & Adolescent Psychiatry* 32(7), 1151–1177.

3 Loades, M. E. et al. (2020). Rapid systematic review: the impact of social isolation and loneliness on the mental health of children and adolescents in the context of COVID-19. *Journal of the American Academy of Child & Adolescent Psychiatry* 59(11), 1218–1239.

4 Psych Central (2022). Borderline personality disorder test. Available at: https://psychcentral.com/quizzes/borderline-test (accessed 10 December 2023).

5 E.g. Zhang, Q., Wang, J. and Neitzel, A. (2023). School-based mental health interventions targeting depression or anxiety: a meta-analysis of rigorous randomized controlled trials for school-aged children and adolescents. *Journal of Youth and Adolescence* 52(1), 195–217.

6 Gómez-Odriozola, J. and Calvete, E. (2021). Effects of a mindfulness-based intervention on adolescents' depression and self-concept: the moderating role of age. *Journal of Child and Family Studies* 30, 1501–1515.

7 Harvey, L. J. et al. (2023). Investigating the efficacy of a dialectical behaviour therapy-based universal intervention on adolescent social and emotional well-being outcomes. *Behaviour Research and Therapy* 169, 104408.

8 Guzman-Holst, C. et al. (2022). Research review: do antibullying interventions reduce internalizing symptoms? A systematic review, meta-analysis, and meta-regression exploring intervention components,

moderators, and mechanisms. *Journal of Child Psychology and Psychiatry* 63(12), 1454–1465.

9 Harari, L., Oselin, S. S., and Link, B. G. (2023). The power of self-labels: examining self-esteem consequences for youth with mental health problems. *Journal of Health and Social Behavior.* doi: 10.1177/00221465231175936.

10 Foulkes, L. and Andrews, J. L. (2023). Are mental health awareness efforts contributing to the rise in reported mental health problems? A call to test the prevalence inflation hypothesis. *New Ideas in Psychology* 69, 101010.

11 Instagram (2023). health–anxiety. Reminder it's okay if your holiday season doesn't feel jolly. https://www.instagram.com/p/C0s1LX0goay/.

12 TikTok (2021). @drjulie. Hidden signs of depression. https://www.tiktok.com/@drjulie/video/6926555339819126022.

13 Damour, L. (2023). *The Emotional Lives of Teenagers* [Kindle edn]. Allen & Unwin.

14 Rifkin, L. S. et al. (2021). Attention, rumination and depression in youth with negative inferential styles: a prospective study. *Journal of Affective Disorders* 291, 209–217.

15 Stone, L. B. et al. (2011). Co-rumination predicts the onset of depressive disorders during adolescence. *Journal of Abnormal Psychology* 120(3), 752.

16 Alho, J. et al. (2024). Transmission of mental disorders in adolescent peer networks. *JAMA Psychiatry.* doi: 10.1001/jamapsychiatry.2024.1126.

17 Inequality, city living, eco-anxiety: Choudhury, S., Piera Pi-Sunyer, B. and Blakemore, S. J. (2023). A neuroecosocial perspective on adolescent development. *Annual Review of Developmental Psychology* 5, 285–307. Obesity, academic pressure: Boer, M. et al. (2023). National-level schoolwork pressure, family structure, internet use, and obesity as drivers of time trends in adolescent psychological complaints between 2002 and 2018. *Journal of Youth and Adolescence* 52(10), 2061–2077.

18 Von Soest, T., Luhmann, M. and Gerstorf, D. (2020). The development of loneliness through adolescence and young adulthood: its nature, correlates, and midlife outcomes. *Developmental Psychology* 56(10), 1919. The increase was in direct measures of loneliness and in emotional loneliness; social loneliness fell.

**19** Laursen, B. and Hartl, A. C. (2013). Understanding loneliness during adolescence: developmental changes that increase the risk of perceived social isolation. *Journal of Adolescence* 36(6), 1261–1268.

**20** Anderson, A. S. et al. (2021). Relations between maternal coping socialization, adolescents' coping, and symptoms of anxiety and depression. *Journal of Child and Family Studies* 30, 663–675.

**21** Zwierzynska, K., Wolke, D. and Lereya, T. S. (2013). Peer victimization in childhood and internalizing problems in adolescence: a prospective longitudinal study. *Journal of Abnormal Child Psychology* 41, 309–323.

**22** Eisenberger, N. I., Lieberman, M. D. and Williams, K. D. (2003). Does rejection hurt? An fMRI study of social exclusion. *Science* 302(5643), 290–292.

**23** Lucas-Thompson, R. G., Lunkenheimer, E. S. and Dumitrache, A. (2017). Associations between marital conflict and adolescent conflict appraisals, stress physiology, and mental health. *Journal of Clinical Child & Adolescent Psychology* 46(3), 379–393.

**24** Buist, K. L., Deković, M. and Prinzie, P. (2013). Sibling relationship quality and psychopathology of children and adolescents: a meta-analysis. *Clinical Psychology Review* 33(1), 97–106.

**25** Compas, B. E. et al. (2017). Coping, emotion regulation, and psychopathology in childhood and adolescence: a meta-analysis and narrative review. *Psychological Bulletin* 143(9), 939–991.

**26** Anderson et al. (2021).

**27** Compas et al. (2017).

**28** Lobo, F. M. et al. (2021). Parental emotion coaching moderates the effects of family stress on internalizing symptoms in middle childhood and adolescence. *Social Development* 30(4), 1023–1039.

**29** Main, A. et al. (2019). Timing of adolescent emotional disclosures: the role of maternal emotions and adolescent age. *Emotion* 19(5), 829.

**30** Rejaän, Z., van der Valk, I. E. and Branje, S. (2022). The role of sense of belonging and family structure in adolescent adjustment. *Journal of Research on Adolescence* 32(4), 1354–1368.

**31** Yap, M. B. H. et al. (2014). Parental factors associated with depression and anxiety in young people: a systematic review and meta-analysis. *Journal of Affective Disorders* 156, 8–23.

**32** Manuele, S. J. et al. (2023). Associations between paternal versus maternal parenting behaviors and child and adolescent internalizing problems: a systematic review and meta-analysis. *Clinical Psychology Review*, 102339.

**33** Buckholdt, K. E., Parra, G. R. and Jobe-Shields, L. (2014). Intergenerational transmission of emotion dysregulation through parental invalidation of emotions: implications for adolescent internalizing and externalizing behaviors. *Journal of Child and Family Studies* 23, 324–332.

**34** Bodner et al. (2018).

**35** Bidler, D. on Chatterjee, R. (Host). (2023, 6 December.) #408 How Changing Your Lifestyle Can Fix Your Mental Health & Why Depression and Anxiety Are Not Disorders with David Bidler [Audio podcast episode]. In *Feel Better, Live More with Dr Rangan Chatterjee*. https://podcasts.apple.com/gb/podcast/feel-better-live-more-with-dr-rangan-chatterjee/id1333552422.

**36** Lovato, N. and Gradisar, M. (2014). A meta-analysis and model of the relationship between sleep and depression in adolescents: recommendations for future research and clinical practice. *Sleep Medicine Reviews* 18(6), 521–529.

**37** Zhang, Y. et al. (2020). The association between green space and adolescents' mental well-being: a systematic review. *International Journal of Environmental Research and Public Health* 17(18), 6640.

**38** Zielińska, M. et al. (2022). The Mediterranean diet and the Western diet in adolescent depression: current reports. *Nutrients* 14(20), 4390.

**39** Oberste, M. et al. (2020). Physical activity for the treatment of adolescent depression: a systematic review and meta-analysis. *Frontiers in Physiology* 11, 185.

**40** Lyell, K. M. et al. (2020). Parent and peer social support compensation and internalizing problems in adolescence. *Journal of School Psychology* 83, 25–49.

**41** Johnson, S. R. L., Blum, R. W. and Cheng, T. L. (2014). Future orientation: a construct with implications for adolescent health and wellbeing. *International Journal of Adolescent Medicine and Health* 26(4), 459–468.

42 Giollabhui, N. M. et al. (2018). The development of future orientation is associated with faster decline in hopelessness during adolescence. *Journal of Youth and Adolescence* 47, 2129–2142.

43 Damon, W., Menon, J. and Bronk, K. C. (2003). The development of purpose during adolescence. *Applied Developmental Science* 7(3), 119–128.

44 Data tables were downloaded from the GIDS website before the service closed in March 2024. GIDS (2023). Number of referrals to GIDS. Available at: https://gids.nhs.uk/about-us/number-of-referrals/ (accessed 7 December 2023; now removed).

45 ONS (2023). Gender identity: age and sex, England and Wales: Census 2021. Available at: https://www.ons.gov.uk/peoplepopulationandcommunity/culturalidentity/genderidentity/articles/genderidentityageandsexenglandandwalescensus2021/2023-01-25#how-gender-identity-differed-by-age (accessed 7 December 2023).

46 Calculated from ONS (2023). 16–17 year old population: All persons: 000s. Available at: https://www.ons.gov.uk/employmentandlabourmarket/peopleinwork/employmentandemployeetypes/timeseries/jn5p/lms (accessed 7 December 2023).

47 E.g. GIRES (2015). Lesson plan for the Penguin Land Books: gender diversity for nursery and primary school children. Available at: https://www.gires.org.uk/classroom-lesson-plans/ (accessed 18 January 2024).

48 Cass, H. (2024). *Independent Review of Gender Identity Services for Children and Young People: Final Report*. The Cass Review.

49 For example, Hanna et al. (2022). Continuation of gender-affirming hormones in transgender people starting puberty suppression in adolescence: a cohort study in the Netherlands. *The Lancet Child & Adolescent Health* 6(12), 869–875; Carmichael et al. (2021). Short-term outcomes of pubertal suppression in a selected cohort of 12 to 15 year old young people with persistent gender dysphoria in the UK. *PLOS One* 16(2), e0243894. Both studies showed the same continuation rate.

50 Bachmann, C. J. et al. (2024). Gender identity disorders among young people in Germany: prevalence and trends, 2013–2022. An analysis of nationwide routine insurance data. *Deutsches Ärzteblatt International* 121, 370–371.

51 Calculated from Holt, V., Skagerberg, E. and Dunsford, M. (2016). Young people with features of gender dysphoria: demographics and associated difficulties. *Clinical Child Psychology and Psychiatry* 21(1), 108–118. To compare this nationally, we can look at data from the Office for National Statistics for sixteen- to twenty-four-year-olds, which is the youngest age group for which it reports sexual orientation. This shows us that 8% of young people are same-sex attracted or bisexual. Source: Office for National Statistics (2022). Sexual orientation, UK: 2012 to 2020. [Data set.] Data is reported for the most recently available year (2020). Available at: https://www.ons.gov.uk/peoplepopulationandcommunity/culturalidentity/sexuality (accessed 24 July 2024).

52 Calculated from Kaltiala-Heino, R. et al. (2018). Gender dysphoria in adolescence: current perspectives. *Adolescent Health, Medicine and Therapeutics* 9, 31.

53 Becerra-Culqui, T. A. et al. (2018). Mental health of transgender and gender nonconforming youth compared with their peers. *Pediatrics* 141(5).

54 Milano, W. et al. (2020). Gender dysphoria, eating disorders and body image: an overview. *Endocrine, Metabolic & Immune Disorders* 20(4), 518–524.

55 They make up 4.9% of service referrals but only 0.6% of children in England. Matthews, T. et al. (2019). Gender dysphoria in looked-after and adopted young people in a gender identity development service. *Clinical Child Psychology and Psychiatry* 24(1), 112–128.

56 Thoma, B. C. et al. (2021). Disparities in childhood abuse between transgender and cisgender adolescents. *Pediatrics* 148(2).

57 Gosling, M. (2022). Gender-questioning teenagers: puberty blockers and hormone treatment vs placebo. *Teenagers and Gender Identity: The Evidence Base*. Sex Matters. Available at: https://sex-matters.org/wp-content/uploads/2022/12/Teenagers-medication-vs-placebo.pdf (accessed 20 September 2024).

58 Gosling (2022). Gender-questioning teenagers.

59 The Safe Zone Project (2015). Genderbread person & LGBTQ umbrella. Available at: http://thesafezoneproject.com/wp-content/uploads/2015/08/GenderbreadPersonLGBTQUmbrella.pdf (accessed 10 December 2023).

**60** Walton, J. (2016). *Introducing Teddy*. Bloomsbury.

**61** Hancox, L. (2022). *Welcome to St Hell: My Trans Teen Misadventure*. Scholastic.

**62** E.g. r/trans, Capitainefox (2023). Did the bingo :). Reddit. https://www.reddit.com/r/trans/comments/18ev8h8/did_the_bingo/.

**63** E.g. Marsh, J. (2023, 23 November). You don't have to ♥ #lgbtq #nonbinary #trans #free #healing #selfcare #emotional health. TikTok: https://www.tiktok.com/@thejeffreymarsh/video/7304414661691165994.

**64** Marsh, J. (2020, 10 May). Being the internet mom [Video]. YouTube. https://www.youtube.com/watch?v=UVoIT3Dc160.

**65** Ayad, S., Marchiano, L. and O'Malley, S. (2023). *When Kids Say They're Trans*. Swift Press.

**66** https://sex-matters.org/resources/resources-for-parents/

**67** Beutel, M. E. et al. (2017). Childhood adversities and distress: the role of resilience in a representative sample. *PLOS One* 12(3), e0173826.

**68** Otte, C. et al. (2005). Association between childhood trauma and catecholamine response to psychological stress in police academy recruits. *Biological Psychiatry* 57(1), 27–32.

**69** Malhi, G. S. et al. (2019). Modelling resilience in adolescence and adversity: a novel framework to inform research and practice. *Translational Psychiatry* 9(1), 316.

**70** Mansfield, C. D. and Diamond, L. M. (2017). Does stress-related growth really matter for adolescents' day-to-day adaptive functioning?. *The Journal of Early Adolescence* 37(5), 677–695.

**71** Malhi et al. (2019).

**72** Reilly, S. and Semkovska, M. (2018). An examination of the mediatory role of resilience in the relationship between helicopter parenting and severity of depressive symptoms in Irish university students. *Adolescent Psychiatry* 8(1), 32–47.

**73** Parker, K. J. et al. (2007). Early life stress and novelty seeking behavior in adolescent monkeys. *Psychoneuroendocrinology* 32(7), 785–792.

**74** Luecken, L. J. and Gress, J. L. (2010). Early adversity and resilience in emerging adulthood. In J. W. Reich, A. J. Zautra and J. S. Hall (eds), *Handbook of Adult Resilience*. Guilford Press, pp. 238–257.

75 Shiner, R. L. and Masten, A. S. (2012). Childhood personality as a harbinger of competence and resilience in adulthood. *Development and Psychopathology* 24(2), 507–528.

76 Wu, G. et al. (2013). Understanding resilience. *Frontiers in Behavioral Neuroscience* 7, 10.

77 Fritz, J. et al. (2018). A systematic review of amenable resilience factors that moderate and/or mediate the relationship between childhood adversity and mental health in young people. *Frontiers in Psychiatry* 9, 230.

78 Mansfield, C. D. and Diamond, L. M. (2017). Does stress-related growth really matter for adolescents' day-to-day adaptive functioning? *Journal of Early Adolescence* 37(5), 677–695.

79 Mansfield and Diamond (2017).

80 Hampel, P., and Petermann, F. (2006). Perceived stress, coping, and adjustment in adolescents. *Journal of Adolescent Health* 38(4), 409–415.

81 Silk, J. S., Steinberg, L. and Morris, A. S. (2003). Adolescents' emotion regulation in daily life: links to depressive symptoms and problem behavior. *Child Development*, 74(6), 1869–1880.

82 Felton, J. W. et al. (2018). Distress tolerance interacts with negative life events to predict depressive symptoms across adolescence. *Journal of Clinical Child & Adolescent Psychology* 48(4), 633–642.

83 Fritz et al. (2018).

84 Muris, P. et al. (2019). Self-compassion and adolescents' positive and negative cognitive reactions to daily life problems. *Journal of Child and Family Studies* 28, 1433–1444.

85 Muris et al. (2019).

86 Green, L. M. et al. (2018). Empathy, depressive symptoms, and self-esteem in adolescence: the moderating role of the mother–adolescent relationship. *Journal of Child and Family Studies* 27, 3964–3974.

87 Alfieri, S. et al. (2018). Gratitude as a variable of mediation between parental support and self-esteem in adolescence. *Journal of Child and Family Studies* 27, 1394–1401.

88 Petrocchi, N. and Couyoumdjian, A. (2016). The impact of gratitude on depression and anxiety: the mediating role of criticizing, attacking, and reassuring the self. *Self and Identity* 15(2), 191–205.

**89** Alfieri et al. (2018).

**90** Otterpohl, N. et al. (2020). The intergenerational continuity of parental conditional regard and its role in mothers' and adolescents' contingent self-esteem and depressive symptoms. *Social Development* 29(1), 143–158.

**91** Fu, X., Padilla-Walker, L. M. and Brown, M. N. (2017). Longitudinal relations between adolescents' self-esteem and prosocial behavior toward strangers, friends and family. *Journal of Adolescence* 57, 90–98.

**92** Gosling, M. (2022). Part 1: Why might teenagers start to question their gender? *Teenagers and Gender Identity: The Evidence Base.* Sex Matters; Gosling, M. (2022). Part 2: Treatment and outcomes. *Teenagers and Gender Identity: The Evidence Base.* Sex Matters; Gosling, M. (2022). Gender-questioning teenagers: puberty blockers and hormone treatment vs placebo. *Teenagers and Gender Identity: The Evidence Base.* Sex Matters. All available on the Sex Matters website: https://sex-matters.org/posts/category/publications/for-parents/.

## Body

**1** Farello, G. et al. (2019). Review of the literature on current changes in the timing of pubertal development and the incomplete forms of early puberty. *Frontiers in Pediatrics* 7, 147.

**2** Cheng, T. S. et al. (2022). Longitudinal associations between prepubertal childhood total energy and macronutrient intakes and subsequent puberty timing in UK boys and girls. *European Journal of Nutrition* 61(1): 157–167.

**3** Jackson, S. and Goossens, L. (eds) (2020). *Handbook of Adolescent Development.* Psychology Press.

**4** E.g. Pomerantz, H. et al. (2017). Pubertal timing and youth internalizing psychopathology: the role of relational aggression. *Journal of Child and Family Studies* 26(2), 416–423.

**5** Patton, G. C. and Viner, R. (2007), cited in Sawyer, S. M., et al. (2018). The age of adolescence. *The Lancet Child & Adolescent Health* 2(3), 223–228.

**6** Jackson and Goossens (2020).

**7** Royal College of Paediatrics and Child Health (2012). Girls UK Growth Chart 2–18 Years. Available at: https://www.rcpch.ac.uk/sites/

default/files/Girls_2–18_years_growth_chart.pdf (accessed 13 December 2023).

**8** Royal College of Paediatrics and Child Health (2012). Boys UK Growth Chart 2–18 Years. Available at: https://www.rcpch.ac.uk/sites/default/files/Boys_2–18_years_growth_chart.pdf (accessed 13 December 2023).

**9** Siervogel, R. M. et al. (2003). Puberty and body composition. *Hormone Research* 60 (Suppl. 1), 36–45.

**10** Jackson and Goossens (2020).

**11** Hunter, S. K. et al. (2023). The biological basis of sex differences in athletic performance: consensus statement for the American College of sports Medicine. *Translational Journal of the American College of Sports Medicine* 8(4), 1–33.

**12** Chaput, J. P. et al. (2020). 2020 WHO guidelines on physical activity and sedentary behaviour for children and adolescents aged 5–17 years: summary of the evidence. *International Journal of Behavioral Nutrition and Physical Activity* 17, 1–9.

**13** Eime, R. M. et al. (2013). A systematic review of the psychological and social benefits of participation in sport for children and adolescents: informing development of a conceptual model of health through sport. *International journal of Behavioral Nutrition and Physical Activity* 10(1), 1–21.

**14** Nagata, J. M. et al. (2021). Adolescent body mass index and health outcomes at 24-year follow-up: a prospective cohort study. *Journal of the American College of Cardiology* 77(25), 3229–3231.

**15** Naveed, S., Lakka, T. and Haapala, E. A. (2020). An overview on the associations between health behaviors and brain health in children and adolescents with special reference to diet quality. *International Journal of Environmental Research and Public Health* 17(3), 953–973.

**16** Twenge, J. M. et al. (2021). Worldwide increases in adolescent loneliness. *Journal of Adolescence* 93, 257–269.

**17** Orchard, F. et al. (2020). Self-reported sleep patterns and quality amongst adolescents: cross-sectional and prospective associations with anxiety and depression. *Journal of Child Psychology and Psychiatry* 61(10), 1126–1137.

**18** Van Sluijs, E. M. et al. (2021). Physical activity behaviours in adolescence: current evidence and opportunities for intervention. *The Lancet* 398(10298), 429–442.

**19** Fleary, S. A. and Ettienne, R. (2019). The relationship between food parenting practices, parental diet and their adolescents' diet. *Appetite* 135, 79–85.

**20** Wang, J. and Fielding-Singh, P. (2018). How food rules a home influence independent adolescent food choices. *Journal of Adolescent Health* 63(2), 219–226.

**21** Baiocchi-Wagner, E. A. and Talley, A. E. (2013). The role of family communication in individual health attitudes and behaviors concerning diet and physical activity. *Health Communication* 28(2), 193–205.

**22** Rimal, R. N. (2003). Intergenerational transmission of health: the role of intrapersonal, interpersonal, and communicative factors. *Health Education & Behavior* 30(1), 10–28.

**23** Fitzgerald, A. et al. (2013). Self-efficacy for healthy eating and peer support for unhealthy eating are associated with adolescents' food intake patterns. *Appetite* 63, 48–58.

**24** Baum, K. T. et al. (2014). Sleep restriction worsens mood and emotion regulation in adolescents. *Journal of Child Psychology and Psychiatry* 55(2), 180–190.

**25** Crowley, S. J., Acebo, C. and Carskadon, M. A. (2007). Sleep, circadian rhythms, and delayed phase in adolescence. *Sleep Medicine* 8(6), 602–612.

**26** Hansen, M. et al. (2005). The impact of school daily schedule on adolescent sleep. *Pediatrics* 115(6), 1555–1561.

**27** Preckel, F. (2013). Morningness-eveningness and educational outcomes: the lark has an advantage over the owl at high school. *British Journal of Educational Psychology* 83(1), 114–134.

**28** Adan, A. et al. (2012). Circadian typology: a comprehensive review. *Chronobiology International* 29(9), 1153–1175.

**29** Vink, J. M. et al. (2001). Genetic analysis of morningness and eveningness. *Chronobiology International* 18(5), 809–822.

**30** Dutil, C. et al. (2022). Sleep timing and health indicators in children

and adolescents: a systematic review. *Health Promotion and Chronic Disease Prevention in Canada: Research, Policy and Practice* 42(4), 150.
31  Bartel, K. A., Gradisar, M. and Williamson, P. (2015). Protective and risk factors for adolescent sleep: a meta-analytic review. *Sleep Medicine Reviews* 21, 72–85.
32  Suni, E. and Vyas, N. (2023). *Mastering Sleep Hygiene: Your Path to Quality Sleep*. Sleep Foundation.
33  Bartel, Gradisar and Williamson (2015).
34  Shochat, T., Cohen-Zion, M. and Tzischinsky, O. (2014). Functional consequences of inadequate sleep in adolescents: a systematic review. *Sleep Medicine Reviews* 18(1), 75–87.
35  Arora, T. et al. (2014). Associations between specific technologies and adolescent sleep quantity, sleep quality, and parasomnias. *Sleep Medicine* 15(2), 240–247.
36  Hysing, M. et al. (2015). Sleep and use of electronic devices in adolescence: results from a large population-based study. *BMJ Open* 5(1), e006748.
37  Misiunaite, I., Eastman, C. I. and Crowley, S. J. (2020). Circadian phase advances in response to weekend morning light in adolescents with short sleep and late bedtimes on school nights. *Frontiers in Neuroscience* 14, 99.
38  Sabiston, C. M. et al. (2022). Body image self-conscious emotions get worse throughout adolescence and relate to physical activity behavior in girls and boys. *Social Science & Medicine* 315, 115543.
39  Rodgers, R. F. and Melioli, T. (2016). The relationship between body image concerns, eating disorders and internet use, part I: a review of empirical support. *Adolescent Research Review* 1, 95–119.
40  Rodgers and Melioli (2016).
41  Voelker, D. K., Reel, J. J. and Greenleaf, C. (2015). Weight status and body image perceptions in adolescents: current perspectives. *Adolescent Health, Medicine and Therapeutics* 6, 149–158.
42  Boursier, V., Gioia, F. and Griffiths, M. D. (2020). Objectified body consciousness, body image control in photos, and problematic social networking: the role of appearance control beliefs. *Frontiers in Psychology* 11, 147.

**43** Murray, S. B. et al. (2018). Boys, biceps, and bradycardia: THE hidden dangers of muscularity-oriented disordered eating. *Journal of Adolescent Health* 62(3), 352–355.

**44** Jackson and Goossens (2020).

**45** Hart, L. M. et al. (2022). Zoomers: videoconferencing, appearance concerns, and potential effects on adolescents. *Current Opinion in Pediatrics* 34(4), 320–325.

**46** Rodríguez-Suárez, B., Manuel Caperos, J. and Ángel Martínez-Huertas, J. (2022). Effect of exposure to thinness ideals in social networks on self-esteem and anxiety. *Behavioral Psychology/Psicologia Conductual* 30(3).

**47** Voelker, Reel and Greenleaf (2015).

**48** Gioia, F., Griffiths, M. D. and Boursier, V. (2020). Adolescents' body shame and social networking sites: the mediating effect of body image control in photos. *Sex Roles* 83, 773–785.

**49** Paxton, S. J., McLean, S. A. and Rodgers, R. F. (2022). 'My critical filter buffers your app filter': social media literacy as a protective factor for body image. *Body Image* 40, 158–164.

**50** Burnette, C. B., Kwitowski, M. A. and Mazzeo, S. E. (2017). 'I don't need people to tell me I'm pretty on social media:' a qualitative study of social media and body image in early adolescent girls. *Body Image* 23, 114–125.

**51** Tylka, T. L. and Wood-Barcalow, N. L. (2015). What is and what is not positive body image? Conceptual foundations and construct definition. *Body Image* 14, 118–129.

**52** Dailey, R. M., Thompson, C. M. and Romo, L. K. (2014) and Puhl, R. M. and Himmelstein, M. S. (2018), cited in Dahill, L. M. et al. (2023). An exploration of how adolescents experience and reason their parents' comments on their weight, shape, and eating. *Journal of Adolescence* 95, 1488–1504.

**53** Dahill, L. et al. (2021). Prevalence of parental comments on weight/shape/eating amongst sons and daughters in an adolescent sample. *Nutrients* 13(1), 158.

**54** Berge, J. M. et al. (2013). Parent conversations about healthful eating and weight: associations with adolescent disordered eating behaviors. *JAMA Pediatrics* 167(8), 746–753.

55 Bray, I. et al. (2018). Promoting positive body image and tackling overweight/obesity in children and adolescents: a combined health psychology and public health approach. *Preventive Medicine* 116, 219–221.

56 Dahill et al. (2023).

57 Gugliandolo, M. C. et al. (2020). Adolescents and body uneasiness: the contribution of supportive parenting and trait emotional intelligence. *Journal of Child and Family Studies* 29, 2453–2462.

58 De Vries, D. A., Vossen, H. G. and van der Kolk–van der Boom, P. (2019). Social media and body dissatisfaction: investigating the attenuating role of positive parent–adolescent relationships. *Journal of Youth and Adolescence* 48, 527–536.

59 Roberts, T. A. et al. (2022). 'Intermission!' A short-term social media fast reduces self-objectification among pre-teen and teen dancers. *Body Image* 43, 125–133.

60 Fernández-Bustos, J. G. et al. (2019). Effect of physical activity on self-concept: theoretical model on the mediation of body image and physical self-concept in adolescents. *Frontiers in Psychology* 10, 1537.

61 Wang, S. B. et al. (2019). Fifteen-year prevalence, trajectories, and predictors of body dissatisfaction from adolescence to middle adulthood. *Clinical Psychological Science* 7(6), 1403–1415.

62 Huang, Q., Peng, W. and Ahn, S. (2021). When media become the mirror: a meta-analysis on media and body image. *Media Psychology* 24(4), 437–489.

63 Voelker, Reel and Greenleaf (2015).

64 Heany, S. J. et al. (2016). A quantitative and qualitative review of the effects of testosterone on the function and structure of the human social-emotional brain. *Metabolic Brain Disease* 31, 157–167.

65 Duke, S. A., Balzer, B. W. R. and Steinbeck, K. S. (2014). Testosterone and its effects on human male adolescent mood and behavior: a systematic review. *Journal of Adolescent Health* 55(3), 315–322.

66 Rosen, N. L. and Nofziger, S. (2019). Boys, bullying, and gender roles: how hegemonic masculinity shapes bullying behavior. *Gender Issues* 36, 295–318.

67 Tolman, D. L., Davis, B. R. and Bowman, C. P. (2016). 'That's just how it is.' A gendered analysis of masculinity and femininity ideologies in

adolescent girls' and boys' heterosexual relationships. *Journal of Adolescent Research* 31(1), 3–31.

**68** Östberg, V. et al. (2015). The complexity of stress in mid-adolescent girls and boys. *Child Indicators Research* 8, 403–423.

**69** Shih, J. H. et al. (2006). Differential exposure and reactivity to interpersonal stress predict sex differences in adolescent depression. *Journal of Clinical Child and Adolescent Psychology* 35(1), 103–115.

**70** OECD (2023). *Gender, Education and Skills: The Persistence of Gender Gaps in Education and Skills.* OECD Skills Studies.

**71** Rosen and Nofziger (2019).

**72** Van der Graaff, J. et al. (2014). Perspective taking and empathic concern in adolescence: gender differences in developmental changes. *Developmental Psychology* 50(3), 881.

**73** Renk, K. et al. (2005). Gender and age differences in the topics of parent-adolescent conflict. *The Family Journal* 13(2), 139–149. Data was pooled together between mothers and fathers. Behaviour differences were statistically significant for both groups; friendship differences ('peer group') were statistically significant for fathers, but not for mothers. No significant differences in conflict topics were reported other than for behaviour and peer groups.

**74** Flynn, H. K. (2018). Friendships of adolescence. In G. Ritzer and C. Rojek (eds), *The Blackwell Encyclopedia of Sociology*. Wiley.

**75** Archer, J. (2004). Sex differences in aggression in real-world settings: a meta-analytic review. *Review of General Psychology* 8(4), 291–322.

**76** Various sources, cited in Fortenberry, J. D. (2013). Puberty and adolescent sexuality. *Hormones and Behavior* 64(2), 280–287.

**77** Way, N. et al. (2014). 'It might be nice to be a girl… then you wouldn't have to be emotionless': boys' resistance to norms of masculinity during adolescence. *Psychology of Men and Masculinity* 15(3), 241–252.

**78** Rosen and Nofziger (2019).

**79** Weissbourd, R. et al. (2017). *The Talk: How Adults Can Promote Young People's Healthy Relationships and Prevent Misogyny and Sexual Harassment.* Making Caring Common Project & Harvard Graduate School of Education.

80 Ormerod, A. J., Collinsworth, L. L. and Perry, L. A. (2008). Critical climate: relations among sexual harassment, climate, and outcomes for high school girls and boys. *Psychology of Women Quarterly* 32(2), 113–125.

81 Horn, S. S. and Poteat, V. P. (2023). Developmental changes in young people's evaluations of sexual harassment. *Journal of Social Issues* 79(4), 1174–1192.

82 Salomon, I. and Brown, C. S. (2021). Engage, ignore, stand up: exploring how (and why) early adolescents respond to sexual harassment. *Journal of Adolescent Research* 36(3), 219–246.

83 Horn and Poteat (2023).

84 Driesmans, K., Vandenbosch, L. and Eggermont, S. (2014). Playing a videogame with a sexualized female character increases adolescents' rape myth acceptance and tolerance toward sexual harassment. *Games for Health Journal* 4(2). doi: 10.1089/g4h.2014.0055.

85 Kaltiala-Heino, R., Fröjd, S. and Marttunen, M. (2016). Sexual harassment and emotional and behavioural symptoms in adolescence: stronger associations among boys than girls. *Social Psychiatry and Psychiatric Epidemiology* 51, 1193–1201. There were five measures of sexual harassment, and in all but one of them (sexual name-calling) the link was stronger in boys.

86 Ormerod, Collinsworth and Perry (2008).

## Risk and reward

1 Winnicott, D. W. (2001). *The Family and Individual Development*. Brunner Routledge, p. 84.

2 Willoughby, T. et al. (2021). Is adolescence a time of heightened risk taking? An overview of types of risk-taking behaviors across age groups. *Developmental Review* 61, 100980.

3 Shulman, E. P. et al. (2016). The dual systems model: review, reappraisal, and reaffirmation. *Developmental Cognitive Neuroscience* 17, 103–117.

4 Office for National Statistics (2022). Deaths registered in England and Wales: Dataset. Available at: https://www.ons.gov.uk/

peoplepopulationandcommunity/birthsdeathsandmarriages/deaths/datasets/deathsregisteredinenglandandwalesseriesdrreferencetables, table 10a (accessed 13 November 2023).

**5** Kloep, M. et al. (2009), cited in Defoe, I. N., Rap, S. E. and Romer, D. (2022). Adolescents' own views on their risk behaviors, and the potential effects of being labeled as risk-takers: a commentary and review. *Frontiers in Psychology* 13, 945775.

**6** MacArthur, G. J., Hickman, M. and Campbell, R. (2020). Qualitative exploration of the intersection between social influences and cultural norms in relation to the development of alcohol use behaviour during adolescence. *BMJ Open* 10(3), e030556.

**7** E.g. Siegel, D. J. (2014). *Brainstorm: The Power and Purpose of the Teenage Brain* [Kindle edn]. Scribe.

**8** Peters, L. W. H. et al. (2009). A review of similarities between domain-specific determinants of four health behaviors among adolescents. *Health Education Research* 24, 198–223.

**9** Siegel (2014).

**10** França, T. F. and Pompeia, S. (2023). Reappraising the role of dopamine in adolescent risk-taking behavior. *Neuroscience & Biobehavioral Reviews* 147, 105085.

**11** Shulman et al. (2016).

**12** Jackson, S. and Goossens, L. (2020). *Handbook of Adolescent Development.* Psychology Press.

**13** Blakemore, S. J. (2018). Avoiding social risk in adolescence. *Current Directions in Psychological Science* 27(2), 116–122.

**14** Leung, R. K., Toumbourou, J. W. and Hemphill, S. A. (2014). The effect of peer influence and selection processes on adolescent alcohol use: a systematic review of longitudinal studies. *Health Psychology Review* 8(4), 426–457.

**15** Fergusson, D. M., Swain-Campbell, N. R. and Horwood, L. J. (2002). Deviant peer affiliations, crime and substance use: a fixed effects regression analysis. *Journal of Abnormal Child Psychology* 30, 419–430.

**16** Reynolds, E. K. et al. (2014). Analogue study of peer influence on risk-taking behavior in older adolescents. *Prevention Science* 15, 842–849.

**17** Logue, S. et al. (2014). Adolescent mice, unlike adults, consume more alcohol in the presence of peers than alone. *Developmental Science* 17(1), 79–85.

**18** Defoe, I. N. et al. (2016). The unique roles of intrapersonal and social factors in adolescent smoking development. *Developmental Psychology* 52(12), 2044.

**19** Cooper, M. L. et al. (2016). Motivational models of substance use: a review of theory and research on motives for using alcohol, marijuana, and tobacco. In Sher, K. J. (ed.), *The Oxford Handbook of Substance Use and Substance Use Disorders*. Oxford University Press, pp. 375–421.

**20** Scholes-Balog, K. E. et al. (2015). Relationships between substance use and depressive symptoms: a longitudinal study of Australian adolescents. *The Journal of Early Adolescence* 35(4), 538–561. The link with illegal drugs was only significant in girls.

**21** Whitesell, M. et al. (2013). Familial, social, and individual factors contributing to risk for adolescent substance use. *Journal of Addiction*. doi: 10.1155/2013/579310.

**22** Defoe, Rap and Romer (2022).

**23** Albert, D. and Steinberg, L. (2011). Judgment and decision making in adolescence. *Journal of Research on Adolescence* 21(1), 211–224.

**24** Schepis, T. S., Adinoff, B. and Rao, U. (2008). Neurobiological processes in adolescent addictive disorders. *American Journal on Addictions* 17(1), 6–23.

**25** Khurana, A., Loan, C. M. and Romer, D. (2022). Predicting cigarette use initiation and dependence in adolescence using an affect-driven exploration model. *Frontiers in Psychology* 13, 887021.

**26** Ryan, S. M., Jorm, A. F. and Lubman, D. I. (2010). Parenting factors associated with reduced adolescent alcohol use: a systematic review of longitudinal studies. *Australian & New Zealand Journal of Psychiatry* 44(9), 774–783.

**27** Yurasek, A. M. et al. (2019). The effects of parent, sibling and peer substance use on adolescent drinking behaviors. *Journal of Child and Family Studies* 28, 73–83.

**28** Poor-quality relationships and poor communication: Ryan, Jorm and Lubman (2010). Low levels of monitoring: Villarreal, D. L. and Nelson, J. A.

(2018). Parental monitoring and adolescent risk behaviors: the moderating role of adolescent internalizing symptoms and gender. *Journal of Child and Family Studies* 27, 3627–3637. Psychological control: Plummer Lee, C., Beckert, T. and Marsee, I. (2018). Well-being and substance use in emerging adulthood: the role of individual and family factors in childhood and adolescence. *Journal of Child and Family Studies* 27, 3853–3865.

29 Harris-McKoy, D. (2016). Adolescent delinquency: is too much or too little parental control a problem? *Journal of Child and Family Studies* 25, 2079–2088.

30 Suldo, S. and Huebner, E. (2004). The role of life satisfaction in the relationship between authoritative parenting dimensions and adolescent problem behavior. *Social Indicators Research* 66(1/2), 165–195.

31 Chan, T. and Koo, A. (2011). Parenting style and youth outcomes in the UK. *European Sociological Review* 27(3), 385–399.

32 Romer, D. (2010). Adolescent risk taking, impulsivity, and brain development: Implications for prevention. *Developmental Psychobiology* 52(3), 263–276.

33 Thomas, S. A. et al. (2019). Moderated mediation of the link between parent-adolescent conflict and adolescent risk-taking: The role of physiological regulation and hostile behavior in an experimentally controlled investigation. *Journal of Psychopathology and Behavioral Assessment* 41, 699–715.

34 Molina, B. S. G. and Pelham, W. E. (2003), cited in Spirito, A. et al. (2015). Improving parenting and parent-adolescent communication to delay or prevent the onset of alcohol and drug use in young adolescents with emotional/behavioral disorders: a pilot trial. *Journal of Child & Adolescent Substance Abuse* 24(5), 308–322.

35 E.g. Falk, E. B. et al. (2014). Neural responses to exclusion predict susceptibility to social influence. *Journal of Adolescent Health* 54(5), S22–S31.

36 Bray, J. H. et al. (2022). Parental monitoring, family conflict, and adolescent alcohol use: a longitudinal latent class analysis. *Journal of Family Psychology* 36(7), 1154–1160.

37 Willems, Y. E. et al. (2020). Out of control: examining the association between family conflict and self-control in adolescence in a genetically

sensitive design. *Journal of the American Academy of Child & Adolescent Psychiatry* 59(2), 254–262.

**38** Arım, R. G. et al. (2011). The family antecedents and the subsequent outcomes of early puberty. *Journal of Youth and Adolescence* 40, 1423–1435.

**39** Vermeersch, H. et al. (2008). The role of testosterone in aggressive and non-aggressive risk-taking in adolescent boys. *Hormones and Behavior* 53(3), 463–471.

**40** Albert and Steinberg (2011).

**41** Schuster, R. M., Mermelstein, R. and Wakschlag, L. (2013). Gender-specific relationships between depressive symptoms, marijuana use, parental communication and risky sexual behavior in adolescence. *Journal of Youth and Adolescence* 42, 1194–1209.

**42** Biglan, A. and Cody, C. (2003), cited in Romer, D. (2010).

**43** YouGov (2023). YouGov Survey Results, Sex Partners and Virginity Loss. Available at: https://d3nkl3psvxxpe9.cloudfront.net/documents/YouGov_-_Sex_partners_and_virginity_loss_age.pdf (accessed 17 November 2023). Includes data tables as well as author's calculations.

**44** Collins, W. A. and Steinberg, L. (2008). Adolescent development in interpersonal context. In W. Damon and R. M. Lerner (eds), *Child and Adolescent Development: An Advanced Course*. Wiley, pp. 551–590.

**45** Not her real name, obviously.

**46** Collins and Steinberg (2008).

**47** Coley, R. L. et al. (2013). Sexual partner accumulation from adolescence through early adulthood: the role of family, peer, and school social norms. *Journal of Adolescent Health* 53(1), 91–97.

**48** Epstein, M. et al. (2018). Adolescent age of sexual initiation and subsequent adult health outcomes. *American Journal of Public Health* 108(6), 822–828.

**49** Kahn, N. F. and Halpern, C. T. (2018). Associations between patterns of sexual initiation, sexual partnering, and sexual health outcomes from adolescence to early adulthood. *Archives of Sexual Behavior* 47(6), 1791–1810.

**50** Weissbourd, R. et al. (2017). *The Talk: How Adults Can Promote Young People's Healthy Relationships and Prevent Misogyny and Sexual Harassment*.

# ENDNOTES

Making Caring Common Project & Harvard Graduate School of Education.

51 Coley et al. (2013).

52 Cox Jr, R. B. et al. (2015). Parenting, peers, and perceived norms: what predicts attitudes toward sex among early adolescents? *Journal of Early Adolescence* 35(1), 30–53.

53 Online dating and chat rooms: Vandenbosch, L. et al. (2016). Online communication predicts Belgian adolescents' initiation of romantic and sexual activity. *European Journal of Pediatrics* 175, 509–516. Cannabis and alcohol: Young, H., Burke, L. and Gabhainn, S. N. (2018). Sexual intercourse, age of initiation and contraception among adolescents in Ireland: findings from the Health Behaviour in School-aged Children (HBSC) Ireland study. *BMC Public Health* 18, 1–17.

54 Rodgers, K. B. et al. (2019). Adolescents' sex-related alcohol expectancies and alcohol advertisements in magazines: the role of wishful identification, realism, and beliefs about women's enjoyment of sexualization. *Journal of Health Communication* 24(4), 395–404.

55 Young, Burke and Gabhainn (2018).

56 Patton, G. C. et al. (2016). Our future: a Lancet commission on adolescent health and wellbeing. *The Lancet* 387(10036), 2423–2478.

57 Farré, J. M. et al. (2020). Pornography use in adolescents and its clinical implications. *Journal of Clinical Medicine* 9(11), 3625.

58 Kreager D. A. et al. (2016). The double standard at sexual debut: gender, sexual behavior and adolescent peer acceptance. *Sex Roles* 75, 377–392.

59 Garceau, C. and Ronis, S. T. (2019). A qualitative investigation of expected versus actual initial sexual experiences before age 16. *Journal of Adolescence* 71, 38–49.

60 Marshall, E. A. and Miller, H. A. (2019). Consistently inconsistent: a systematic review of the measurement of pornography use. *Aggression and Violent Behavior* 48, 169–179.

61 Grubbs, J. B. and Perry, S. L. (2019). Moral incongruence and pornography use: a critical review and integration. *The Journal of Sex Research* 56(1), 29–37.

**62** Pathmendra, P. et al. (2023). Exposure to pornography and adolescent sexual behavior: systematic review. *Journal of Medical Internet Research* 25, e43116.

**63** Farré et al. (2020).

**64** Lim, M. S. et al. (2017). Young Australians' use of pornography and associations with sexual risk behaviours. *Australian and New Zealand Journal of Public Health* 41(4), 438–443.

**65** Alexandraki, K. et al. (2018). Adolescent pornography use: a systematic literature review of research trends 2000–2017. *Current Psychiatry Reviews* 14(1), 47–58.

**66** Peter, J. and Valkenburg, P. M. (2016). Adolescents and pornography: a review of 20 years of research. *Journal of Sex Research* 53(4–5), 509–531.

**67** Alexandraki et al. (2018).

**68** Mes, C., Van Oosten, J. M. F. and Vandenbosch, L. (2022). Adolescents' digital media interactions within the context of sexuality development. In J. Nesi, E. H. Telzer and M. J. Prinstein (eds), *Handbook of Adolescent Digital Media Use and Mental Health.* Cambridge University Press, pp. 135–161.

**69** Owens, E. W. et al. (2012). The impact of internet pornography on adolescents: a review of the research. *Sexual Addiction & Compulsivity* 19(1–2), 99–122.

**70** Farré et al. (2020).

**71** Hornor, G. (2020). Child and adolescent pornography exposure. *Journal of Pediatric Health Care* 34(2), 191–199.

**72** Owens et al. (2012).

**73** Perry, S. L. (2020). Pornography and relationship quality: establishing the dominant pattern by examining pornography use and 31 measures of relationship quality in 30 national surveys. *Archives of Sexual Behavior* 49, 1199–1213.

**74** Rostad, W. L. et al. (2019). The association between exposure to violent pornography and teen dating violence in grade 10 high school students. *Archives of Sexual Behavior* 48, 2137–2147.

**75** @parentingteenagersuntangled (2023, 15 November.) *How to: Talk to your kids about porn, with Dr Mandy Sanchez of Culture Reframed* [Video]. YouTube. https://www.youtube.com/watch?v=UwYRIzWUihA.

## ENDNOTES

76 Le Conte, M. [@youngvulgarian]. (2023, 10 March). not especially thrilled to be sticking my head above the parapet on this one... [Tweet]. X. https://twitter.com/youngvulgarian/status/1634163046108082176.

77 Edwards, S. S. (2020). Consent and the 'rough sex' defence in rape, murder, manslaughter and gross negligence. *Journal of Criminal Law* 84(4), 293–311.

78 Brown, J. D. and L'Engle, K. L. (2009). X-rated: sexual attitudes and behaviors associated with US early adolescents' exposure to sexually explicit media. *Communication Research* 36(1), 129–151.

79 Peter and Valkenburg (2016).

80 Peter, J. and Valkenburg, P. M. (2007). Adolescents' exposure to a sexualized media environment and their notions of women as sex objects. *Sex Roles* 56, 381–395.

81 Hornor (2020).

82 @parentingteenagersuntangled (2023).

83 Lejars, V. O. B., Bélanger, C. H. and Razmak, J. (2020). Exploring new measures of online sexual activities, device use, and gender differences. *Computers in Human Behavior* 108, 106300.

84 Mes, Van Oosten and Vandenbosch (2022).

85 Döring, N. (2014). Consensual sexting among adolescents: risk prevention through abstinence education or safer sexting. *Cyberpsychology: Journal of Psychosocial Research on Cyberspace* 8(1), 9.

86 Eleuteri, S., Saladino, V. and Verrastro, V. (2017). Identity, relationships, sexuality, and risky behaviors of adolescents in the context of social media. *Sexual and Relationship Therapy* 32(3–4), 354–365.

87 Handschuh, C., La Cross, A. and Smaldone, A. (2019). Is sexting associated with sexual behaviors during adolescence? A systematic literature review and meta-analysis. *Journal of Midwifery & Women's Health* 64(1), 88–97.

88 Mori, C. et al. (2019). Association of sexting with sexual behaviors and mental health among adolescents: a systematic review and meta-analysis. *JAMA Pediatrics* 173(8), 770–779.

89 Titchen, K. E. et al. (2019). Sexting and young adolescents: associations with sexual abuse and intimate partner violence. *Journal of Pediatric and*

*Adolescent Gynecology* 32(5), 481–486. Links were shown with being a victim of sexual abuse for both girls and boys; with intimate partner violence, the significant link for girls was being a victim and for boys was being a perpetrator.

90 Mori et al. (2019).

91 Eleuteri, Saladino and Verrastro (2017).

92 Ringrose, J. et al. (2013) Teen girls, sexual double standards and 'sexting': gendered value in digital image exchange, *Feminist Theory* 14(3): 305–323.

93 Madigan, S. et al. (2018). Prevalence of multiple forms of sexting behavior among youth: a systematic review and meta-analysis. *JAMA Pediatrics* 172(4), 327–335.

94 Farré et al. (2020).

95 Gassó, A. M. et al. (2019). Sexting, mental health, and victimization among adolescents: a literature review. *International Journal of Environmental Research and Public Health* 16(13), 2364.

96 Machimbarrena, J. M. et al. (2018). Internet risks: an overview of victimization in cyberbullying, cyber dating abuse, sexting, online grooming and problematic internet use. *International Journal of Environmental Research and Public Health* 15(11), 2471.

97 Döring (2014).

98 Hopwood, K. on Shone, J. and Sertin, J. (Hosts). (2020, 24 January.) Talking Teenagers – Season 1 – Technology & Teens with Karl Hopwood [Audio podcast episode]. In *Talking Teenagers*. https://podcasts.apple.com/gb/podcast/talking-teenagers/id1500452887?i=1000466954355.

99 @parentingteenagersuntangled (2023).

100 Rothman, E. F., Daley, N. and Alder, J. (2020). A pornography literacy program for adolescents. *American Journal of Public Health* 110(2), 154–156.

101 Rothman, Daley and Alder (2020).

102 Rothman, E. (2023). Talking with teens and preteens about pornography: tips and scripts to promote healthy communication and development. Common Sense Media. Available at: https://www.commonsensemedia.org/articles/talking-with-teens-and-preteens-about-pornography (accessed 27 December 2023).

103 Padilla-Walker, L. M., Rogers, A. A. and McLean, R. D. (2020). Is there more than one way to talk about sex? A longitudinal growth mixture model of parent–adolescent sex communication. *Journal of Adolescent Health* 67(6), 851–858.

104 Ashcraft, A. M. and Murray, P. J. (2017). Talking to parents about adolescent sexuality. *Pediatric Clinics* 64(2), 305–320.

105 Garceau and Ronis (2019).

106 Flores, D. et al. (2019). 'It's almost like gay sex doesn't exist': parent-child sex communication according to gay, bisexual, and queer male adolescents. *Journal of Adolescent Research* 34(5), 528–562.

107 Padilla-Walker, Rogers and McLean (2020).

108 Parkes, A. et al. (2011). Is parenting associated with teenagers' early sexual risk-taking, autonomy and relationship with sexual partners? *Perspectives on Sexual and Reproductive Health* 43(1), 30–40.

109 Ashcraft and Murray (2017).

110 Dutch study: Overbeek, G., van de Bongardt, D. and Baams, L. (2018). Buffer or brake? The role of sexuality-specific parenting in adolescents' sexualized media consumption and sexual development. *Journal of Youth and Adolescence* 47, 1427–1439.

111 Internet Matters (n.d.). Prevent harm to children: How to prevent access to online pornography. Available at: https://www.internetmatters.org/issues/online-pornography/protect-your-child/ (accessed 27 December 2023).

112 Hornor (2020).

113 Ashcraft and Murray (2017).

114 Children's Society (2023). County lines and criminal exploitation: What is county lines? Available at: https://www.childrenssociety.org.uk/what-we-do/our-work/child-criminal-exploitation-and-county-lines/what-is-county-lines (accessed 27 December 2023).

115 Ivison Trust (2024). What is county lines? Available at: https://ivisontrust.org.uk/criminal-exploitation/what-is-county-lines/ (accessed 2 August 2024).

116 National Crime Agency (2023). County lines. Available at: https://www.nationalcrimeagency.gov.uk/what-we-do/crime-threats/drug-trafficking/county-lines (accessed 27 December 2023).

117 Ivison Trust (2024). Ask for help. Available at: https://ivisontrust.org.uk/criminal-exploitation/ask-for-help/ (accessed 2 August 2024).

118 Johnston, L. D. et al. (2023). *Monitoring the future national survey results on drug use 1975–2022: overview, key findings on adolescent drug use.* Institute for Social Research, University of Michigan.

119 Johnston et al. (2023).

120 Johnston et al. (2023).

121 Johnston et al. (2023).

122 Branstetter, S. A. and Furman, W. (2013). Buffering effect of parental monitoring knowledge and parent-adolescent relationships on consequences of adolescent substance use. *Journal of Child and Family Studies* 22, 192–198.

123 Whitesell et al. (2013).

124 Branstetter and Furman (2013).

125 NHS (2023). Alcohol poisoning. Available at: https://www.nhs.uk/conditions/alcohol-poisoning/ (accessed 26 December 2023).

126 Chadi, N., Hadland, S. E. and Harris, S. K. (2019). Understanding the implications of the 'vaping epidemic' among adolescents and young adults: a call for action. *Substance Abuse* 40(1), 7–10.

127 Vrinten, C. et al. (2023). Patterns of cigarette and e-cigarette use among UK adolescents: a latent class analysis of the Millennium Cohort Study. *European Journal of Public Health* 33(5), 857–863. Missing data was excluded from calculations.

128 Leventhal, A. M. et al. (2019). Flavored e-cigarette use and progression of vaping in adolescents. *Pediatrics* 144(5).

129 Zhu, S. H. et al. (2014). Four hundred and sixty brands of e-cigarettes and counting: implications for product regulation. *Tobacco Control* 23(Suppl. 3), iii3.

130 Tattan-Birch, H. (2023). Rapid growth in disposable e-cigarette vaping among young adults in Great Britain from 2021 to 2022: a repeat cross-sectional survey. *Addiction* 118(2), 382–386. Note that while the confidence intervals for each age range did not overlap, they were very wide, suggesting we can't have much confidence in the magnitude of the gap.

131 Goldenson, N. I. et al. (2017). Associations of electronic cigarette

nicotine concentration with subsequent cigarette smoking and vaping levels in adolescents. *JAMA Pediatrics* 171(12), 1192–1199.

**132** Jonas, A. (2022). Impact of vaping on respiratory health. *BMJ* 378, e065997.

**133** McConnell, R. et al. (2017). Electronic cigarette use and respiratory symptoms in adolescents. *American Journal of Respiratory and Critical Care Medicine* 195(8), 1043–1049.

**134** Tobore, T. O. (2019). On the potential harmful effects of e-cigarettes (EC) on the developing brain: the relationship between vaping-induced oxidative stress and adolescent/young adults social maladjustment. *Journal of Adolescence* 76, 202–209.

**135** Bush, A. et al. (2021). E-cigarettes as a growing threat for children and adolescents: position statement from the European Academy of Paediatrics. *Frontiers in Pediatrics* 9, 698613.

**136** Jonas, A. M. and Raj, R. (2020). Vaping-related acute parenchymal lung injury: a systematic review. *Chest* 158(4), 1555–1565.

**137** Freeman, T. P. et al. (2021). Changes in delta-9-tetrahydrocannabinol (THC) and cannabidiol (CBD) concentrations in cannabis over time: systematic review and meta-analysis. *Addiction* 116(5), 1000–1010.

**138** Gersh, E. et al. (2018). Adolescent health risk behaviors: parental concern and concordance between parent and adolescent reports. *Academic Pediatrics* 18(1), 66–72. Statistically significant differences (see Table 1) are reported.

**139** Campbell, R. et al. (2008). An informal school-based peer-led intervention for smoking prevention in adolescence (ASSIST): a cluster randomised trial. *The Lancet* 371(9624), 1595–1602.

**140** Samek, D. R. et al. (2015). Parent involvement, sibling companionship, and adolescent substance use: a longitudinal, genetically informed design. *Journal of Family Psychology* 29(4), 614–623.

**141** Martínez-Casanova, E., Molero-Jurado, M. D. M. and Pérez-Fuentes, M. D. C. (2024). Self-esteem and risk behaviours in adolescents: a systematic review. *Behavioral Sciences* 14(6), 432.

**142** Pederson, C. A. et al. (2022). The relationship between neighborhood safety and adolescent substance use: the role of self-esteem and social support. *Journal of Child and Family Studies* 31(11), 3234–3246.

**143** Ryan, Jorm and Lubman (2010).

**144** Littlecott, H. J. et al. (2023). Perceptions of friendship, peers and influence on adolescent smoking according to tobacco control context: a systematic review and meta-ethnography of qualitative research. *BMC Public Health* 23(1), 424–445.

**145** Moore, G. F. et al. (2016). E-cigarette use and intentions to smoke among 10–11-year-old never-smokers in Wales. *Tobacco Control* 25(2), 147–152.

**146** Vahedi, Z., Sibalis, A. and Sutherland, J. E. (2018). Are media literacy interventions effective at changing attitudes and intentions towards risky health behaviors in adolescents? A meta-analytic review. *Journal of Adolescence* 67, 140–152.

**147** Hamann, C. J. et al. (2014). Parent and teen agreement on driving expectations prior to teen licensure. *American Journal of Health Behavior* 38(1), 13–21.

**148** McCartt, A. T., Shabanova, V. I. and Leaf, W. A. (2003). Driving experience, crashes and traffic citations of teenage beginning drivers. *Accident Analysis and Prevention* 35, 311–320.

**149** Siegel (2014).

**150** Drummond, A. on Shone, J. and Sertin, J. (Hosts). (2020, 24 January.) Talking Teenagers – Season 1 – Teen Tips with Alicia Drummond [Audio podcast episode]. In *Talking Teenagers*. https://podcasts.apple.com/gb/podcast/talking-teenagers/id1500452887?i=1000466651700.

**151** Romer (2010).

**152** Spargo-Mabbs, F. on Drummond, A. (Host). (2019, 17 July.) Drugs – Part 2. In *Teen Tips*. https://podcasts.apple.com/gb/podcast/drugs-part-2/id1386679368?i=1000444717944.

**153** https://addictionfamilysupport.org.uk.

## Equipping a future adult

**1** Winter, C. on Wills, H. (Host). (2022, 8 November.) Sleep Tips for Teenagers [Audio podcast episode]. In *Teenage Kicks*. https://podcasts.apple.com/gb/podcast/sleep-tips-for-teenagers/id1501488455?i=1000585419904.

# ENDNOTES

**2** Salusky, I. et al. (2014). How adolescents develop responsibility: What can be learned from youth programs. *Journal of Research on Adolescence* 24(3), 417–430.

**3** Salusky et al. (2014).

**4** Allemand, M., Job, V. and Mroczek, D. K. (2019). Self-control development in adolescence predicts love and work in adulthood. *Journal of Personality and Social Psychology* 117(3), 621.

**5** Duckworth, A. L. et al. (2015). Will not want: Self-control rather than motivation explains the female advantage in report card grades. *Learning and Individual Differences* 39, 13–23.

**6** Li, J. B. et al. (2019). Parenting and self-control across early to late adolescence: A three-level meta-analysis. *Perspectives on Psychological Science* 14(6), 967–1005.

**7** Crocetti, E. et al. (2016). The dynamic interplay among maternal empathy, quality of mother-adolescent relationship, and adolescent antisocial behaviors: new insights from a six-wave longitudinal multi-informant study. *PLOS One* 11(3), e0150009.

**8** Wray-Lake, L. and Syvertsen, A. K. (2011). The developmental roots of social responsibility in childhood and adolescence. *New Directions for Child and Adolescent Development* 2011(134), 11–25.

**9** Gottlieb, Z. (2023, 10 December). Opinion: Listen up. The closing of the teenage mind is almost complete [News article]. *Los Angeles Times*. Available at: https://www.latimes.com/opinion/story/2023-12-10/los-angeles-high-school-cancel-culture-free-speech (accessed 14 December 2023).

**10** Knight Foundation (2022). Future of the First Amendment 2022: High schooler views on speech over time. *Knight Free Expression Research (KFX) Series Report.*

**11** Wolf, T. and Franks, S. (2020). *Get Out of My Life: But First Take Me and Alex into Town* [Kindle edn]. Profile Books, 4th Edition.

**12** González, M. et al. (2015). Adolescents' perspective on their participation in the family context and its relationship with their subjective well-being. *Child Indicators Research* 8, 93–109.

**13** Salusky et al. (2014).

**14** Lam, C. B., Greene, K. M. and McHale, S. M. (2016). Housework time from middle childhood through adolescence: links to parental work hours and youth adjustment. *Developmental Psychology* 52(12), 2071.

15  Offer, S. (2013). Family time activities and adolescents' emotional well-being. *Journal of Marriage and Family* 75(1), 26–41.

16  Lam, Greene and McHale (2016).

17  DuBois, D. L. and Silverthorn, N. (2005). Characteristics of natural mentoring relationships and adolescent adjustment: evidence from a national study. *Journal of Primary Prevention* 26, 69–92.

18  Núñez, J. C. et al. (2015). Relationships between perceived parental involvement in homework, student homework behaviors, and academic achievement: differences among elementary, junior high, and high school students. *Metacognition and Learning* 10, 375–406.

19  Gottfried, A. E., Fleming, J. S. and Gottfried, A. W. (2001). Continuity of academic intrinsic motivation from childhood through late adolescence: a longitudinal study. *Journal of Educational Psychology* 93(1), 3.

20  Wang, M., Hill, N. and Hofkens, T. (2014). Parental involvement and African American and European American adolescents' academic, behavioral, and emotional development in secondary school. *Child Development* 85(6), 2151–2168.

21  Adachi, P. J. and Willoughby, T. (2013). More than just fun and games: the longitudinal relationships between strategic video games, self-reported problem solving skills, and academic grades. *Journal of Youth and Adolescence* 42, 1041–1052.

22  Cullinane, C. and Montacute, R. (2017). *Life Lessons: Improving Essential Life Skills for Young People.* Sutton Trust.

23  Hart, D. et al. (2007). High school community service as a predictor of adult voting and volunteering. *American Educational Research Journal* 44(1), 197–219.

24  Loderup, C. L. et al. (2021). How do parents teach their children about work? A qualitative exploration of household chores, employment, and entrepreneurial experiences. *Journal of Family and Economic Issues* 42, 73–89.

25  Mortimer, J. T. (2010). The benefits and risks of adolescent employment. *The Prevention Researcher* 17(2), 8.

# ENDNOTES

**26** Gardiner, L. (2020). *Never Ever: Exploring the Increase in People Who've Never Had a Paid Job.* Resolution Foundation.

**27** Mortimer (2010).

**28** Mortimer (2010).

**29** Staff, J. et al. (2013). Identifying good and bad jobs in adolescence. In C. W. Runya et al. (eds), *Health and Safety of Young Workers: Proceedings of a U.S. and Canadian Series of Symposia.* US Department of Health and Human Services, Centers for Disease Control and Prevention, and National Institute for Occupational Safety and Health.

**30** Mortimer (2010).

**31** Melman, S., Little, S. G. and Akin-Little, K. A. (2007). Adolescent overscheduling: the relationship between levels of participation in scheduled activities and self-reported clinical symptomology. *The High School Journal* 90(3), 18–30.

**32** Pickering, L. E. and Vazsonyi, A. T. (2002). The impact of adolescent employment on family relationships. *Journal of Adolescent Research* 17(2), 196–218.

**33** Lukina, A. K. and Volkova, M. A. (2021). How adolescents today imagine adulthood and their future: research review. *European Proceedings of Social and Behavioural Sciences.* doi: 10.15405/epsbs.2021.09.02.179.

**34** Schmid, K. L. and Lopez, S. J. (2011). Positive pathways to adulthood: the role of hope in adolescents' constructions of their futures. *Advances in Child Development and Behavior* 41, 69–88.

**35** Snyder, C. R. (1995). Conceptualizing, measuring, and nurturing hope. *Journal of Counseling & Development* 73(3), 355–360.